# Cultural Diversity
## in Sexual Abuser Treatment

### Issues and Approaches

*Alvin D. Lewis, Ed.D.*
editor

Safer Society Press
PO BOX 340 • BRANDON • VT 05733

Developmental Editor: Euan Bear

Cover design: Carrie Fradkin

Production management: Jenna Dixon
Copyediting: Linda Lotz
Typesetting: Sam Sheng, CompuDesign
Proofreading: Beth Richards

Printed in the United States of America by Malloy Lithographing, Inc.

ISBN 1-884444-49-0 / $22.00
Bulk discounts available.

**Safer Society Press**
Safer Society Press
PO Box 349
Brandon VT 05733
(802) 247-3132

∞ The paper used in this publication meets the minimum requirements of the American National Standard for Information Sciences—Permanence of Paper for Printed Library Materials, ANSI Z39.48-1984.

*Library of Congress Cataloging-in-Publication Data*
  Cultural diversity in sexual abuser treatment : issues and approaches / Alvin
  D. Lewis, editor.
        p.      cm.
    Includes bibliographical references and index.
    ISBN 1-884444-49-0 (alk. paper)
    1. Minority sex offenders—Rehabilitation.  2. Minority sex offenders—
  Mental health services.  I. Title.
    RC560.S47L49    1999
    616.85'8306—dc21                                              98-35773

08 07 06 05 04 03 02 01 00 99    10 9 8 7 6 5 4 3 2 1    1st Printing 1999

# Contents

# Foreword

## I. State of the Field

Over the past 25 years, our society has increasingly focused attention on individuals who commit sexual offenses. Hardly a day goes by without our reading in the newspaper or seeing on TV a report of a sex offense committed against a vulnerable victim. Historically, sex abusers who were caught and convicted were incarcerated and ultimately released without benefit of treatment. More recently, clinical researchers have developed therapeutic interventions for the treatment of sexual offenders. Today, treatment programs can be found in almost every community, and some prison programs provide treatment for their sex offender populations.

National organizations have been formed to spread knowledge to the professionals who will intervene with both adult and juvenile sex offenders, the Association for the Treatment of Sexual Abusers (ATSA) and the National Task Force on Juvenile Sexual Offending among them. These organizations offer forums in which the most up-to-date scientific and clinical findings can be disseminated.

In attempts to make our communities safer, legislatures have been extremely active in passing laws that embody social control policies, including sex offender registration, community notification, lifetime probation, and sexual predator laws. Some of these policies affect communities in ways that are not yet well understood.

While there has been an increasing body of empirical literature on treatment interventions, risk assessments, therapy outcome studies, and offender typologies, there has been a dearth of literature on the assessment and treatment of culturally diverse populations. It is past time for us to move from the "one-size-fits-all" approach to intervening with individuals who have sexual behavior disorders and to focus on what assessment and treatment modalities are appropriate for the heterogeneous populations with which we work.

*Cultural Diversity in Sexual Abuser Treatment: Issues and Approaches* does just that. Gender, ethnicity, and culture are all important considerations when approaching the assessment and treatment of individuals. We are all products of the experiences we have had in our families and communities. Those experiences and values are not left behind when an individual enters treatment. The men, women, and children we treat deserve treatment providers who have knowledge of and sensitivity to the cultural base from which they come. It is important that we be aware of gender issues, what is considered normative and non-normative within various cultures, subtleties of verbal and body language that may be lost in translation, the degree of acculturation to the dominant culture, different family structures and traditions, relationships to authority figures, and attitudes toward sexuality.

It is incumbent upon us as treatment providers to educate ourselves in the cultural backgrounds of our clients. We can begin by recognizing the presence and effects of our own built-in cultural biases, by reading about various cultures and traditions, and by consulting with colleagues who know and understand specific cultures. By so doing, we will be taking the appropriate first steps to providing culturally sensitive, effective, relevant treatment in the service of our ultimate goal: preventing further sexual abuse and making society safer.

*Judith V. Becker, Ph.D.*
Tucson, Arizona

# II. A Personal Journey

I vividly recall beginning my career in the field of sexual abuse prevention and treatment as a clinician treating juvenile and adult sexual abusers back in 1978. The state hospital program in which I worked as a clinician housed a diverse group of patients, many of whom were Black Americans or of Hispanic background and origin. Then and for many years afterwards, it never dawned on me that my lack of understanding about individual clients' and patients' backgrounds and cultures would directly affect my ability to be an effective helping professional. Several years later, after the Mariel boat lift from Cuba, the number of Cuban sexual abusers coming into Florida prisons increased significantly. Thinking back, I must admit that I probably lost any chance of establishing rapport with hundreds of potential clients during interviews and screening procedures due to my lack of cultural knowledge and sensitivity. Sadly, I cannot turn back the clock.

During the last decade or so, but especially during the past six or seven years, sensitivity to the cultural differences of our clients has emerged and begun to grow among many of my colleagues in the field of sexual abuser treatment. We now understand how our lack of cultural sensitivity can foster denial and resistance in our clients. We recognize the need to acknowledge traditions, customs, and lifestyles in the different cultural and minority groups represented in our client populations. We better understand the need to incorporate traditional non-Western mental health approaches, resources, rituals, and treatments in our practice with people of color and of religious, ethnic, and cultural backgrounds that differ from our own.

As I worked as a consultant to several state departments of corrections in the late 1980s, it became apparent that as professionals we must pay close attention to customs and traditions of various cultures. Treating all clients alike and making them participate in group therapy while maintaining "eye contact" and talking about "feelings" was problematic for many incarcerated sexual abusers. The system's inability to allow such offenders to practice cultural rites, rituals, customs, and traditions that are important to them can have a strong negative effect on their ability to feel comfortable in the treatment environment and to maximize their potential for growth and change. Even something as "insignificant" as refusing to allow clients to meet their "hunger" for traditional foods from their culture affects their willingness to trust and participate in treatment. Certain traditions and basic resources are directly tied to healing practices of many peoples.

During the past decade I have searched the literature to find ways of developing my knowledge of different cultures and improving my understanding of how I might best serve these clients and patients. I found a limited number of articles, books, and published professional literature that addressed my interests and concerns. There was a definite void of specialized literature. *Cultural Diversity in Sexual Abuser Treatment: Issues and Approaches* is the Safer Society Foundation's initial attempt to help fill that void and address an extremely important issue for our field. As helping professionals we are most effective when we are adequately informed and armed with the necessary material, knowledge, and tools to forge ahead in helping others and work toward making a safer society. It is for these reasons and others that I decided this book was necessary.

Through our mutual friend Dr. Judith Becker, I met Dr. Alvin Lewis and asked him if he would be interested in heading up this project and editing the resulting book. He agreed. We brainstormed ideas and topics and then went about finding the people who were most knowledgeable to write specialized chapters on the populations that *Cultural Diversity in Sexual Abuser Treatment* addresses. We are both very pleased with the results. The authors of the chapters that follow have worked hard to provide the most recent thinking regarding cultural issues and sensitivity in the treatment of sexual abusers.

These pages are filled with interesting and stimulating information about many different cultures and groups of people that I only wish I had the foresight and wisdom to pursue 20 years ago. It is truly a delight to read this volume, and I am excited that this project — started almost three years ago — is now complete as a snapshot of where we are now. I encourage you to read this book from cover to cover and to pay particular attention to and reread the chapters that address the cultures of clients you may be treating in your program or practice. There is much to learn and generations of wisdom to respect from some of the leaders in our field who know about "their" people, customs, traditions, and lifestyles and readily share this information to enrich our lives as clinicians, administrators, and concerned persons. Yet perhaps the most important piece of wisdom in these pages is not specific information on a particular culture but the message to all of us as professionals to remain open, to become aware of and acknowledge our own cultural biases, and to show genuine respect for the cultures of our clients.

Our world is filled with knowledge about the similarities and differences between cultures and communities. Our respect for life and its many traditions and customs must be applied to everyone, including the sexual abusers we work with as patients and clients, as each has his or her own unique story to tell. Each has his or her personal background, however rich or poor, to be understood, respected, and worked with. We no longer have to worry about turning back the clock in a desperate need to understand, as

*Cutural Diversity in Sexual Abuser Treatment* provides us with the opportunity to learn and move forward in our understanding of the many people, cultures, and traditions that make up the rich environment of the world we live in and the diversity of clients we may treat.

My heartfelt thanks to all the contributors and to Dr. Alvin Lewis for making this volume possible.

*Robert E. Freeman-Longo, M.R.C., L.P.C*
The Safer Society Foundation, Inc.
Brandon, Vermont

# Dedication

To my wife Bee Bee and sons Affindi and Azlan. Thanks for your loving support of this project.

# Acknowledgments

My deep gratitude to the authors who contributed their best to this project. My heartfelt thanks to my family for their support, the staff at The Pines Residential Treatment Center, Dr. John Hunter, Dr. Judith V. Becker, Rob Freeman-Longo, Shay Kelly, Georgia Gray, Leslie Mitchell, and Bonita Webster. Special thanks to Matt Markovich, Helen Acevedo, Euan Bear, and Dr. Sherry Rosenthal for their support and technical assistance.

# About the Contributors

JUDITH V. BECKER, PH.D., is an associate dean in the School of Behavioral and Social Sciences at the University of Arizona in Tucson. She is also a professor in the Psychology Department and the School of Medicine. She is a past president of the Association for the Treatment of Sexual Abusers and has published numerous articles and book chapters on sexually abusive behaviors and sexual disorders.

CHARLES S. BROADFIELD, PH.D., is a consultant in private practice, with over 30 years' experience in working with various mental-health populations. He holds graduate degrees in psychology and has a special interest in forensics.

ERIC CUESTAS-THOMPSON, M.A. is a therapist with the HIV Clinic at El Rio Behavioral and Medical Services in addition to his work with the Southern Arizona Mental Health Corporation and his private practice in Tucson, Arizona. He has worked with sex offenders for eight years and recently published a journal article. He holds graduate degrees from the University of Arizona and is pursuing another from Arizona State University.

KEN CULLEN, M.S.W., is a senior staff member with the Sex Offender Treatment Program affiliated with CAP Behavior Foundation in New York City. He has worked in several sex offender programs.

ROBERT E. FREEMAN-LONGO, M.R.C., L.P.C., C.C.J.S., is a consultant to the Safer Society Press, part of the private, nonprofit Safer Society Foundation, Inc. He also has established an international consultancy on sexual abuser assessment, treatment, and program development, called Sexual Abuse Prevention & Education Resources International. He cofounded and was the first president of the Association for the Treatment of Sexual Abusers.

ROGER GRAVES, PH.D., works for the South Central Foundation in Alaska and has worked with Alaska Native groups for several years. He is a clinical psychologist with a special interest in forensics.

DAVID HILLMAN, PH.D., is currently a psychologist with Psychological Services, Department of Corrections, in the Te Piriti Special Treatment Unit in a prison in New Zealand.

STEPHEN M. HUDSON, PH.D., is a senior lecturer with the Department of Psychology, University of Canterbury in Christchurch, New Zealand. He also consults with the Kia Marama Special Treatment Unit in the Department of Corrections and has written numerous articles and book chapters on sexual offenders.

SAUNDRA D. JOHNSON, B.A., is in private practice in Denver, Colorado. She has many years of experience in the public and private sectors with victims and perpetrators of sexual abuse. She is a board member of the Association for the Treatment of Sexual Abusers.

ROBIN L. JONES, M.A., DIP. CLIN. PSYCH., has worked with adult and adolescent sex offenders in New Zealand and the United States. At present, she is a consultant and trainer in New York City. She was formerly the clinical director of a sex offender program in New York.

JILLIAN LARSEN, PH.D., is senior psychologist with Psychological Services, Department of Corrections. She is currently with the Victoria Therapy Centre and the Kia Marama Special Treatment Unit of the Department of Corrections in New Zealand.

PHILIP LACLAIRE, M.A., works as a therapist at a private mental-health center. In the past, he was employed at a treatment center for sexual offenders. He holds degrees in psychology. Recently, he returned to school at Chapman University to pursue another degree.

ALVIN D. LEWIS, ED.D., is a faculty member at Pima Community College and in private practice in Tucson, Arizona. For several years he was the associate clinical director of a residential treatment program for juvenile sex offenders. He is a returned Peace Corps volunteer and has presented papers throughout the United States on diversity and multiculturalism. Dr. Lewis received his M.S.W. from Temple University and doctorate from Nova Southeastern University.

CARLOS M. LOREDO, PH.D., has treated and assessed physical and sexual abuse cases for 23 years, beginning with his work at a child and family agency. He earned his Ph.D. in 1978 and has been a licensed practicing psychologist for 20 years. He has conducted a juvenile sex offender program for Travis County Juvenile Court (Austin, Texas) for 15 years and has a private practice where he sees children, adolescents, adults, and families.

GARRY H. MCFARLANE-NATHAN, M.A., DIP. CLIN. PSYCH., is a psychologist with Psychological Services, Department of Corrections, in Auckland, New Zealand. He has worked with sex offenders for many years and has been affiliated with a special prison program for the major population.

GAYANE MINASIAN, M.A., received her undergraduate degree in psychology from UCLA and her M.A. in psychology from San Diego State University. She is a doctoral candidate in the School of Psychology with a minor in clinical psychology at the University of Arizona. Currently she is a therapist with Southern Arizona Mental Health Center in Tucson, Arizona.

PAUL ROBERTSON, PH.D., is affiliated with the Te Piriti Special Treatment Unit, Psychological Services, Department of Corrections and the National Centre for Treatment Development (Alcohol, Drugs & Addiction) at the Christchurch School of Medicine in New Zealand.

KAREN THOMASSON, M.D., received her medical degree from the University of Arizona. For several years, she worked with the Navajo Nation and provided psychiatric and counseling services to sex offenders. Currently, she is in private practice in Farmington, New Mexico.

SHELDON TRAVIN, M.D., is associate director of the Department of Psychiatry at the Bronx-Lebanon Hospital Center. He is interested in cultural aspects in the treatment of sex offenders and has coauthored several articles on sex offenders.

MARY H.S. WELCH, ED.D., is a clinical psychologist in private practice and works as a school psychologist on the East Coast of the United States.

MYRNA WYSE, L.C.S.W., is a clinical social worker in private practice in Cortez, Colorado. She received her graduate education at the University of Denver and has specialized in family therapy since 1962. Initially involved in working with victims of sexual abuse, she has turned her attention to the treatment of sexual offenders. In addition to her private practice in Cortez, she is currently working at the Northern Navajo Medical Center in Shiprock, New Mexico, where she is implementing a program for the treatment of sexual offenders.

# Part I
# *Overview*

# 1 A Paradigm for Culturally Relevant Sexual Abuser Treatment: An International Perspective

Robin L. Jones, M.A., Dip. Clin. Psych.
Carlos M. Loredo, Ph.D.
Saundra D. Johnson, B.A.
Garry H. McFarlane-Nathan, M.A., Dip. Clin. Psych.

Some noticeable gaps and paradoxes become apparent in the sexual abuser treatment field when we raise the issue of cultural diversity. First, despite a healthy and proliferating literature on issues such as etiology, treatment, and prevention of sexual abuse, there has been scant attention to culture-specific contributions and influences for different ethnic groups. Second, while a vast majority of the architects of the sexual abuser treatment field in Western countries are members of the dominant cultural group (Anglo-European), it is ethnic minority and socioeconomically disadvantaged peoples who are significantly overrepresented in the criminal justice system and the sexual offender client group. Third, despite numerous studies evaluating the efficacy of sexual abuser treatment, little attention has been paid to its relative outcomes for different ethnic groups. Equal effectiveness across cultures cannot be assumed; indeed, outcome studies of traditional psychotherapy (which has evolved within an Anglo-European values base) consistently indicate poorer treatment outcomes for minority and socioeconomically disadvantaged clients. There is no obvious reason to suggest that the sexual offense–specific segment of psychotherapy fares any better.

These observations raise some important questions. What barriers have prevented a diversity of cultural perspectives from being integrated into existing sexual offender literature and knowledge? What alternative cultural processes, thus far obscured or marginalized, need to be articulated in the mainstream literature on sexual offending? How might the barriers be overcome, to facilitate an inclusive knowledge base and nurture programs that are responsive to cultural differences?

This chapter offers some preliminary concepts and frameworks for integrating cultural knowledge into the sexual offender treatment field. It draws from the knowledge and experiences of the authors, representing four different ethnic groups and six different sexual offender treatment settings in two different countries.

Due to space constraints, we have taken the view that minority groups share similar experiences within an Anglo-European–dominated society. Culture-specific examples are offered as illustrations of key points rather than as extensive sources of culture-specific information that stands alone. Other chapters in this book offer the necessary levels of detail specific to a range of minority ethnic groups, including those of the African-American, Latino, and New Zealand Māori contributors to this chapter.

# Barriers to the Development of Cross-Cultural Knowledge in the Sexual Offender Treatment Field

*Institutional Racism*

Institutional racism may be defined as organizational culture and management systems that operate according to a monocultural perspective. It permeates all the institutions in our society, including education, mental health, and the criminal justice system. In sexual offender work, institutional racism supports the status and power differences that determine minority overrepresentation in the client population and minority underrepresentation in higher positions, both educationally and occupationally. Thus it is one of the primary vehicles by which minority cultures and people are marginalized. It is also the most fundamental of all barriers to the development and integration of diverse values and perspectives within the sexual offender treatment field.

Institutional racism perpetuates itself in myriad ways. For example, if sexual offender treatment outcomes are — as we later predict — poorer for minority clients, status differences between minorities and members of the dominant culture will mediate against this disparity being rapidly articulated or remediated, since minority persons, to whom the unaddressed needs will be most immediately evident, are likely to hold the least power and influence in the system. At the same time, it will be members of the dominant culture who, in spite of coming from a position of less experiential knowledge of minority issues, will have greater power to determine the organization's position on cultural issues and the direction and rate of change.

At a broader level, when the largest institutions in our society, such as the federal and state governments, do not allocate resources in ways that benefit the members of society in greatest need, minority peoples will be disproportionately affected. The current political climate of cutbacks in government funding for social service and criminal justice programs threatens the survival of many sexual offender treatment programs. Since minorities are often overrepresented in these systems, this process of inequitable resource distribution represents another form of institutional racism. Even programs with staff who are highly motivated to address cultural issues will not be in a strong position to do so, since the development of cultural initiatives in programs generally requires a small but significant increase in program resources (e.g., salaries of cultural consultants or advisors). When programs are struggling on existing budgets that are already too slim, an outlay of money and staff time to address cultural issues in the program is likely to appear unrealistic.

*Ethnocentrism*

In any society that tolerates institutional racism, we contend that ethnocentrism is a primary process by which nondominant cultural knowledge is marginalized. Brislin (1990) defines ethnocentrism as the process of using standards from one's own cultural background to judge and draw conclusions about people from other cultures. Although it is often described as a culturally universal phenomenon, minority social scientists have often cautioned that because of power differences between dominant and minority groups and minority self-deprecation or idealization of the dominant culture, ethnocentrism is generally stronger among members of the dominant group (e.g., McFarlane-Nathan, 1994; Comas-Díaz & Griffith,

1988). The following sections briefly examine how, at both systemic and individual levels, ethnocentrism has inhibited the integration of minority cultural knowledge into contemporary models of sexual abuser treatment.

## SYSTEMIC AND PROFESSIONAL ETHNOCENTRISM

Psychology as a discipline has often been charged with ethnocentrism to the core of its defining assumptions, concepts, and methods (Brislin, 1990; Comas-Díaz & Griffith, 1988; Warwick, 1980). In particular, psychology has tended to de-emphasize culture-specific factors in favor of variables assumed to be culture-general or universal, while at the same time representing and relying upon a predominantly Anglo-European knowledge base and values orientation. While professional psychology has recently begun to address the need for training in multiculturalism, such initiatives are still usually limited to a small part of the curriculum. Since multiculturalism in professional psychology is clearly in its infancy, we can expect sexual offender treatment to be fundamentally ethnocentric to the extent that it has evolved from culturally encapsulated disciplines.

Certainly it is true that contemporary models of sexual abuser treatment have been developed within Anglo cultural frameworks. Due to minority overrepresentation in the criminal justice system, these models have been applied cross-culturally, even though the cultural backgrounds of minority clients differ not only from those of most treatment providers but also from the treatment models themselves. Whether this has occurred due to ethnocentrism at a higher systemic level (e.g., programs were not sufficiently funded to offer services specific to the needs of minority clients) or due to a more directly visible ethnocentric belief among Anglo academics and practitioners that "what works for us should work for you," the net result has been the same. Anglo-oriented treatment models have been delivered to minorities on the untested and unstated assumption that they will be similarly effective.

This process has been especially prevalent in adult sexual offender treatment, which has generally converged upon psychology's highly Anglicized cognitive behavioral methods as the treatment of choice. Ethnocentric bias is a little less apparent in treatment models for younger (juvenile) sexual offenders, which, although arguably less coherent at a theoretical level, have had a more interdisciplinary genesis and thus offer multisystemic approaches that are potentially compatible with a wider range of cultural values and worldviews than a strictly cognitive-behavioral approach.

It is also important to consider that the problem with applying Western conceptual models cross-culturally may not always stem from the models themselves, but rather from their application within the dominant cultural context, thereby making them less valid for the belief systems and behavioral repertoire within which other-culture clients operate. Clinicians may, therefore, use their own cultural norms as criteria to assess other-cultural behaviors, cognitive distortions, and precipitants to offense behaviors. This brings us to the issue of individual ethnocentrism.

## INDIVIDUAL ETHNOCENTRISM

Ethnocentrism also operates at an individual level, by which people explicitly or implicitly judge others according to their own standards and worldviews. It most often occurs in sexual offender treatment when members of the dominant culture use methods and techniques from their own cultural context in their work with minority clients and assume that they will be equally meaningful and relevant.

This stance reflects a range of ethnocentric assumptions and processes. One is the idea that the issues and concerns being dealt with in treatment somehow transcend cultural differences or operate purely at the level of cultural universals ("after all, everyone has thoughts, feelings, and behaviors; every sexual offender, regardless of race, color, or creed, is still a sexual offender").

Another process is an unawareness of the existence of other perspectives on issues related to one's work. Many Anglo clinicians and academics simply have not had the level of cross-cultural experience to realize that their perspective has a culture-specific basis of its own and that other cultural perspectives exist that could produce different theories, methods, or techniques. One example is the reluctance of most contemporary Anglo models of treatment to address the spiritual dimension, in spite of repeated indications from many minority groups that spirituality is a legitimate and important part of their worldview. This "blindness" to other worldviews is part of the essence of ethnocentrism among members of the dominant culture, especially when class differences are operating as well, since the "exclusivity" associated with the middle and upper middle class further insulates members of the dominant culture from minority people. It is important to note that this position produces outcomes indistinguishable from an explicit stance of cultural superiority, even if it arises out of unawareness rather than intentional racism.

Also contributing to ethnocentrism at an individual level may be assumptions about the scope of empathy as a therapeutic tool. While empathy overcomes many areas of difference between therapists and their clients, and is therefore one of the most effective ingredients of psychotherapy, we contend that empathy is necessary but not sufficient to overcome cultural differences between therapists and their clients. The construct of empathy involves not only emotional concern about a person's situation but also the ability to accurately view that situation from the other person's perspective (Marshall, Hudson, Jones, & Fernandez, 1994). In turn, accurate perspective-taking demands a depth of knowledge and understanding of the other person's worldview, which is likely to be constricted in cross-cultural situations due to (1) the fact that persons from the dominant culture are not required to adapt to minority cultures for basic survival, and can therefore substantially choose whether or not to learn about minority perspectives; and (2) the existence of systemic ethnocentric biases in education and the workplace, which means that even those motivated to learn about minority perspectives will be unlikely to have access to extensive culture-specific training in their education or on the job and thus must rely largely on life experience. Renfrey (1992) identifies this situation as contextual illiteracy, noting that one cannot empathize with, assess, or treat processes of which one is unaware.

In a similar vein, Bennett (1996) points out how empathy is often ethnocentrically conceived according to the "golden rule" that one should "treat others as you would have them treat you," a rule that is insufficient in cross-cultural interactions, because it assumes similarities in values, experiences, and needs that may not exist. Thus Bennett offers the "platinum rule" for cross-cultural work: "treat others as they would have you treat them." This rule allows for the existence of differences and demands that the therapist step outside of an ethnocentric position by actively learning about the client's worldview — essentially, to become "contextually literate."

## The Apparent Success of Sexual Offender Treatment

The lack of direct attention to cultural factors in models of sexual offender treatment, especially for adults, may also be accounted for at least in part by the moderate levels of success reported for existing models of sexual offender treatment overall (Marshall, Ward, Jones, Johnson, & Barbaree, 1991). Given that minority offenders are generally present in treatment populations, professionals in the field may have assumed that the treatment was working as satisfactorily for them as for others. However, it is also possible that a positive response by nonminority offenders has masked a poorer treatment response for minorities. The lack of cross-cultural differentiation in outcome studies makes this an open question, and at least two factors support it as a hypothesis.

First, we can expect greater treatment success for clients whose cultural values and worldview are supported by the treatment model and knowledge base of the therapy staff. Currently this continuity exists for most Anglo clients in contemporary sexual abuser treatment programs, but not for most minority offenders. Second, for Anglo clients there is less need to articulate cultural factors in the etiology of offending. Culture-specific variables are less likely to have explanatory value for Anglo clients, since membership in the dominant culture is likely to be a protective factor rather than a source of potential vulnerability toward any form of social ill, be it substance abuse, suicide, or sexual abusing.

## Insufficient Cross-cultural Knowledge and Skills

Many members of the dominant culture working in the field of sexual abuser treatment increasingly recognize that their treatment strategies need to reflect the cultural values and worldviews of the clients they serve, but when faced with a diverse client group, they still lack the knowledge and skills to develop and provide such services. The enduring effects of institutional racism and systemic ethnocentrism reinforce this deficit by curtailing the breadth of available learning opportunities. For example, program directors and researchers are unlikely to have many minority colleagues or superiors who can advise them in this area, since their Anglo colleagues are unlikely to have that cultural depth of knowledge. And the literature still offers little practical or theoretical material in the sexual offender treatment field on these issues.

## Emotional Responses to "the Race Issue"

One of the authors is reminded of an interaction between two colleagues in New York: A Jewish man in his 20s and an African-American man in his 40s were commenting on the extent of poverty among many of the African-American families referred. The conversation turned to the historical backdrop, including the legacy of slavery, and the efforts of the civil rights movement. The Jewish psychologist said that he was frustrated by the fact that his people had been active in the civil rights movement despite not having even been in America during much of the period of slavery, yet were still accused of perpetrating institutional racism. The African-American psychologist responded that despite their political activism, the Jewish people could still return home from the protests to safe neighborhoods, whereas the dangerous streets were the only homes the Black Americans had. Thus, even when people were making the effort to right the wrongs, at a material level the usual inequities continued to prevail.

In culturally diverse countries, nearly everyone has to develop a point of view about "race," because ethnicity, like gender, is such a fundamental part of human identity. It is an emotionally charged subject, due to the differing, sometimes opposing, stakes that people hold in regard to it. Therefore, efforts to address cultural issues in the workplace — such as in sexual offender treatment programs — will be likely to arouse emotional responses in people. The nature of the feelings generated may be very different for members of the dominant culture, compared with the minority view.

For Anglo professionals, the prospect of developing greater cultural competence may be associated with anxiety about unfamiliarity and change. For some, this might include fear that a lack of knowledge or discriminatory attitudes and beliefs will be exposed, or concern about professional identity. Thus the easiest option for some nonminority staff may be to maintain an ethnocentric stance, which does not acknowledge the need for change, but rather expects minority clients (and staff) to assimilate. Persons maintaining this position may hold on to the belief that "science is objective" and therefore that psychological models of treatment are unbiased, despite mounting evidence to the contrary; or they may simply assign a low priority to the need to address cultural issues in their work.

While some resistance is to be expected, there will obviously be a range of levels of commitment and awareness of the need for such change among Anglo professionals in the field. Anglo staff who have developed an informed multicultural commitment may be in a particularly strong position to initiate change among their more resistant Anglo colleagues, since their views will be less easily dismissed as "pulling the race card" or appealing purely to self-interest.

Minority professionals may also feel some anxieties, but for very different reasons. For example, in New Zealand, Māori professionals may be concerned that they are expected unconditionally to have a breadth and depth of cultural knowledge, in spite of the fact that Māori deculturation has been a direct — and historically intended — result of European colonization. Or minority staff may be concerned that they will be expected to produce impossible amounts of change in environments where they are culturally isolated and already overworked from being assigned all the minority cases.

Others, especially those who do possess a wealth of knowledge about their culture, may fear that the information, if shared, will be naively applied by nonminorities, or even deliberately misused to further discriminate against minority clients (Fontes, 1995). For example, in one part of a bicultural therapy project in New Zealand (described in Larsen, Robertson, Hillman, & Hudson, 1998), Māori elders and healers have been training Anglo psychologists who work with Māori clients as an interim measure until enough Māori are in the system to do this work themselves. There was significant Māori opposition to this concept at first. Accordingly, very specific parameters have been defined for the project, to guard against Māori knowledge being misused.

Minority people may also feel an accompanying sense of acknowledgment, validation, and support if the efforts to address cultural issues are well managed in the workplace. In the early and mid-1990s, for example, all government departments in New Zealand launched widespread bicultural training initiatives. Since participation was mandatory, the programs managed to reach even those least motivated to voluntarily address cultural issues in their work. The programs directly addressed people's anxieties and concerns and used strategies deliberately designed to reduce defensiveness, such as nonjudgmental but honest accounts of history and participatory, collaborative planning for change.

## Cultural Influences and Processes in Sexual Offender Treatment

This section highlights some culture-specific issues and concerns for minority clients that either have a role in the development and maintenance of sexual offending or are likely to have an impact on the treatment process itself. Many of these issues do not exist in the same way for nonminority clients. Due to barriers such as those outlined in the previous section, many culture-specific issues have not been sufficiently visible or accessible to social scientists from the dominant culture.

As well as identifying a new range of offense precursors and treatment needs, a clear understanding of cultural factors will also illuminate particular areas of strength and resilience that have enabled minority peoples to survive in spite of the previously noted barriers and difficulties. This resilience and strength can be utilized and reinforced in the treatment effort and can become a useful tool for the clinician. There is a considerable need for issues such as these to be integrated into mainstream literature on sexual offending in order to better meet the needs of minority clients.

We would like to emphasize that the issues discussed below are just a subset of the true range of cultural contributors that exist. We have confined our discussion to those that have been most immediately evident in our work and to those that have already been articulated in broader psychotherapy but not yet tailored to the sexual offender literature.

### Sociohistorical Factors, Acculturation, and Racism

Most minority groups in countries such as the United States and New Zealand live with a common historical theme of cultural loss and marginalization, arising from histories of colonization, slavery, and/or migration. This is coupled with the need for minorities to acculturate to the dominant society in order to survive. We contend that, for minority sexual offenders, the residues of these histories and the ongoing acculturation stresses are integrally related to their propensity to offend. If unaddressed, these issues may inhibit a positive response to treatment. Residues from historical trauma become visible in the form of poorer adjustment and performance for minorities on almost every economic and social indicator, as statistics on poverty, school failure, unemployment, crime, child abuse, and other social problems attest.

Studies on acculturation stress have identified a range of moderating variables: degree of similarity between the two cultures, extent to which culturally valued traditions can be maintained in the new country, voluntariness of the intercultural contact, and degree of acceptance of the minority group by the dominant group. The latter is a particularly important moderating variable. It determines the extent and accessibility of positive acculturative opportunities and, correspondingly, the level of institutional (and personal) racism that minority groups will face. It is also a factor over which minority groups themselves have little or no control. Insufficient access to quality affordable housing, health care, education, and employment and discriminatory immigration and criminal justice policies are just a few examples of ongoing vehicles for institutional racism in the United States, which continue to contribute to the acculturation stress of minorities. The minority groups who are doing least well socially and economically are those for whom the moderating variables for acculturation stress have failed to provide a protective influence.

For example, when we consider these factors for African Americans, we see that few if any of the moderating factors provide a protective influence. The legacy of slavery caused many culturally valued African traditions to be lost. Intercultural contact with Europeans was involuntary. People of African descent were placed into a culture that differed radically from their own. Black status in the new country was defined on explicitly racist principles, including an assumption of racial inferiority. All these factors continue to have a significant impact on African Americans today.

Or, for Māori in New Zealand, the history of colonization caused intercultural contact with Europeans that was involuntary, and the colonization process damaged culturally important traditions in interconnected areas such as land, language, spirituality, family organization, and economic livelihood. Under conditions such as these, the process of acculturating to the dominant society is much more perilous than, say, for Irish, Dutch, Italian, or Polish immigrants to the United States or New Zealand, who migrated voluntarily and did not face racism based on color, and whose cultures of origin overlapped to some extent with the culture of the dominant group.

For many minority persons, the above factors combine to create a pattern of responses variously referred to as "inherited anger" (Ertz, 1994) or "historical hostility" (Vontress & Epp, 1997), involving emotions and behaviors associated with anger, hopelessness, and a paranoid perception of discrimination in most cross-racial encounters. At the heart of this anger is an ever-present fear of the pain of oppression. Consistent with this view is the observation from several sociopolitical authors (e.g., Cose, 1993; Steele, 1991) that the ability to respond nondestructively to high levels of anger is a challenge facing potentially all minority persons, on account of constant and ongoing experiences of racism.

Although the preceding analysis helps demonstrate that a vast range of stresses is uniquely associated with minority status, the relevance to minority sexual offending still needs to be articulated. We contend that these influences contribute directly to the predisposing factors in the etiological model and then filter down to become part of the precipitating and maintaining factors as well.

The sexual offender treatment field has long recognized a perceived need for power and control as one of the core factors motivating sexual aggression. Legacies of marginalization and loss have stripped away traditionally sanctioned means for gaining power and control in minority communities, and this has had an especially destructive effect upon minority men. In African-American culture, the need to regain power and control has become a significant preoccupation for young males, resulting in the development of increasingly violent definitions of masculinity. Extreme manifestations of sexual aggression and violence in Black communities represent increasingly distorted and desperate efforts to compensate for this lack of power and control. These dynamics are often misunderstood by lawmakers, treatment providers, and other system representatives, resulting in prejudiced or misguided responses that perpetuate the cycle of oppression and inherited anger and contribute to the maintenance of compensatory behaviors such as sexual offending.

Institutional racism also dictates that minority offenders will be more likely to be living in poverty. Especially when combined with acculturation stresses, racism, and the corrosive effects of historical hostility, many psychosocial problems associated with poverty translate quite directly into vulnerabilities toward offending. Family chaos, neglect, victimization, exposure to violence and abuse, substance abuse, and higher rates of traumatic experiences of all kinds are just a few examples. These factors produce higher rates of cognitive styles associated with offense risk, such as impulsive decision making, low empathy, and an external locus of control. They also produce high-risk emotional states such as anger, loneliness, and feelings of powerlessness and inadequacy, which again fuel the need for compensatory behaviors such as sexual offending and violence.

Thus there are multiple pathways by which factors associated with culture-specific history, acculturation, and racism may converge and contribute to sexual offending. It is important to note that while these factors produce some offense precursors that are substantially the same as those of nonminority offenders (e.g., exposure to violence, victimization history, anger), their origins are different, and effective treatment responses need to acknowledge and be responsive to these differences. There are also some offense precursors that are tied so directly to the stress of minority status that they simply do not exist for sexual offenders from the dominant culture and thus may have been substantially overlooked in existing treatment responses. These include historical hostility, language barriers, ethnic identity conflicts, and intergenerational differences in the rate of acculturation to dominant society norms and values on issues such as sexuality.

### Racial/Ethnic Identity Issues in Treatment

The identity concerns of members of the dominant culture differ from the identity concerns of minorities. Minority individuals are especially vulnerable to ethnic identity conflicts, due to the deep and lasting effects of racism and cultural discontinuity arising from histories of slavery, colonization, and migration. Ethnic identity concerns are also of special significance to biracial clients — a growing demographic group — due to the complexities of identifying with two distinct ethnic groups.

Theoretical literature on identity development has implications for sexual offender treatment in at least two areas: first, the potential role of ethnic identity conflicts in the development and maintenance of sexual offending, and second, the issue of culture matching between therapists and clients in the delivery of sexual offender treatment services.

Weinrich (1988) defines ethnic identity as a dynamic set of processes by which people construct and reconstruct their view of themselves, in relation to their own cultural and racial group. The nature of one's ethnic identity thus depends on what types of identifications people make with their own people and with people from other cultures. Ethnic identity conflict arises when there are too many conflictual identifications that cannot be easily resolved. Examples include empathizing with someone similar to oneself while at the same time wishing to be dissociated from what that person represents, or gaining a sense of pride from membership in one's ethnic group while at the same time seeing that group denigrated in the media. These are commonplace experiences for minority peoples. A conflicted ethnic identity may be a very natural response to repeated experiences of racism and has obvious negative implications for self-esteem and social functioning, both of which are strongly associated with a propensity toward sexual offending.

Ethnic identity issues also have implications for culture matching in the delivery of clinical services of all kinds, including sexual offender treatment. These implications are clearly articulated for general psychotherapy in a five-stage model of racial/cultural identity development proposed by Sue and Sue (1990). The model reflects a gradual (not necessarily linear) transition from racial self-deprecation and idealization of the dominant culture in the first stage, to appreciation of one's own cultural group and selective appreciation of the dominant culture in the final stage, accompanied by an awareness of how White racism also damages White people. The model also has implications for White identity development, with pure ethnocentrism characterizing the first stage and a positive, nonracist White identity defining the final stage.

Clients' preferences about the ethnicity of the therapist they wish to see and the nature of identity concerns that need to be addressed in treatment are significantly determined by the client's stage of ethnic identity development. At the same time, the therapist's own stage of ethnic identity development has a powerful influence on his or her ability to meet the client's needs. Thus Sue and Sue's model points to the need for staff education and training on cultural identity to include a self-examination component for therapists. This would allow decisions about culture matching to be based not only on client preference but also on therapist capacity to meet clients' needs.

## Sociopolitical Sources of Mistrust

For a range of reasons, minority clients may mistrust treatment to a greater extent than Anglo clients. Minority clients are more likely to have had prior interactions with the criminal justice system, welfare services, and other governmental bodies. These interactions are more likely to have been experienced as negative, coercive, or invasive. Due to the criminal nature of sexual offending and the reluctance of most offenders to seek help, there is a necessarily coercive aspect to sexual offender treatment. Coercion, however, has more salience for minority offenders than for non-minorities, as it carries more negative connotations based on past experience. This may cause minority offenders to be more hostile, suspicious, or passively resistant toward treatment, at least initially.

Another common source of mistrust arises from the fact that traditional therapy has been developed within Anglo institutions and frameworks. Some minorities therefore view therapy as "something that White people do," contributing to distrust about the motives of those offering it to their people. When placed in a broad perspective, minority people's suspicion and skepticism are not misplaced. In neglecting to take contextual factors into account, traditional therapy has at times been drastically misused in cross-cultural contexts, for example, by "helping" families and individuals adjust to poverty or by offering solutions that impose dominant cultural values while marginalizing or ignoring clients' culture-specific values and needs.

Also, there are cultural differences in the ways clients assess therapists' credibility. Clients from the dominant culture often assess therapist credibility according to reputation, education, and technical competence, whereas minority clients are more likely to assess credibility according to demonstrated level of comfort with, knowledge about, and understanding of the client's worldview. Indeed, an emphasis on reputation and training may sometimes have the reverse effect for minorities and contribute to distrust by emphasizing the therapist's immersion in a system to which minority clients may feel they do not belong.

For minority sexual offenders in treatment, mistrust of the dominant culture has serious implications for rapport, program completion, and treatment success. Treatment models, processes, and goals must be culturally appropriate and relevant if this mistrust is to be overcome. Culturally competent therapists will recognize such sources of mistrust and explore them as a first step in developing a therapeutic relationship, thus creating another gateway for minority clients to respond positively to treatment. Our challenge in the sexual offender treatment field is to modify and expand existing treatment approaches until they prove their relevance and appropriateness for minority clients.

*Differences in Values Orientations*

Values are part of what define and distinguish cultures from one another. While values may differ between cultures on any number of dimensions, empirical international studies by Hofstede (1984) found that the individualism-collectivism continuum explains an especially large proportion of intercultural variance. Anglo culture highly values individualism (an orientation that requires wealth), whereas many minority groups subscribe to collectivist value systems, which have their origins in economic necessity.

Cultural differences on the individualism-collectivism continuum have strong implications for therapy and sex offender treatment, since many social norms associated with sexuality, family, and social functioning are determined by values in this area. For example, in collectivist cultures, the expectation of interdependence with family and extended family is strong. Thus family problems commonly seen among sexual offenders (such as intergenerational conflicts about sexuality, or estrangements on account of sexual abuse) may have an added dimension of significance for minority clients compared with those from the dominant culture. Vertical loyalties within collectivist families are strongest; thus behavior change is more likely if superiors are consulted. This has implications about including extended family in treatment, especially on matters involving safety, such as enforcing victim access restrictions or using relapse prevention strategies. Minority clients may expect a longer-term relationship with their therapist and a higher level of intimacy than do

Anglo clients, which has implications for how professional boundaries are defined. Minority clients may also be more comfortable with unequal status relationships, which raises questions about how rapport is established. Togetherness may be valued over privacy, which may affect the appropriateness of our assumptions about our clients' social and personal needs. Future considerations may be linked more strongly to the past, which again highlights the importance of acknowledging the role of history and sociocultural issues. One clinical implication is to draw parallels between the minority group's broader experiences of oppression and the continuation of oppression within the minority client's family and community through the perpetration of sexual abuse.

Differences in help-seeking behavior may also be evident. Traditional collectivist values often dictate responses to social and mental health problems that differ vastly from the European conceptualizations of therapy. For example, rather than seeking therapy, many Latino and African-American people frequently turn to spiritual resources such as churches, mosques, or traditional healers. In New Zealand, Māori conceptualizations of health are holistic, and Māori therapy explicitly acknowledges the dimensions of *tinana* (body), *wairua* (spirituality), *hinengaro* (mind), *whānau* (family), and *turangawaewae* (land, place to stand).

A final consideration for this section is the intersection between class-bound values and culture-bound values. Given the higher rates of socioeconomic hardship among minorities, values associated with poverty and oppression are often a significant part of the clinical picture when working with minority clients. For example, Fontes (1995) notes the child-raising norms of corporal punishment and unquestioning obedience to authority in African-American, Caribbean, and Puerto Rican communities. While appearing to be "part of the culture," these characteristics may have emerged in an effort to help children survive racism, slavery, and the ongoing dangers of living in poverty. Other values associated with poverty and oppression include a present-oriented time perspective, impulsive decision making, an external locus of control, low empathy, a desire for immediate gratification, and low frustration tolerance (Taylor-Gibbs & Huang, 1989). Many of these values are associated with a propensity toward delinquency and crime, including some forms of sexual offending, and call for a different repertoire of therapeutic techniques from those needed for clients who endorse middle-class values such as delayed gratification, restraint, and future orientation. For example, immediate, action-oriented, and experiential forms of therapy, rather than more cognitively focused approaches, could become methods of choice for clients who endorse values associated with poverty such as those outlined above.

### Dimensions of Worldviews

Sue and Sue (1990) identified locus of control and locus of responsibility as two constructs of particular importance in understanding the worldviews of people from different cultural backgrounds, since they vary according to culturally mediated values and experiences. These constructs are also important to understand when doing sexual offender work, since mainstream treatment models and methods emphasize the development of an internal locus of control and an internal locus of responsibility for one's behaviors and experiences.

Studies have consistently shown that minorities score higher on external locus of control than do Anglo subjects; however, a crucial distinction between ideological control (consistent with the dominant culture's values) and personal control (the opportunity to apply these values in one's own life) has rarely been made. It turns out that minorities do not differ from Whites on control ideology, but they are more external than Whites on personal control. This reflects that although they have internalized the dominant culture's value on internal control, it cannot always be applied to their own situations, due to racism and discrimination.

In a similar way, the assumption that an internal locus of responsibility is the most adaptive worldview can be inappropriate for minority clients, especially when acculturation and discrimination are taken into account. While effective treatment must always ensure that sexual offenders do not make excuses or shift the blame for their actions, the distinction between *excuse* and *explanation* may have particular salience in understanding minority offending. Racism, discrimination, and other pressures associated with acculturation and minority status clearly are not the responsibility of minority offenders, but for many, these processes contributed directly or indirectly to their decisions to offend.

For example, many of the youthful Latino sexual offenders treated in a New York program came from first-generation migrant families in which a single parent attended school and worked one or more jobs to send money back to extended family, leaving their teenagers unsupervised and sometimes resentful of the expectation that they care for younger siblings or relatives. When other problems such as overcrowding, presence of sexually abusive adults, exposure to violence, or substance abuse also existed within these families, the teenagers' propensities to offend were directly increased. In working with the parents, it was then very helpful to utilize Taylor-Gibbs and Huang's (1989) "cultural re-frame," in which some of the predisposing factors were viewed as being due to the acculturation process rather than parental failure. This does not detract from the youth's being responsible for the final decision to offend, but it does encourage the development of an external locus of responsibility for the parts of the clinical picture where this is appropriate.

Indeed, Sue and Sue (1990) point out that to encourage an internal locus of responsibility under circumstances in which clients are dealing with acculturation, racism, and other stresses associated with minority status is to encourage a marginalized worldview in which they must accept the dominant culture's emphasis on self-responsibility, while at the same time having little real control over how they are defined by others. This in turn breeds denial of racism and a tendency toward racial self-hate, due to blaming the plight of minority people entirely on their own actions. Sue and Sue (1990) identify the ideal worldview as incorporating an internal locus of control that allows minority people to believe that they can shape events in their own lives if given the opportunity, along with an external locus of responsibility in areas of their lives where systemic barriers are operating. This worldview is not incompatible with contemporary sexual offender treatment approaches; it simply requires a broader range of underlying assumptions about personal control and responsibility.

## Differences in Language and Communication Styles

A common circumstance in the United States is the referral of a Latino family for services where the children are bilingual but the parents are not fluent in English. The New Zealand parallel is for Pacific Island families who recently migrated from islands such as Samoa or Tonga. Several issues arise if there is not a fluently bilingual member of the treatment team. Use of an interpreter or translator, even if professionally trained, is not recommended. The very need for an interpreter communicates that the therapist is not equipped to work with the client, hence compromising the therapist's credibility. This has clear implications for rapport and treatment effectiveness. Also, attempting to communicate through an interpreter is time-consuming, labor-intensive, and imprecise, given all the nonequivalencies and nuances in word meanings and tonality.

There are also difficulties when the client is expected to communicate as well as possible in his or her second language. Sexual offender treatment involves talking about highly personal, emotionally charged issues. The subject matter is at times very distressing, embarrassing, or unfamiliar to clients. Efforts to verbalize in these areas is difficult enough in a familiar language. To expect clients to do so in an unfamiliar language is setting them up to fail. In addition, many minority clients who are not fluent in the language of the dominant culture feel self-conscious about their lack of fluency, further compromising rapport and communication. These concerns highlight the need for culturally diverse, multilingual direct-service staff.

Even when the language is the same, communication styles and preferences often vary considerably between different cultural groups. Sue and Sue (1990) note how most Anglo-European groups communicate in "low-context" ways, defined as direct, linear, and more dependent on verbal and written cues, whereas communication for many minority groups is highly context-dependent, relying more on nonverbal cues, symbolic communication, and affective expression. Imagery, metaphors, and stories may be especially powerful forms of communication for minority peoples, especially if their culture originally depended on an oral tradition.

For example, whether or not they are fluent in their native language, many Māori in New Zealand intersperse Māori words into English phrases to add an emphasis or meaning for which there is no English equivalent. For African Americans, there are many subtle differences in word meanings between standard English and Black English. For some groups, there is also a proliferation of rapidly evolving street terms and phrases, generated especially by youth, that are unfamiliar to many nonminorities.

There are also considerable differences in nonverbal norms such as level of affective expressiveness and meanings attributed to such expressions. For example, emotional expressiveness may seem unreasoned or aggressive when viewed within low-context communication norms, whereas a high-context interpretation would view the same communication as indicating sincerity and commitment. Such differences in language and communication styles inevitably have an impact on cross-cultural therapy.

## Overcoming the Barriers

Thus far, we have identified a range of barriers that have inhibited the development of effective treatment responses for minority sexual offenders. We have also articulated some of the culture-specific issues and concerns that have implications for sexual offender treatment that have been largely obscured or ignored in our field. What remains is the identification of strategies to overcome the barriers, so that this diverse knowledge can be effectively integrated into the field. The enhancement of "cultural competence" is at the heart of this matter.

Lewis (1994) defined cultural competence as "a set of congruent behaviors, attitudes and policies that come together in a system or an agency, or among professionals that enable them to work effectively in cross-cultural situations" (p. 7). Lewis identified several mechanisms by which cultural competence can be increased, including promoting attitudes and beliefs that respect and value diversity; increasing cultural knowledge, resources, and skills; adapting service delivery; empowering minority people in the change process; and building in mechanisms to continually assess the impact of cultural competence initiatives in the workplace. Cultural competence thus requires systemic initiatives that not only promote and nurture change at all levels within a given setting but also measure its impact and effectiveness.

In the sections that follow, a distinction has been made between organizational initiatives and those specific to sexual offender treatment environments. The desired outcome of these efforts, at the very least, is an improvement in minority offender treatment response. Thus improvement in cultural competence is an important avenue within the field for preventing the perpetration of further sexual abuse.

*Systemic and Organizational Initiatives*

Systemic and organizational initiatives in the area of cultural competence often require policy changes, such as providing resources to expand program structure and content or revising staff hiring, promotion, and training criteria.

Without broader systemic and organizational support, individual and program-specific efforts, which affect minority clients most directly, are unlikely to have the desired level of impact. They may also come at considerable cost to the individuals attempting to initiate and maintain the changes. Many minority professionals have had this experience in work environments, where their efforts were not supported or appropriately acknowledged by the broader organization.

### DEVELOP A MISSION STATEMENT AND CULTURAL PERSPECTIVES POLICIES

Mission statements and cultural perspectives policies can be developed by institutions and organizations to reflect the importance of the cultural dimensions of the work. These can provide a blueprint for the development and implementation of multicultural initiatives within the system and can help integrate diverse perspectives into program and agency philosophy.

For example, Larsen and Hillman (1996) provided a detailed cultural perspectives policy with explicitly stated goals and objectives to guide a bicultural therapy model in New Zealand. Goals included the development of an environment that is culturally supportive of all staff, enhancement of staff's bicultural knowledge, and development of culturally relevant processes for Māori clients. Specific, clearly defined objectives were established, providing a range of mechanisms by which the goals could be achieved. The principles of this approach could be adapted to the U. S. context.

### INCREASE MINORITY REPRESENTATION AND INFLUENCE

In addition to offering a direct, immediately visible cultural connection for minority clients, strong minority presence in the workplace provides a direct source of cross-cultural learning and dialogue for nonminority staff. Fontes (1995) identified the need for Anglo professionals to seek friendships and professional relationships with healthy members of minority groups, to serve as cultural advisors and informants. The workplace may be one of the most obvious settings in which to develop such connections.

Systemic barriers continue to cause minority professionals to be underrepresented in sexual offender treatment environments. Minority staff are more likely to be in frontline positions, often in paraprofessional roles, with few opportunities to influence policy. The low numbers of and the high demand for minorities with academic qualifications considered necessary for clinical, supervisory, and management positions also contribute to this situation. This points to the need for additional (and sometimes unconventional) efforts to increase minority representation in positions of responsibility and influence.

First, recruiting efforts could be extended beyond traditional methods. For example, positions could be advertised in more than one language. Recruitment efforts could be made through minority professional organizations, colleges, media, and community outreach. Word of mouth through existing minority colleagues may be especially helpful.

Second, sufficient value needs to be placed on culture-specific knowledge when hiring. Viewing it as an essential rather than a desirable set of skills and aligning job descriptions with this emphasis may attract minority candidates with the requisite knowledge. This requires organizations to identify and assess the characteristics of cultural competence and the needs of minority clients. Having diverse interview panels would assist in this area. This has become policy on the dimensions of both race and gender for hiring in the government service in New Zealand. In New York, in a community-based setting for youth, case management positions were defined in ways that increased the likelihood of attracting minority candidates. In this program, successful past experience working with minority youth, fluency in Spanish, and knowledge of resources within the African-American and/or Latino communities were considered as important as formal educational qualifications.

Third, minority scholarships and internships could be offered to existing minority staff as an incentive for them to continue their studies if they do not already have graduate degrees. For example, in a New Zealand correctional facility, a Māori cultural consultant was hired on the strength of his bicultural competence to assist and advise a predominantly Anglo team in the provision of sex offender treatment to Māori clients. He completed his social work qualification during his first two years in the job. Since his appointment, more Māori and Pacific staff have been hired, and the bicultural competence of the non-Māori staff has increased considerably (D. Hillman, personal communication, January 1997).

Fourth, supervision and accountability structures can be developed that directly acknowledge and utilize the cultural knowledge of minority persons, both within and beyond the organization. This is discussed later in a separate section.

Once workplaces begin to succeed in diversifying their staff, a variety of new considerations will become important. First, there will be a vast range of immediate, positive effects for minority clients. In many instances, these will include more rapid development of rapport between staff and clients, the transformation of assessment and intervention procedures into language and concepts that are familiar to the client, the ability to challenge (from an informed perspective) culturally based excuses for offending, and a greater knowledge of indigenous or culture-specific resources. In addition, the very presence of minority individuals in the treatment setting will illustrate many positive things to minority clients, including the staff person's own way of negotiating systemic barriers, cultural identity issues, and the demands to be bicultural.

A second consideration is that minority staff, unlike their colleagues from the dominant culture, will be affected to varying degrees by the stresses of minority status. For example, they are likely to be exposed to a larger number of significant life stressors, either directly or through close family and friends. There will also be unique issues arising in their work with minority clients, such as "vicarious pain" and countertransference when seeing clients whose traumatic experiences are similar to their own. Or there may be complex issues having to do with trust in relationships with some clients, such as the perception that the minority clinician has compromised his or her loyalty to the group by working within a system that has oppressed minorities. Or the client may perceive barriers based on socioeconomic or identity differences between the worker and client. Thus minority staff will have a range of culture-specific supervision and support needs that must be addressed.

Third, the presence of minority staff will rapidly bring into focus the level of cultural competence of the organization and the individuals who work within it. Areas of strength and weakness will be rapidly exposed. This will have implications at both an individual level and a systemic level within the organization.

At an individual level, minority presence in the workplace will provide support and exchange of knowledge for other minority colleagues. For Anglo staff seeking to increase their knowledge, it will provide positive avenues for cross-cultural information and advice. For some, especially those who have not yet addressed their own ethnocentrism, it may also raise concerns about "reverse discrimination." Such objections fail to recognize that racial preferences have always operated in Anglo institutions — favorable to members of the dominant culture — a fact that is abundantly clear to most minority people. Such objections from members of the dominant culture underscore the need for ongoing diversity training in the workplace. It may help to emphasize that increasing minority representation is not about racial quotas or biasing job selection according to skin color or racial identification. Rather, it recognizes and affirms that all people have experiential knowledge of the cultural group to which they belong. It also acknowledges that cultural competence, like education and relevant work experience, is a necessary qualification for working cross-culturally, and that increasing minority representation is just one of several strategies for doing so.

At an organizational level, increasing minority influence will expose the "readiness" of the organization to meet the needs of minority professionals in the workplace. Organizations that are not developing in this area will not only fail to meet the needs of their minority staff but also present systemic barriers that limit their ability to effect positive change. Organizations working to increase their competence may also fail to meet the needs of minority staff, but for different reasons, such as inadvertently placing too much responsibility on them. In situations in which the number of minority staff is low, there is a high potential for burnout, not only because of a lack of cultural connections and support within the workplace but also because one person may be expected to work with all the minority clients and/or initiate all cultural initiatives for the organization. This may be due to well-intentioned but misapplied principles or to a supervisor's lack of understanding of how best to utilize minority staff, or it may arise from an avoidant or token response to the identified need. Alternatively, minority staff can be utilized in ways that are appropriate to their own needs and the needs of the organization, by contributing to the development of cultural perspectives policies, by assisting nonminority staff to increase their cross-cultural skills, and by helping to recruit more minority staff. This approach would enhance the cultural competence of the whole organization and at the same time generate support systems for minority staff. Only organizations with a high level of competence will be fully equipped to offer challenging, rewarding positions for minority staff, in well-supported situations.

INSTITUTIONALIZE DIVERSITY TRAINING

Diversity training is an important vehicle for increasing the cultural competence of staff from all ethnic backgrounds. It can have the effect of raising the cultural competence of the entire organization. It can lend new significance to the work that frontline staff are already doing with minority clients and educate managers and policy makers about other systemic changes that need to be made.

Efforts to increase bicultural or multicultural competence may be especially important for nonminority staff because their ethnocentric bias is likely to be stronger and their cross-cultural skills less developed; however, the needs of minority staff in this area should not be overlooked, in relation to both their own culture of origin and the cultures of other minority groups. Deculturation is a significant issue for many members of ethnic groups with histories of colonization or forced migration. Oppression has often contributed to interethnic conflicts or misconceptions between minority groups.

For Anglo participants, it is essential that the consciousness-raising dimension of diversity training include self-exploration of their own culture, assumptions, and racism. Anglo culture has often been neglected in such discussions or not fully recognized as a culture of its own, because its dominance allows it to surround its members so completely. For example, it may surprise many Anglo people to consider that a characteristic of their own culture is that it suffers at times from the narrowness of its own assumptions (Fontes, 1995), or that it has produced a confusing division between media portrayals of sexuality and violence and expectations about individual sexual conduct. Often, it is not until Anglo people have a clear and comprehensive understanding of their own culture that they can accurately identify and appreciate the ways in which other cultures differ from their own.

Sue and Sue (1990) identify three important features of effective diversity training. First, the material must be tailored to the needs of the participants. In our field, the information must therefore be specific to sexual offending and treatment. Training topics could include values about family and sexuality, gender roles, communication styles, culturally mediated responses to norms violations and crises such as sexual abuse, and the ability to identify and interpret the significance of broader systemic barriers in the clinical picture for minority clients. A small but growing number of trainers on diversity issues come from within the sexual offender treatment field and are thus able to tailor the issues specifically to the needs of staff working with this client group (e.g., Johnson, 1996; Loredo, 1994; Ertz, 1994).

Second, effective diversity training must combine affective, cognitive, experiential, and skills-building components. The affective component will build participants' motivation to learn. The cognitive component will facilitate the acquisition of knowledge. The experiential and skills-building components will translate knowledge into culturally competent behavior. For example, the affective component of Saundra Johnson's (1996) training materials includes video resources illustrating the links between the history of slavery and oppression and the present-day conditions that contribute to violence and sexual aggression for African-American clients. Her approach also demonstrates some of the areas of resiliency that can be harnessed in culturally appropriate treatment and affirms some of the African legacies that contribute to contemporary Black American culture and identity.

Third, effective diversity training needs to be an ongoing, mandatory, and regular aspect of people's work. Much as we would not expect our clients to learn and change their behavior on the basis of a single session, the enhancement of cultural competence among ourselves requires multiple, cumulative training opportunities for all members of staff. This may be one of the most neglected aspects of diversity training, and it is dangerous to assume that a single training opportunity or voluntary participation will produce a significant impact on the cultural competence of an organization.

Other avenues of learning can supplement diversity training. Reading and adapting cross-cultural information in the general

psychotherapy literature are useful. Broader sociopolitical literature can educate nonminority staff about the perspectives of
minority individuals, in turn allowing empathy to more effectively
bridge the cultural gap between therapist and client. Some excellent
works are those by Shelby Steele (*The Content of Our Character*),
Ellis Cose (*The Rage of a Privileged Class*), and Andrew Hacker
(*Two Nations: Black and White, Separate, Hostile, Unequal*).
Affiliation with multicultural organizations such as the Association
for Multicultural Counseling and Development or the ethnic
minority division of the American Psychological Association may
also be helpful, by providing access to valuable literature and training resources.

To help the change process gain momentum, staff incentives can
be created at an organizational level. For example, certain indices
of cultural sensitivity and expertise could be built into staff goals,
objectives, and work performance evaluations, such as the expectation that a certain number of hours of diversity training be attended
each year, or a certain number of performance targets include a
culture-specific dimension. Sue and Sue (1990) contend that the key
characteristics of cross-culturally skilled therapists fall into three
areas: self-awareness variables, the ability to understand diverse
worldviews, and the use of appropriate techniques, which are
expanded upon in their book. These could be used as a framework
for ongoing assessment of individual staff improvement and change.

### DEVELOP ALTERNATIVE SUPERVISION AND ACCOUNTABILITY STRUCTURES

The development of culturally appropriate supervision and accountability structures is part of the process of improving organizational
cultural competence. These structures provide the necessary support for minority staff and provide another avenue for enhancing
the cultural competence of all staff. They give priority and visibil-
ity to cultural issues so that they can be safely and productively
addressed in the workplace. Although the form of these structures
will depend on the specific needs and resources available in different treatment settings, they can generally be expected to include
mechanisms for peer supervision and/or consultancy.

Peer supervision opportunities specifically for the discussion of
cultural issues could be facilitated in the workplace through staff
retreats or as a part of regular team meetings. For example, in

New Zealand, Māori psychologists have a national network, and regular meetings for the local "chapters," which serves as a support system. A multiethnic team working with adolescent sexual offenders in New York utilized some of the regular staff meeting time to share and discuss sociopolitical information that had implications for working with the youth, and they discussed cultural issues and concerns for clients as a matter of course in case reviews.

Cultural consultants could be hired specifically to assist with the enhancement of cultural competence. For example, at a sexual offender treatment facility in New Zealand, the responsibilities of a Māori cultural consultant included facilitating a weekly Māori caucus with clients and staff (non-Māori could also attend), developing Māori protocols and procedures in the unit, observing all treatment groups, and advising staff on culture-specific issues arising for the Māori clients.

Senior staff could seek culture-specific supervision to guide decision making and policy development through peer supervision with minority colleagues, or they could seek regular consultation with multiethnic committees with special expertise in multicultural consulting. External supervision sources could also assist with efforts to assess and evaluate the impact of cultural initiatives.

For a comprehensive approach to developing appropriate treatment, supervision, and accountability structures with regard to both culture and gender, the reader is referred to the "Just Therapy" approach pioneered by Tamasese and Waldegrave (1993). Many of the preceding principles are consistent with their Just Therapy model.

*Program and Direct-Service Considerations*

Systemic and organizational commitment to the enhancement of cultural competence should create the mechanisms necessary for sexual offender treatment programs to specifically address the culture-specific needs of their clients. In general, this calls for an expansion, rather than a complete revision, of existing treatment models, processes, and goals. This reflects that some factors involved in sexual offending and treatment are relevant to people of all cultural backgrounds, while others are more culture-bound. It also affirms that therapeutic issues, even when similar, need to be delivered in ways that are consistent with the different value dimensions and worldviews of diverse peoples.

Program-specific areas needing expansion or adaptation include program structure, environment, content, methods, and evaluation systems. Many other chapters in this book provide culture-specific illustrations of these concepts; the following sections offer some broad principles to help guide this process of change.

EXPAND PROGRAM PHILOSOPHY AND STRUCTURE

The published literature on sexual offender treatment is dominated by a cognitive-behavioral treatment orientation, often combined with family therapy, psychoeducational, and pharmacological approaches for some populations. The general cross-cultural therapy literature, in contrast, emphasizes ecological and multisystemic approaches that, on account of acknowledging and responding to broader contextual factors, are "culturally mobile." The challenge is to identify and keep the aspects of existing treatment approaches that have good utility with minority clients, while also extending into new and sometimes unfamiliar territory. We contend that many aspects of contemporary treatment models are potentially appropriate for minority sexual offenders but that they need to be located, structurally and philosophically, within a multisystems framework.

For example, it has been frequently noted in the cross-cultural literature that active, directive treatment approaches that include the family are more compatible with minority values and norms than insight-oriented or nondirective approaches. Many aspects of cognitive-behavioral and family therapy are therefore potentially highly appropriate. The collectivist and family-oriented values of many minority groups may lend themselves especially well to the external supervisory dimension of relapse prevention.

Successfully delivering these forms of treatment to minority clients will require some changes in program structure and philosophy. For example, the therapy will need to be provided by diverse and culturally competent clinicians, and a broader range of settings may need to be considered (e.g., the home, the school, or the family's place of worship). Flexible hours may need to be offered to accommodate work schedules that a family member or offender cannot financially afford to disrupt. The clinician's definition of family may need to be expanded to include several generations and/or nonblood kin. The definition of the intervention itself may need to be broadened to include a concrete service component to assist with basic needs such as housing, drug treatment, or negotiating the legal system. Issues related to spirituality may also be important, regarding both service provision (e.g., use of clergy or indigenous healers) and client symptoms (e.g., distinguishing psychosis from a culture-bound reaction to stress).

In a similar vein, Dewey Ertz (1994), in his illuminating work with Native American sexual offenders, refers to Maslow's hierarchy of needs to illustrate how interventions for Native American clients need to be appropriately targeted. Many traditional forms of Anglo-European therapy assume that people are struggling with the higher-order "self-esteem, love and belongingness needs," whereas many minority clients, on account of economic and sociohistorical influences, are still struggling with more primary needs for physiological and psychological security, such as adequate material means and physical safety. This again emphasizes the need for treatment models that include a concrete service component.

Mechanisms to help translate these ideas into action include stating explicitly the multisystems focus in the program's mission statement and policy information and defining appropriate staffing structures with roles and responsibilities that facilitate these kinds of initiatives. For example, in New Zealand the inclusion of a cultural consultant and two community and family workers in the staffing structure for a correctional treatment facility allowed a breadth and depth of Māori protocols and practices to be incorporated into the program (D. Hillman, personal communication, January 1997). In a youthful sexual offender program in New York, half the staff were clinicians and half were intensive case managers. The case managers not only addressed the families' concrete service needs but also closely supervised and monitored the youth in the community, developed a life skills component, and co-led the therapy groups for youth and parents. A more comprehensive description of this program is available in an upcoming book (Jones, Winkler, Kacin, Salloway, & Weissman, in press). For a comprehensive account of how to integrate various treatment approaches into a multisystems framework, the reader is referred to Boyd-Franklin (1989).

ADAPT PROGRAM ENVIRONMENT

Adaptations to program environments can be an immediate and visible signal that a program can "walk its talk" about diversity issues. The key environmental principle is to communicate to minority clients that this service is able to reach out specifically to them, rather than being just another part of an impersonal social or criminal justice bureaucracy, which may be perceived as intimidating or insensitive to their needs. This message can be communicated environmentally in a range of ways.

Location is important. For community-based programs serving high proportions of minority clients, attendance tends to be better if the service is offered within the minority group's own geographic community, or within easy access to public transport. If the service is at a residential or correctional facility, family members of clients may need financial assistance to cover the cost of transport if they travel to the institution for family sessions.

The physical environment will be much more welcoming to minority clients if its design and decoration details cater to their interests and needs. Helpful touches include having telephone messages and signs in more than one language, culturally relevant posters and displays on the walls, and magazines in the waiting area that are written with minority readership in mind. In community-based settings and those serving youthful sexual offenders, a "family-friendly" environment is important. Activities and resources could be made available for children and teens, such as toys, books, computer games, or a supervised play area.

Providing food and drink can also be helpful for increasing client rapport and comfort levels, especially if the food preferences of the minority groups can be made available. Sharing food is a culturally universal way of providing hospitality and communicating that visitors and clients are valued. Food is a necessity for programs serving teen offenders, since for developmental reasons they tend to be constantly hungry. Providing food also creates opportunities to teach clients about nutrition as part of the lifestyle balance and self-care components of relapse prevention and provides a concrete response to the problem of poor nutrition commonly seen among people dealing with economic hardship. For example, one community-based youth program was located in an agency with a fully equipped kitchen, so food was always available when clients came in after school, and the parent group meetings always started or finished with an evening meal.

DIVERSIFY PROGRAM CONTENT AND METHODS

The diversification of program content and methods will evolve fairly naturally, if enough of the foregoing cultural competence initiatives are in place. Picture an organization that actively supports diversity initiatives according to clearly defined cultural perspectives policies and that makes resources available to assist programs with their own specific cultural initiatives. Picture within this organization a sexual offender treatment program with a diverse staff in both frontline and senior positions, with regular diversity education and training, and with an explicitly stated multisystems approach to treatment. Bring these people together and charge them with the task of defining and delivering services that will meet the culture-specific needs of a diverse client group, and it will become a realistic and achievable process.

Of course, for many reasons, not the least of which is the erosion of governmental support for criminal justice and social service programs, the above situation is not currently realistic in many treatment environments. Thus we are left with the prospect of making what changes we can, within the limits of existing systemic and organizational support. An overarching axiom to help guide efforts in this area is to ensure that culture-specific treatment processes are in synchrony with culture-specific treatment goals, no matter how modest the processes and goals may need to be. If the processes are appropriate but the goals are not, then an ethnocentric definition of success is imposed by the program. An example would be when minority staff are hired but they must follow a set curriculum and do not have the organization's support to address issues such as ethnic identity or acculturation. If the goals are appropriate but the processes to achieve them are not, then the treatment methods may inadvertently violate the norms of the client. This would occur, for example, if staff attempt to incorporate culture-specific matters into their treatment model but lack the requisite cultural competence themselves to carry it through and do not have access to appropriate culture-specific supervision. In both cases, the quality of services for minority clients would be severely compromised.

Following are suggestions for how the content of sexual offender programs might be altered to better meet the needs of minority clients, especially those whose ethnic groups endorse collectivist values:

1. Develop strengths-based assessment strategies, and include relevant aspects of the minority group's traditional cultural values and belief systems, such as culturally relevant risk factors and supports. For example, appropriate assessment will identify the

significance and role of issues such as ethnic identity conflict, acculturation stress, access to extended family or spiritual resources, and the influence of other systems.

2. Avoid culturally biased assessment methods, such as psychometric tests that have not been cross-culturally validated.

3. Be aware that physiological assessment methods such as plethysmography and polygraphy, invasive for clients of all ethnic backgrounds, raise additional concerns for minority clients. At a practical level, these concerns may include language differences and the cultural appropriateness of stimulus materials. At a more fundamental level, such methods may compound minority clients' existing feelings of systemic abuse or may contravene culturally mediated norms about sexuality and privacy. Decisions about whether to use physiological measures with minority clients must therefore include an understanding of the culture-specific implications.

4. Build sociocultural factors into clinical formulations and be clear about issues to do with locus of control and locus of responsibility (refer to the previous section "Dimensions of Worldviews").

5. Specify cultural needs and concerns in treatment plans and case reviews, to keep them visible.

6. Due to trust and rapport issues, do not expect to gain as much assessment information from minority clients as from Anglo clients upon initial contact. Expect a range of attitudes to authority, ranging from unquestioning deference on account of the clinician's position to hostility or challenges to the therapist's credibility on account of previous negative experiences with helping institutions. Provide crisis intervention or concrete services early in the process, if needed. This will not only help develop rapport but also provide important assessment information in alternative ways.

7. Provide information early and demystify therapy. Use collaborative, direct, practical, solution-focused methods.

8. Make special efforts to include and extend respect to male relatives and elders, such as fathers of youthful African-American or Latino offenders, or *kuia* and *kaumatua* (older and wiser women and men affiliated through family, extended family, or tribes for Māori). Especially in the African-American context, sociohistorical factors have had a particularly virulent effect on males, resulting in higher levels of estrangement from their families. Thus some programs may overlook "absent" fathers in family therapy, even though in many cases they are still potentially accessible in the

broader community. A fathers' group distinct from the usual parent groups could be a useful addition to youth programs.

9. Build traditional cultural practices into the treatment context. For example, at a New Zealand institution, all group sessions began with a traditional Māori *karakia* (prayer, proverb, or poem), which had the desired effect of focusing people on the significance of the group process. Completion of treatment was marked by a *poroporoake*, a traditional Māori farewell ceremony, incorporating song, prayer, speeches, and the sharing of traditional food.

10. Let the values of the minority culture guide aspects of the therapeutic relationship and therapeutic methods, when appropriate. For example, the importance of external, socially mediated controls over behavior and the issues of family shame arising from the offenses of some clients may be harnessed in all kinds of ways in the therapeutic process (e.g., to increase the treatment motivation of a reluctant client, to expand the scope of victim empathy, or to enlist family support for a client's relapse prevention plan).

11. Be prepared to negotiate conflicts between standard intervention practices and the cultural values of clients, especially when these conflicts are potentially counterproductive to effective treatment. The definition of professional boundaries is one area in which such conflicts often arise. One example is about gift giving. In many cases, agency policies, licensing standards, and/or professional codes of ethics prohibit therapists from accepting gifts from clients. In some cultures, such as Latino, Native American, and Māori, the offer of a gift signifies respect and appreciation for a person (in this case, the therapist). Refusal of such a gift could be considered highly insulting, although cultural standards could preclude discussion of the "insult," since it would be considered insensitive to confront such an issue. Similarly, invitations to social functions and ceremonies within Latino and other cultures represent an acceptance as "family." Again, there may be practice proscriptions against clinicians attending "social" functions with their clients. These invitations to outsiders are not lightly offered and represent a high regard for someone outside their social circle. Refusal of such an honor can be detrimental to the therapeutic process and can significantly close off therapists' access to clients and their families.

12. Be aware of cultural influences on sexual attitudes and beliefs, including gender issues in the therapeutic relationship.

13. Utilize existing culture-specific resources that have already been articulated in the field; for example, Tikanga Māori therapy

principles for Māori offenders in New Zealand (McFarlane-Nathan, 1994), or Saundra Johnson's (1996) Tree Life Cycle as an analogy for the offense cycle and the treatment process for African-American offenders.

14. When teaching skills, especially in group settings, use methods that are consistent with traditional and contemporary methods of acquiring knowledge for the cultures represented in the group. For example, youthful offenders of all ethnicities may be receptive to video as a medium and the use of role playing and videotaped feedback. Many youth, especially minorities, may be especially familiar with the use of rhyming and rapping. They may also prefer active, demonstrative methods such as psychodrama and art over more traditional reading and writing tasks, at least partly because they are more likely than nonminority youth to have negative associations with school. Adult offenders may respond especially well to methods that are traditional to their culture (such as storytelling) or to the use of imagery and metaphor or to exploring parallels between their sexually abusive behavior and their history as a people, especially if treatment can be conducted in their language of origin.

15. Incorporate culturally relevant local events into the therapeutic process to illustrate or explore certain points for offenders of all ages. For nonminority staff, this may mean accessing minority media such as newspapers and magazines geared toward a cultural group that is not their own to gain more than one slant on a particular issue and to find out about events not publicized in the mainstream media. Incidents such as the deaths of Tupac Shakur and Biggie Smalls and a 1996 case of police brutality against an African-American youth in Brooklyn are examples of incidents that provided extensive material in youth group sessions in a New York program on issues as diverse as anger management, empathy, problem solving, and values clarification.

16. Maintain a flexible approach to the program curriculum to accommodate new treatment processes and goals, in response to the identification of additional needs. For example, a youth program in New York found it necessary to incorporate some specific material on coping with grief and loss, since so many of the youth and families had lost parents and significant others to drug abuse, HIV infection, and incarceration.

17. Provide an effective response to significant culture-specific issues. Issues related to deculturation are likely to be especially relevant for indigenous, colonized peoples such as Native Americans in the United States and Māori in New Zealand. The endorsement of

destructive "cultural" and gender norms is an issue for many African-American youth. Acculturation stress and intergenerational conflicts are often significant for migrant groups such as Latino peoples in the United States, and Pacific peoples in New Zealand. One possibility would be to have a separate group devoted to strengthening ethnic identity and enhancing clients' resilience to systemic barriers. The use of indigenous persons within and beyond the organization who can educate people about their own culture and offer positive strategies for acculturation is central to such a group. Linking progress in these areas to relapse prevention principles is also important.

## UNDERTAKE RESEARCH AND EVALUATION OF CULTURAL INITIATIVES

At least two issues arise with regard to research and evaluation of cultural initiatives. First, how shall we determine ethnic differences in the response to existing forms of sexual offender treatment? The thesis of this chapter rests on the assumption that minority sexual offenders' treatment response is consistent with the generally poorer response of minority client populations reported in the general psychotherapy literature. And while this commonsense assumption also reflects a vast body of minority literature, knowledge, and experience, for several reasons it still needs to be scientifically quantified and understood directly within our field. One reason is that empirical evidence is one of the key vehicles by which theories are validated in Anglo-oriented social science. Empirical research will thus strengthen the commitment to diversity and cultural competence initiatives within the dominant culture. Also, such research will create a clearly specified baseline against which the impact of future cultural competence efforts can be measured.

A second issue is how best to measure the impact of cultural initiatives as they become more broadly implemented in the field. Such evaluation is a vehicle by which competence initiatives can be refined and improved to continually upgrade services to minority clients.

The fact that these questions have not already been substantially addressed within the sexual offender treatment field brings us back to the points made at the beginning of this chapter and reflects the ethnocentrism of disciplines that have contributed to our field. Evaluation research on cultural initiatives brings an empirical dimension to an area that has been neglected but at the same time politicized and has thus been vulnerable to distortions and mis-conceptions that scientific research should help to ameliorate.

Recent interest in addressing cultural needs in treatment and research demonstrates a welcome step in the direction of multicul-tural development and change in disciplines such as psychology. At the same time, there are a range of ways in which scientific method and its findings can be brought to bear on cross-cultural matters. Concerns about the imposition of ethnocentric methods in treat-ment apply also to research. Thus it is very important not to repeat history by inadvertently using research in ways that contribute to the ongoing oppression of minority peoples.

For example, if empirical studies were to confirm (as we suspect) that minority clients generally respond less well to community-based treatments and relapse at higher rates, the information could be misused to argue in favor of longer and more severe sentences for minority offenders (a sentencing practice that already exists) or to support theories about racial inferiority. Alternatively, such research findings could be positively used in innumerable ways; for example, to demonstrate unequivocally the need for greater cul-tural competence in treatment settings, to identify and articulate existing programmatic weaknesses and needs, to highlight the role of systemic barriers that have a differential impact on minorities, or to identify resiliency factors in the minority clients for whom the treatment outcome was positive.

In spite of existing gaps, the sexual offender treatment field is in a strong position to address the clinical and research issues in the enhancement of cultural competence. Cognitive-behavioral approaches, which dominate the field, lend themselves especially well to research. The community is relatively cohesive and yet international, with annual conferences convened by organizations such as the Association for the Treatment of Sexual Abusers (ATSA) and the National Adolescent Perpetrator Network (NAPN), which attract influential people in the field from all over North America and as far away as Australia, New Zealand, the United Kingdom, and several European countries. National databases are emerging, through both NAPN and the Safer Society Foundation. Such orga-nizations are also in a good position to aggressively promote the development and distribution of research and clinical information on diversity issues in their journals and other materials they choose to publish. A growing number of minority and nonminority pro-fessionals with an active commitment to diversity issues hold influential positions in the field, including many of the contributors to this book. Because minority clients continue to be overrepresented in identified sexual offender populations, the level of need for these initiatives continues to be high.

A recommended starting point in the field would be clear specification of the following, in all evaluative sexual offender research: (1) details of ethnicity for the clients being studied, (2) qualitative information on the extent (if any) to which the program developed cultural initiatives, and (3) treatment outcomes distinguished for ethnicity. This would help provide baseline information and would require very little modification to the content of contemporary research approaches. It would also eventually allow a mini metaanalysis to determine whether effect size for minorities is related to organizational cultural competence.

A wide range of additional existing variables could be measured with little extra effort, such as differential client retention rates according to ethnicity, and differential levels of within-treatment change. It may be, for example, that current approaches to victim empathy training are reasonably effective for many minorities, but anger management approaches are not.

More difficult would be the articulation and measurement of change on more culture-specific variables not yet widely acknowledged in the sexual offender research literature, such as ethnic identity issues for clients or various measures of cultural competence for treatment providers and organizations. The specification of methods by which this information would be gathered is also fraught with potential pitfalls. However, we contend that if the research process is defined and spearheaded by culturally competent social scientists (many of whom will be minorities), contextual illiteracy will be less of a problem, and the research process will be more likely to be consistent with minority needs and values.

In particular, the "emic" and "cultural science" dimensions of research need to be integrated into the "etic" and "natural science" approaches that currently dominate in psychological research. (For detailed accounts of this dichotomy, refer to Guthrie, 1979, or Marsella, 1979.) This expansion of emphasis parallels the expanded vision recommended in the clinical work and, in the research context, entails utilizing the qualitative methods of allied disciplines such as sociology, education, and ethnic psychology to augment more typical quantitative methods.

There will also be a need for some new ethical guidelines when cultural differences are made visible in research. Warwick (1980) provides an excellent outline of ethical considerations when studying minority groups, including guidelines for the responsible inclusion of minority researchers and cultural informants, unique concerns to do with consent and safety, credit and information distribution issues, and the development of methods to make ethnocentric biases and political influences explicit in the work. These guidelines could be reviewed and integrated into professional codes of ethics or tailored specifically to research involving sexual offenders and then disseminated within the field.

Currently being developed in New Zealand is a research framework for evaluating the Bicultural Therapy Project and other corrections programs for Māori. Such evaluations represent a partnership between Māori and Anglo New Zealanders to assess the impact of culturally appropriate treatment strategies currently being developed for incarcerated Māori sexual offenders. Although still in its early stages, drafts currently available (McFarlane-Nathan, 1997; Cunningham & Harris, 1997) provide valuable insights into how some of the above issues are being addressed in one specific setting. For example, evaluation criteria are being developed under four distinct elements: program competence and safety, responsiveness, offender satisfaction, and matching. These elements have been derived from theoretically likely outcomes that have been identified (and are desired) by Māori. Again, these pioneering efforts to operationalize variables in a new area could be adapted to the U.S. context and promulgated through some of the larger organizations in this country dedicated to the continuing evolution and improvement of sexual offender treatment.

Since we represent four different ethnic groups, the material presented integrates a diversity of perspectives on the subject of cultural competence within the field of sexual offender treatment. We chose to focus on key areas of consensus and common ground that emerged in the development of this chapter. When we consider that these vast tracts of common experience came from material spanning two different countries, six different treatment settings and three different ethnic minority groups, the robust nature of our collective observations is clear.

It is our hope that this chapter provides workable directions to improve the quality of services provided for minority sexual offenders.

Along with other developments in our field, the enhancement of cultural competence will increase the effectiveness of our interventions in preventing the perpetration of further sexual abuse. As is summed up in the following Māori proverb, such efforts have the potential to benefit all people.

| | |
|---|---|
| *Kua mai ki ahau* | You ask of me |
| *He aha te mea nui o te ao?* | What is the most important thing in the world? |
| *Maku e kii atu,* | My reply must be, |
| *He tangata, he tangata,* | It is people, it is people, |
| *he tangata.* | it is people. |

# References

Bennett, M. (1996). *Empathy, ethnocentrism and egocentrism.* Keynote address at the 12th annual conference of the National Adolescent Perpetrator Network, Minneapolis, MN.

Boyd-Franklin, N. (1989). *Black families in therapy: A multisystems approach.* New York: Guilford Press.

Brislin, R.W. (Ed.). (1990). *Applied cross-cultural psychology.* Newbury Park, CA: Sage.

Comas-Díaz, L., & Griffith, E.H. (Eds.). (1988). *Clinical guidelines in cross cultural mental health.* New York: John Wiley & Sons.

Cose, E. (1993). *The rage of a privileged class: Why are middle class Blacks angry? Why should America care?* New York: HarperCollins.

Cunningham, C., & Harris, A. (1997). *Measuring the effectiveness of corrections programmes for Māori, part I: Draft criteria.* Research report (draft). Petone, New Zealand: Authors.

Ertz, D. (1994). *Treatment of juvenile sexual offending in Indian country.* Paper presented at the 13th annual Research and Treatment Conference of the Association for the Treatment of Sexual Abusers, San Francisco, CA.

Fontes, L. (Ed.). (1995). *Sexual abuse in nine North American cultures: Treatment and prevention.* Thousand Oaks, CA: Sage.

Guthrie, G.M. (1979). A cross-cultural odyssey: Some personal reflections. In A.J. Marsella, R.G. Tharp, & T.J. Cibrowski (Eds.), *Perspectives on cross-cultural psychology* (pp. 349–368). New York: Academic Press.

Hacker, A. (1995). *Two nations: Black and white, separate, hostile, unequal.* New York: Ballantine Books.

Hofstede, G. (1984). *Culture's consequences: International differences in work-related values.* Newbury Park, CA: Sage.

Johnson, S. (1996). *An effective approach to a more thorough treatment repertoire for African American clients.* Workshop presented at the 12th annual conference of the National Adolescent Perpetrator Network, Minneapolis, MN.

Jones, R.L., Winkler, M.X., Kacin, E., Salloway, W., & Weissman, M. (in press). Community based treatment for African American and Latino sexual offenders. In

W. Marshall, S. Hudson, & T. Ward (Eds.), *Sourcebook of treatment programs with sexual offenders*. New York: Plenum Press.

Larsen, J., & Hillman, D. (1996). *Te Piriti: A bicultural approach to treating sex offenders in Aotearoa, New Zealand*. Paper presented at the 15th annual conference of the Association for the Treatment of Sexual Abusers, Chicago, IL.

Larsen, J., Robertson, P., Hillman, D., & Hudson, S. (1998). Te Piriti: A bicultural model for treating child molesters in Aotearoa/New Zealand. In W. Marshall, S. Hudson, T. Ward, & Y. Fernandez (Eds.), *Handbook of sexual assault: Issues, theories, and treatment of the offender* (pp. 257–275). New York: Plenum.

Lewis, A. (1994). *The importance of culture in the treatment of juvenile sex offenders*. Paper presented at the 13th annual Research and Treatment Conference of the Association for the Treatment of Sexual Abusers, San Francisco, CA.

Loredo, C. (1994). *Working effectively with Hispanic sexual offenders*. Paper presented at the 13th annual Research and Treatment Conference of the Association for the Treatment of Sexual Abusers, San Francisco, CA.

Marsella, A.J. (1979). Cross-cultural studies of mental disorders. In A.J. Marsella, R.G. Tharp, & T.J. Cibrowski (Eds.), *Perspectives on cross-cultural psychology* (pp. 233–262). New York: Academic Press.

Marshall, W., Hudson, S., Jones, R., & Fernandez, Y.M. (1994). Empathy in sex offenders. *Clinical Psychology Review, 15*, 99–113.

Marshall, W., Ward, T., Jones, R.L., Johnson, P., & Barbaree, H. (1991). An optimistic evaluation of treatment outcome with sex offenders. *Violence Update, 1*(7), 8–11.

McFarlane-Nathan, G. (1994). *Cognitive behavior therapy and the Māori client*. Paper presented at the annual conference of the Department of Justice Psychological Services Division, Wellington, New Zealand.

McFarlane-Nathan, G. (1997). The Bicultural Therapy Project: Te Komako. *Social Work Review, 8*(1), 22–27.

Renfrey, G. (1992). Cognitive behavior therapy and the Native American client. *Behavior Therapy, 23*, 321–340.

Steele, S. (1991). *The content of our character*. New York: HarperCollins.

Sue, D.W., & Sue, D. (Eds.). (1990). *Counseling the culturally different: Theory and practice*. (2nd ed.). New York: John Wiley & Sons.

Tamasese, K., & Waldegrave, C. (1993). Cultural and gender accountability in the "Just Therapy" approach. *Journal of Feminist Family Therapy, 5*(2), 29–45.

Taylor-Gibbs, J., & Huang, L.N. (Eds.). (1989). *Children of color: Psychological interventions with minority youth*. San Francisco: Jossey-Bass Social and Behavioral Science Series.

Vontress, C.E., & Epp, L.R. (1997). Historical hostility and the African American client: Implications for counseling. *Journal of Multicultural Counseling and Development, 25*, 170–184.

Warwick, D.P. (1980). The politics and ethics of cross-cultural research. In H.C. Triandis & W.W. Lambert (Eds.), *Handbook of Cross-Cultural Psychology: Vol. 1*. Boston: Allyn & Bacon.

Weinrich, P. (1988). The operationalization of ethnic identity. In J.W. Berry & R.C. Annis (Eds.). *Ethnic psychology: Research and practice with indigenous peoples, immigrants, refugees and sojourners*. Amsterdam: Swetz & Zeitlinger.

# 2  Working with Culturally Diverse Populations

*Alvin D. Lewis, Ed.D.*

Successful models for treating adult sex offenders have existed for the past 20 years, and treatment models have also been developed for adolescent sex offenders in recent years. These models have generally focused on treating offenders as a homogeneous population when, in fact, the population is heterogeneous. Sociocultural and gender issues must be considered in the assessment and treatment of sex offenders. Cultural differences are important variables that have been neglected for too long in the assessment and treatment of sex offenders. Jones (1983) notes that knowledge of the cultural base from which a client is operating is vital for all human service practitioners.

## Preassessment Cultural Considerations

Clinicians must consider several factors before initial contact with the offender. Perhaps the first factor to consider is who should do the assessment. Characteristics of the evaluator are variables that can significantly affect how much information will be given by the offender and the family. For example, if the offender is an adult female, more information may be shared if the interviewer is female than if the interviewer is male. The gender of the offender and the gender of the interviewer represent important variables when determining who should conduct the assessment.

Some individuals or families may request an interviewer of a preferred gender. Others may request that the interviewer be of a certain ethnic or racial group. Whenever possible, such requests should be respected and efforts made to satisfy them; agency or facility staff can ask about the reasons for the request.

The acculturation of the offender and his or her family should be considered as well. Sometimes, based on information obtained about the offender, the interviewer determines how much acculturation the offender has experienced. A recent move from another country may be a clear indicator of the acculturation status of an offender and family. Children generally assimilate into new cultures more quickly than parents and grandparents. Therapists should consider this factor if the offender is an adolescent or sexually reactive child. Acculturation may become a dynamic factor in the assessment and treatment process.

A decision should be made whether an interpreter is needed before the initial interview with the offender and the family. Sometimes, the referral source may clearly articulate the need for an interpreter. Other times, language fluency may not be known, so the therapist should perhaps contact the offender and/or family about this matter. Language concerns are discussed in detail later in this chapter.

Many factors must be considered when deciding who should attend the initial interview. The people who attend the interview would be different for an adult client than for an offender who is an adolescent. Meeting with the offender and family members separately may be appropriate in some situations. This may increase everyone's comfort level and the quality of information obtained from the offender and family. Willis, Dobrec, and Sipes (1992) point out, for example, that sex or sexuality is not an acceptable topic to discuss openly among Native Americans. The therapist should consider gender, race and ethnicity, religion, history, and degree of acculturation when determining participants in the assessment interview.

A final issue that should be considered is what should be modified or not done in the assessment process. A staff member who is a member of the client's racial or ethnic group can help determine what aspects of the assessment should be modified or eliminated. A specialist who knows the culture could be consulted as an alternative.

## Clinical Assessment and Diagnostic Issues

The cultural context of behavior is an important element in a comprehensive evaluation. The offender's family and the family's experience must be considered. Vargas and Koss-Chioino (1992) assert that therapists are often not aware of the cultural content and context in their work. Clearly, what is considered acceptable and unacceptable sexual behavior varies from culture to culture and from one period in time to another (Zastrow, 1993).

The belief that all clients have the same measure of "normal" behavior is a common assumption in the assessment and treatment process. Treatment professionals must be aware of an implied assumption that "normal" is almost universal across social, cultural, and economic or political backgrounds. Behavior that is considered normal differs according to the situation, the cultural background of the person being judged, and the time during which a behavior is displayed or observed (Pedersen, 1987).

The notion of traditional culture and mainstream culture must be examined. Some ethnic and racial groups maintain much of their traditional culture, but others may identify more with mainstream culture. This varies within cultural groups and families as well. McGoldrick, Pearce, and Giordana (1982) emphasize the importance of assessing how much connection a minority client has with the culture of origin. Vargas and Koss-Chioino (1992) point out to therapists that individuals and families are often caught between the conflicting pulls of traditional practices of their own cultural groups and those of the mainstream culture.

CASE EXAMPLE:
B's family came to the United States from Cambodia two years ago. He would have been expected to have very little contact with young women until his early 20s in his country of origin. Much of his free time would have been spent with other young adult males. In Cambodia young adult males often hug, hold hands, and sit close together.

B was enrolled in a large university in his sophomore year after his family's immigration to Detroit. B immediately found himself caught between traditional values and practices and the practices of mainstream culture. His new peers made fun of him for sitting close to other males and wanting to hold their hands. He was in two physical altercations during his first three months at the university. The fights occurred because two classmates thought that B was trying to harass them sexually. Soon, he was being called a "fag" by his peers at the university.

Several months passed, and B began to show an interest in young women. He began sneaking out to meet a young woman because his parents did not approve of his dating, in accordance with traditional practices. Several males at the university told B that if he wanted to prove he was not gay, he had to have sex with the young woman he was seeing. This created much conflict for B.

Eventually, B decided he would try to have sex with the young woman. He pushed to visit the girl's house when her parents were out one evening. B later admitted to date rape. He had done what he thought all young adult American males did. His family felt great shame and wanted to keep his crime a secret. B became depressed and tried to commit suicide. He begged his parents to move back to Cambodia.

## Biculturality

Persons of color in America must learn to function in two environments: their own culture and that of the mainstream society. Biculturality, the ability to function in two worlds, is adaptive (Anda, 1984). It is different from assimilation, which implies total immersion in mainstream culture and having all needs met based on mainstream norms, values, beliefs, and perceptions. The therapist must understand and accept the importance of biculturality for the offender of color. For example, an offender who is Chinese American may celebrate Chinese New Year as a holiday but may also appreciate Christmas.

A young adult offender who is Asian may make eye contact with the therapist during an assessment, but not with his or her parents. The offender who is bicultural understands the importance placed on eye contact in mainstream culture. However, the offender may not make eye contact with his or her parents out of respect, as determined by the culture of origin. The therapist would then need to be culturally sensitive in his or her evaluation of eye contact in the assessment and treatment process.

## Family Tradition and Structure

Family structures vary considerably among ethnic and racial groups. Much intragroup diversity exists. Some groups are more patriarchal, and others are matriarchal. Still others are egalitarian. Minnuchin (1974) did extensive research on family structure and emphasized the importance of understanding family structure and respecting it in the therapeutic process.

Mistakes can be made that lead to the offender and family dropping out of therapy, if a therapist does not understand the importance of family structure. Understanding the father's special role in a patriarchal family structure is very important. The therapist must be careful not to stereotype. The therapist must not hold on to an assumption if the experience with the offender or the family differs. Boyd-Franklin (1989) asserts:

> The clinician must test hypotheses and accept and discard them according to his or her experience of the individual and family. Knowledge about culture is a flexible hypothesis and not a rigidly held thesis. (p. ix)

Role flexibility is an important aspect of some family structures. Many African-American families, for example, maintain more role flexibility between spouses than do White families. Parenting by the oldest child may be accepted in other families of color. He or she may function as a surrogate parent and may be in charge when neither parent is home or available. The child does not carry out this role when a parent is available. Minnuchin (1974) points out that role flexibility is seen as a strength in some racial groups. However, he goes on to say that the extended family structure is quite vulnerable to boundary and role confusion.

Family composition is another aspect of family tradition. I grew up in a home inhabited by parents, siblings, grandparents, nephews, and nonbiologically related adults. The grandparents and unrelated adults had authority to discipline the children.

Parents expect married adult children to live at home for several years before getting their own places in some Asian and Hispanic cultures. I lived with a Chinese family while serving as a Peace Corps volunteer in Malaysia. The family's oldest daughter and her family lived at home. The daughter was a nurse, and her husband owned his own business. At age 40 and 42, respectively, they finally moved into their own home with their two children. The couple had owned two houses for more than 10 years but rented them to tenants. A therapist working with this family would need to be sensitive to this factor and not see the adult children as dependent and irresponsible.

## Degree of Acculturation

The therapist, as part of the assessment, must understand acculturation. Acculturation may be defined as the degree to which a person of color meets his or her needs in the mainstream culture. Degree of acculturation varies from one individual to another and from one family system to another. The therapist must be careful of bias there. That is, the therapist must realize that an individual or family may be bicultural by choice. Needs are met in both the mainstream culture and the culture of origin. For example, some East Indians may stop wearing saris after living in the United States for a few years. Other Indian women may have lived here for 20 years and wear saris but also wear Western clothes. Biculturality may similarly occur regarding holidays. Some individuals or families may celebrate their traditional holidays, but others may celebrate only American holidays.

The therapist can make some preliminary hypotheses during the assessment based on family members' dress, language, and roles. Often, conflicts arise between young adults and parents and grandparents. Young adults frequently want to identify wholly with the mainstream culture, but parents and grandparents might want to be bicultural sometimes. Minnuchin (1974) further stresses that the family structure must change shape, with rules and roles modified to fit their new context.

### Language

The clinical assessment should be conducted in the preferred language of the offender and the family, if possible. Before the assessment, the therapist should have determined what language the offender and family want to use. Arrangements should then be made to use an interpreter who, ideally, is a mental-health professional. The interview is then less cumbersome, and the chances of miscommunication are decreased.

The therapist should *never* use a child to interpret. Often, this is viewed as disrespectful to the family, especially the parents. Other reasons why a child should not interpret include that (1) the family hierarchy is not being considered, (2) children may distort what the therapist says, (3) children may distort what the parents or other family members say, (4) children can be triangulated in the communication process, and (5) exposure to sexual information may be inappropriate for a child.

The therapist must be sensitive to cultural nuances when it is necessary to use an interpreter. The following factors should be considered: (1) gender of the interpreter, (2) comfort level of the interpreter with the nature of the interview and the use of sexual words and phrases, (3) background of the interpreter — professional or layperson — in mental health, (4) inappropriate use of family members as translators, (5) the speed of the therapist's speech to ensure that the interpreter can easily understand, and (6) preliminary meetings with the interpreter to devise a plan to ensure clear communication.

According to Baker (1981):

> The "ideal" interpreting style falls between the extremes of translating every word versus a summary and varies according to the client, circumstances, and the personalities of the worker and interpreter. The key to effective interpreting is for the worker and interpreter to become a close team in their enterprise, using the best qualities of each to help clients more effectively. Thus, the working relationship between them is crucial. (p. 393)

## Help-seeking Behavior

Asking for help from a mental-health professional, in many cultures, is a last resort. The offender may feel that he or she will "lose face" because of the evaluation, if the assessment is mandated. When I was a Peace Corps volunteer, I was aware that any individual or family who met with me was doing so as a last resort. In other words, everything else had failed, including seeing a traditional healer.

The therapist may need to ask the individual or family members how they have already tried to resolve the problem. Also, the therapist may want to find out how the problem would be dealt with within the culture. Lappin (1983) notes that conducting cross-cultural assessments and therapy is a balance.

> The balance has to do with the attitude the therapist conveys — one of asking for the individual or family's help while, at the same time, offering help. Cultural questioning is the start of a process that can begin to challenge old rules, roles, and narrow definitions of self. (p. 125)

Ho (1987) points out that clients' lack of knowledge of help-seeking behavior could cause many therapists to misdiagnose something that is actually a cultural difference as something that is pathological.

## Eye Contact

In mainstream Anglo-American culture, eye contact is highly valued. Many people use a handshake and eye contact to negotiate multimillion-dollar transactions. Much is written about eye contact and other nonverbal behavior in the field of mental health. The evaluator often mentions in clinical assessments whether the client made good or poor eye contact during the interview. Some people associate innocence or guilt with eye contact or the lack of it. However, eye contact is culturally mediated. Adult children in the Chinese culture are not expected to make eye contact with their parents. To do so is considered disrespectful to the parents and elders. A teenager in the African-American culture should not look directly at the parent, especially during a father-son talk when the son is being disciplined or receiving a lecture.

Some cultures hold professionals in very high regard. In other cultures (e.g., India), people of one class or caste cannot look directly at someone from a different socioeconomic class or caste. The therapist must take this factor into consideration in the evaluation process. An offender may not make eye contact with the professional based on his or her cultural background. In some Asian cultures, the client is expected to refrain from eye contact with the therapist out of respect.

## Spirituality and Religion

Spirituality is seen as a complex notion. The therapist needs to have some knowledge of spirituality as it pertains to a culture to do a comprehensive assessment. African Americans, for example, consider spirituality a very important dimension of the community. Many people believe that African Americans endured and survived slavery and other oppressions because of their strong spiritual foundation.

The therapist must try to understand that spirituality may be a guiding factor for the offender and his or her family. Also, the therapist must be able to differentiate between religion and spirituality. Frequently, even mental health professionals see religion and spirituality as the same. Boyd-Franklin (1989) asserts that the role of spirituality has received much attention in the mental-health literature in recent years.

The therapist attempts to understand what the offender is saying with respect to spirituality and religious belief during the assessment. Even before the interview, the therapist may want to do some reading about spirituality or consult with a specialist on the culture who can offer some expertise in this area.

## How Privacy Is Treated in the Family and Culture

Privacy is both cultural and contextual. A Muslim woman covers her body to be modest. This custom is an effort not to appear attractive or provocative toward males. A common belief among Muslims is that Western females dress provocatively and, as a result, increase the chance that they might be sexually abused or raped.

I observed, during service in the Peace Corps, various East Indian family members sleeping on the floor together. Sleeping next to her 16-year-old grandson was common for a grandmother. The culture saw no need for the grandson to have privacy with respect to sleeping arrangements. Muslim families, in the same culture, allowed adult and adolescent males to swim with shorts or trunks but required females to be fully clothed in the water.

I have observed many situations in which Asian adult males and children cover themselves with sarongs or use locked stalls to change clothes in a public rest room. Most American males change clothes and allow their genitalia to be briefly exposed in similar situations.

Many males from Asian and East Indian cultures find it difficult to work with female therapists from the West. The male may be distracted by or uncomfortable with the way the therapist is dressed. This circumstance would make it difficult to create trust and develop a constructive clinical relationship (McGoldrick et al., 1982). Iranian men, in particular, have difficulty following a female therapist's directives and recommendations. They avoid discussing painful issues, including sexual matters (Zastrow, 1993). Therefore, a male therapist probably would need to do the assessment and therapy.

*Social Tolerance for Deviance and*
*Dysfunctional Behavior*

Tolerance for deviant and dysfunctional behavior varies from culture to culture. What is viewed as abhorrent in one society may be socially sanctioned in another society.

Much of the sexual abuse in Native American families involves father-daughter and stepfather-stepdaughter incest. Frequently, the offender is not convicted of a sexual crime and does not receive treatment for a psychosexual disturbance. Instead, he is treated for alcoholism or other substance-abuse problems. The offender's spouse and the community then accept that the "problem" has been addressed.

The African-American culture allows little open discussion about homosexual lifestyles. A person who is lesbian or homosexual is viewed as "sick," and community members think that homosexuals will be "punished by God." A large segment of the population that is highly religious sees AIDS as God's punishment of gays and thinks that if gays "gave up their lifestyle and repented, then they could be saved." Although the mainstream culture no longer views homosexuality as an illness or as deviant behavior, it is still viewed this way in the African-American culture. Although there is no documented connection between homosexuality and sexual offending, this punitive attitude becomes relevant to sex offenders who molest victims of their own gender, decreasing the likelihood that victims or offenders will voluntarily report the incident.

Gagnon and Henderson (1975) found some cultures that accept and others that encourage homosexuality. Today, all males among the Siwans of North Africa are expected to engage in homosexual relationships throughout their lives. Sullivan, Thompson, Wright, Gross, and Spady (1980) reported that among the Aranda of central Australia, relationships take place between young boys and unmarried men, with these liaisons generally ending at heterosexual marriage.

*Paper-and-Pencil Testing*

The assessment process often includes administration of a series of paper-and-pencil tests. However, the therapist must be careful in the interpretation of the results. Most psychological tests and psychosexual instruments were normed on White populations in the United States. Therefore, administering these tests to a person of color may not reveal much useful information.

Although many "culture-fair" or "culture-free" tests have been developed in recent years, few such tests are actually used. The Cattell is a culture-sensitive test of intellectual abilities used with and administered to offenders of color. No studies are available concerning outcomes in use of the Cattell versus the WISC-R or III.

## Choice of Therapist

The choice of a therapist is vitally important in cross-cultural counseling. An offender may ask for a therapist of a specific race or gender. If meeting this request is possible, it should be done. However, the offender should be given a choice. All Mexican Americans should not be assigned to Mexican-American therapists, even if this were possible. The offender (not to mention the treatment provider) may consider it patronizing to be automatically assigned a therapist of the same race.

The interactions between White therapists and minority clients may be more restrained than are those between therapists and clients of the same race (Atkinson, 1983). The same may be true when a male client is working with a female therapist or vice versa. Parloff, Waskow, and Wolf (1978) conclude that cultural matching of a therapist and client is not clearly preferred. Other research also suggests a lack of support for the preference of matching clients and therapists by culture. Helms (1985) reports that clients with the strongest commitment to their own ethnic group are more likely to prefer therapists from the same ethnic background.

Research by Carkhuff and Pierce (1967) shows that counselors who are different from their clients in ethnicity, social class, and gender have the greatest difficulty effecting constructive changes. Atkinson (1983) reports that the preference for counseling style may be more important than racial match between the therapist and African-American, Asian-American, and low-income White clients, but less important with middle-class White clients.

Lambert (1981) suggests the possibility that cross-cultural therapy may be contraindicated in most circumstances. He goes on to say that there are many complications in understanding and communicating with culturally different clients. Client-counselor relationship correlates with therapy outcome (Peoples & Dell, 1975). Therefore, it is extremely important that the therapist is confident and competent to work with the offender and that the offender views the therapist as competent and culturally sensitive.

## Choice of Treatment Modalities and Methodologies

Some aspects of mainstream sex offender treatment may be contraindicated when working with clients from a specific cultural background. Aspects that are contraindicated vary from one culture to another. The constructs of "healthy" and "normal" that guide the delivery of mental-health services are not the same for all cultures. Group therapy may not work well for Asian offenders, for example, who often believe that they will "lose face" by discussing their problems publicly; being in a group would be viewed as "public." Group treatment could be considered if the offender was born in a Western culture or has lived in the West for several years.

Family therapy may not be useful with some minority offenders. Family therapy with Asian families, for example, may be ineffective because of the importance placed on family reputation. Family members often attempt to protect one another and the good reputation of the whole family. Although the family will not question any directives or instructions given by the therapist, little or no work will be done toward implementation because of discomfort and other issues that the family considers inappropriate or shameful to discuss with the therapist.

The therapist may have to meet with the offender and/or family several times to determine appropriate treatment modalities and methods in particular cases. Pedersen (1988) states that the application of standard methods and modalities indiscriminately across cultural groups creates problems. Kavanagh and Kennedy (1992) note:

> Providers are often unfamiliar with appropriate intervention and communication strategies in situations that involve persons or groups dissimilar from themselves or that involve circumstances beyond their own experience. Discomfort based on unfamiliarity

can threaten personal integrity and encourage resistance and defensiveness. (p. 50)

Research findings have generally shown that many people of color are inappropriately or inadequately served by mental-health services. Traditional counseling theory and methods may often run counter to important developmental aspects of indigenous helping models found in various cultural groups. Traditional counseling practices have often failed to meet the needs of people from diverse cultural backgrounds (Sue & Sue, 1990).

Therapists have usually been taught generic techniques in graduate school. These techniques may work well with clients from the mainstream culture. However, they may be ineffective in work with clients of color (Pedersen, 1988). Minnuchin and Fishman (1981) found that many minority clients terminate therapy early because they have no frame of reference for the therapeutic techniques used by the therapist.

The more a therapist knows about a client's culture, the greater the opportunity for success in the therapeutic relationship. Clients are more likely to stay engaged in treatment when they are comfortable with the techniques used. Boyd-Franklin (1989) notes that spiritual reframing is a useful technique with African-American individuals and families. Spiritual beliefs clinically manifest themselves in many different forms and can be used as part of the reframing by a therapist who is aware of them.

Discussing sex offenses with a therapist is difficult for most people. The therapist must understand that for some offenders of color, little disclosure will occur in the first few sessions. The therapist may have to employ the rituals of social amenities between himself or herself and the offender for a longer time than usual, particularly with Native Americans and Asians. The therapist may still need to base the pace on the offender, even when the presenting problem is already known.

A therapist will hear something about traditional healers and/or traditional medicine at some point in therapy. The therapist may lose the offender and the family if the importance of the traditional healer is negated. McGoldrick et al. (1982) assert that the therapist must recognize that therapy may have to include traditional healers as co-therapists or consultants. The nontraditional technique of including elders and traditional healers in therapy can change the course of treatment constructively (Coutoure, 1980).

Using personal experience as a technique takes on a new meaning in work with Asian Americans. The individual and family may expect the therapist to engage in self-disclosure as a way to develop trust. Most therapists have been trained to reveal little about themselves in the therapeutic process. However, if the therapist expects to develop a relationship with an Asian client, revealing a little personal information may be necessary to give the client some perspective about the therapist.

Therapists may have to adapt their communication style in working with Hispanic and Asian clients. The pace for gathering needed information may have to be much slower than with dominant-culture clients. McGoldrick et al. (1982) note that if the client sees the therapist as aggressive, pushy, and insensitive, the client may feel stressed and disengage from treatment.

CASE EXAMPLE:
The Wu family consisted of the parents in their mid-30s, an 11-year-old daughter, and a 16-year-old son. The therapist had a background in work with Asian families and a solid foundation in sex offender treatment. The therapist, therefore, did not insist that the daughter openly express anger toward her father for sexually abusing her. For the daughter to have done so would have been disrespectful.

Even with educational restructuring, the victim, especially a child, probably would not be able to express negative feelings easily. The therapist should not push the victim or family too hard; some families never feel comfortable deviating from this cultural style of expression (Pedersen, 1988).

## Storytelling

Storytelling is a nontraditional technique that has utility for some cultures. In particular, this technique has been used effectively with African Americans and Asian Americans. Storytelling is non-threatening and especially helpful early in therapy when trust and rapport are being established. Boyd-Franklin (1989) notes that establishing the relationship can be the most difficult aspect of therapy with some clients. Storytelling can be used as a joining tool and can be used throughout therapy. Storytelling is a part of Native American culture. Stories are often passed down from one generation to the next. Understanding the importance of story-telling to a culture and being able to recite some well-known stories will serve the therapist well. In African-American and Native American cultures, history was passed on to others through story-telling (Boyd-Franklin, 1989).

## Ritual

Therapists can also employ rituals as a nontraditional technique. There are rituals unique to each culture and some that transcend many cultures. During my training at the Philadelphia Child Guidance Clinic, I observed rituals being used effectively by many therapists in cross-cultural work. Sue and Sue (1990) note that clients become "stuck" when they cannot adapt effectively to the experiences that influence their lives. Rituals can help get a client "unstuck" and move them to a functional level.

## Racism, Prejudice, and Poverty

Any therapist working with an offender of color must understand the historical and current context of a particular group's experiences with racism and poverty. Robinson (1989) "believes that the initial phase of therapy is the point at which the clinician must assess both the impact of race and racism on the process of therapy" (p. 323). If, for example, the offender includes race as a relevant factor in the presenting problem, the therapist must be sensitive to this. Whether overt or covert, racism is often the apparent basis for decisions and actions that will profoundly affect the lives of people of color. By choosing not to elicit or acknowledge the client's perspective regarding race, the therapist risks disrupting the formation of an alliance that the client experiences as empathic (Robinson, 1989).

The experiences of persons of color with racism and prejudice vary from one culture group to another. African Americans, for example, came to this country primarily from West Africa as slaves. Jews were persecuted in Germany and many other European countries. Native Americans were placed on reservations after years of strife with the mainstream culture. The therapist must know the history of the culture and have an understanding of racism, prejudice, and poverty to treat sex offenders of color effectively. Robinson (1989) notes four issues that may significantly affect the effectiveness of treatment: (1) racial congruence of the client, (2) influence of race on the presenting problem, (3) the therapist's racial awareness, and (4) the therapist's therapeutic strategies (p. 323).

CASE EXAMPLE:

J is a 30-year-old African-American male who was convicted of sexual abuse of his girlfriend's 10-year-old daughter. Early in treatment, a session focused on safe sex practices. J and the therapist had very different views about the use of condoms. J admitted that he had sex and did not use condoms, although he sometimes had sex with females other than his girlfriend. J felt that condoms were mainstream culture's way of limiting the population growth of African Americans. J spoke of involuntary sterilizations of African Americans that occurred in the 1930s and 1940s. In J's view, this practice was racist and was done to reduce the African-American population systematically. The therapist was unable to appreciate what J was saying. The therapist did not know the history of African Americans, so he continued to tell J that he would die of sexually transmitted diseases if he did not use condoms.

Pedersen (1987) concludes that therapists display 10 frequent assumptions resulting in cultural bias in counseling. His ninth assumption relates to the importance of history for a proper understanding of contemporary events. Pedersen notes that counselors are more likely to focus on crisis-precipitating events, and if clients talk about their own history or the history of their "people," the counselor is likely to stop listening and wait for clients to "catch up" to current events, which the counselor considers more salient than history. The client's perspectives may require historical background knowledge that the client feels is relevant to the complete description of his or her problem from his or her point of view. In many cultures, the connection between past and present history makes it necessary for counselors to understand clearly a client's historical context to understand his or her present behavior.

The therapist in the preceding case example had little knowledge of the offender's past and therefore could not understand his views about condoms. In that case, even if the therapist were uninformed, he could have consulted someone familiar with the culture or brought it up as an issue with colleagues on the treatment team.

*Spirituality, Religion, Indigenous Healers,*
*and Other Belief Systems*

The issues concerning spirituality and religion in cross-cultural treatment are similar to those described in the assessment section of this chapter. Little emphasis has been placed on religion and other belief systems in sexual abuser treatment. However, multicultural counseling practice may be enhanced if therapists consider the influence of religion or spirituality to be a crucial dynamic in the helping process (Lee, 1991; Boyd-Franklin, 1989). Religious institutions are important sources of psychological support in the cultural traditions of many groups. The therapist must understand the religious and spiritual influences of the abuser and his or her family. Spiritual beliefs are part of a survival system in some cultures. For example, an offender might state that "God will take care of my problem." Therapists need to be sensitive to offenders' belief systems while also requiring them to take responsibility for their abusive behaviors and address their psychosexual problems.

> CASE EXAMPLE:
> Mr. H is a 42-year-old, married father of two children. He is receiving sex offender counseling for abusing two prepubescent boys. The treatment team has recommended to the therapist that masturbatory satiation be part of the treatment protocol. Mr. H tells the therapist that he does not masturbate due to his religious beliefs. Consequently, he says that masturbatory satiation will not help him. The therapist has provided multicultural treatment to sex offenders and their families for several years. Rather than challenge the offender, the therapist validates the offender's religious beliefs. However, over the next several weeks, he also helps the offender understand the efficacy of the treatment. Mr. H eventually agrees to masturbatory satiation for a three-month period. The therapist and the offender monitor his arousal through monthly phallometric assessments. Mr. H is encouraged by the results and therefore agrees to continue beyond the three months.

At times, the therapist must elicit the help of a religious leader or traditional healer to work effectively with an offender and his or her family. African-American families who are very religious often turn to their ministers for support during emotional crises such as divorce, suicide, death, substance abuse, or the impending imprisonment of a loved one (Broadfield, Lewis, & Davis, 1991). The therapist can develop a relationship of trust and respect with the offender and the family if a link is established with their minister.

The therapist needs to have some familiarity with traditional healers of an offender's culture. The offender probably has had contact with a traditional healer, even when an offender is referred for court-ordered treatment. Lemoine (1986) notes that "exploring how a family has used a traditional healer, when to call one, or whether or not to consult one are questions the western psychotherapist has only recently learned to be of value" (p. 171). The therapist may have to delve deeper into the culture to be effective, depending on how the offender and his or her family use the traditional healer.

### Cultural View of Sexual Abuse and Incest

The definitions of sexual abuse vary from one culture to another. Also, incest, though taboo in most Western and Eastern cultures, is viewed differently in remote and less-developed cultures. Zastrow (1993) points out that what is acceptable and unacceptable sexual behavior varies from culture to culture and from one period to another. The sexual relationships between the young boys and unmarried men of the Aranda, as previously described, are a clear example of such differences among cultures.

The therapist must view incest and other sexually abusive behaviors from both cultural and legal contexts. What may have been acceptable in one culture is a crime in another culture. The therapist must help the offender and the family understand that a sexual crime was committed based on laws and statutes when conflicts arise between cultural and legal standards. The therapist needs to help the offender in accepting responsibility for the sexual offense and making a commitment to treatment.

The Native American offender living on a reservation poses a unique challenge. This situation is often complicated if the offender has a substance-abuse problem as well. He or she may well plead for substance-abuse counseling, and the sex-offending behavior may never be addressed. When the offender returns home, the child is then at risk of being sexually abused again.

The therapist needs to be aware that it is common in Native American families for the victim to recant the abuse. Open discussion of sexual issues in these families, including sexual abuse, is a cultural taboo, especially when the family resides on a reservation (S. Paddock, personal communication, 1995).

In many Asian cultures, treatment can be complicated in incestuous families. Often, the incest goes unreported unless the family seeks treatment as a last resort for another problem. If exposed, the Asian offender and family may contend that he or she suffered with "amok" or psychotic violent rage. Therefore, the offender and the family believe that the offender cannot be held accountable for the sexual abuse (Sullivan et al., 1980). One pitfall in working with Asian offenders and families noted earlier was the likelihood that victims may consider it disrespectful to express negative feelings to parents. The cultural traditions might also be such that the offender cannot talk about his or her behavior in the presence of the victim and other children (Chao, 1992).

## Other Culturally Mediated Matters

The Western-trained therapist doing cross-cultural work will come to realize that certain techniques and social gestures are not appropriate or acceptable and are, in fact, culturally dystonic. Silence as a technique is effective with some offenders but not with others. Intensity and confrontation are other techniques that are culturally mediated. Most Asian cultures would find confrontation offensive, resulting in the client providing even less disclosure and dropping out of treatment.

The appropriateness of social touch, including handshakes, is culturally determined. Shaking the hands of Asian women is frequently considered inappropriate. Also, the open expression of affection in public is unacceptable. This factor would affect family and marital counseling when the therapist wants to use experiential therapies. The couple would probably be very uncomfortable with any instruction requiring a public display of affection.

The culturally sensitive therapist is mindful of things such as manners, eye contact, laughter, gestures, and body language. Lappin (1983) notes that, to be effective, therapists should know nuances of group and intragroup differences. While cultural qualities and patterns cannot be reduced into neat categories, forming a knowledge base about the culture with which therapists work is essential. It means becoming attuned to the macro and micro aspects of therapy and the culture. Characteristics such as body posture, voice tone, and facial expressions carry a greater meaning in cross-cultural work.

Therapists working with offenders and their families need to become more knowledgeable about the culture because of the increase in cultural diversity in most Western countries. The therapist must be comfortable with learning about cultural nuances from the offender, the family, and others.

### Culturally Based Belief Systems About Pharmacology

The use of pharmacotherapy with sex offenders has increased in recent years. Medication has been used with sex offenders when other therapies have not decreased the intensity of their deviant arousal. Depo-Provera has been used for several years and, more recently, Depo-Lupron. Medical research has shown some efficacy with Prozac and Paxil.

Many offenders refuse to take such medication because they think that it will prevent them from having a normal sex drive or will make them impotent. Use of medication becomes even more complex in cross-cultural situations. There is a demarcation between Eastern and Western medicine in most Asian cultures. Tung (1980) points out that "as a rule, western medicines are all hot and herb medicines possess more cooling properties" (p. 6). Usually, Asians are cautious about Western medicines because they think the medicines are too potent for their constitutions.

Studies of dosages among Asian and Latino populations have been conducted. Lee (1982) has worked with Asian Americans and states:

> Clinical reports from Asian countries and sporadic reports in the United States suggest that dosages based on Caucasian patient populations may not be readily applicable to Asian populations. Very detailed explanations and clarification of appropriate dosages are necessary. The mixing of Eastern and Western medicines is a concern to many therapists. It is advisable to get a detailed medical history from the client and to advise against the use of internal herbal medicines in conjunction with psychotropic or other drugs. (p. 549)

The therapists and physicians who believe that offenders can benefit from hormonal therapy must consider the cultural implications of such medicine. Clinicians must move slowly to try to help offenders understand the potential benefit of the treatment in the management of sexual problems.

## Maintenance and Aftercare

Offenders must accept that maintenance or aftercare is an essential part of their treatment. The therapist who is treating a person of color must take into consideration cultural factors that affect the offender's participation in maintenance and aftercare. Some factors include (1) offenders' belief systems about maintenance, (2) choice of a therapist, (3) choice of modalities, and (4) language and need for an interpreter.

## Strategies for Providing Culturally Sensitive and Relevant Sex Offender Treatment

McGoldrick et al. (1982) point out that no therapist can become an expert on all racial and ethnic groups. What is essential is to develop an openness to cultural variability. Recommended strategies include:

1. Be an explorer; be willing to form hypotheses and test them.
2. Be open to consulting with colleagues who are familiar with an offender's culture.
3. Understand that the offender and his or her family will need to teach the therapist about some aspects of their culture.
4. Ask about the obvious if you do not understand it (e.g., why do Muslim women cover their bodies?).
5. Use an interpreter, if necessary, to help with the language and as an expert on the culture.
6. Remain aware that some communication styles and therapeutic techniques will be more effective than others in cross-cultural work.
7. Be aware of subjects that are taboo and bring them up only when the client seems ready to discuss them.
8. Learn to appreciate and work with the offender's natural helping system and indigenous healers when appropriate.

9. Honor and respect cultural diversity and differences.

10. Increase awareness and understanding of the contributions of various cultures.

Incorporation of more knowledge about diversity and culture into the current model is needed. Using a generic model to treat sex offenders of color is no longer acceptable as sex offender–specific treatment develops. Therapists must adapt their skills and increase their knowledge base to serve minority offenders effectively. This improvement can be achieved through training, consultation, and a willingness to learn from the offender and his or her family.

# References

Anda, D. (1984, March/April). Bicultural socialization factors affecting the minority experience. *Social Work*, 101–107.

Atkinson, D. (1983). Ethnic similarity in counseling psychology: A review of research. *The Counseling Psychologist, 11*(3), 79–92.

Baker, N. (1981, September). Social work through an interpreter. *Social Work*, 391–397.

Boyd-Franklin, N. (1989). *Black families in therapy: A multi-systems approach*. New York: Guilford.

Broadfield, C., Lewis, A., & Davis, J. (1991). Substance abuse in the African-American community. *Forum*, pp. 5–7.

Carkhuff, R., & Pierce, R. (1967). Differential effects of therapist race and social class upon patient depth of self-exploration in the initial clinical interview. *Journal of Counseling Psychology, 31*, 632–634.

Chao, C. (1992). The inner heart: Therapy with Southeast Asian families. In L. Vargas & J. Koss-Chioino (Eds.), *Working with culture* (pp. 157–181). San Francisco: Jossey-Bass.

Coutoure, J. (1980). *Next time try a medicine man*. Unpublished manuscript.

Gagnon, B., & Henderson, J. (1975). *Human sexuality: The age of ambiguity*. Boston: Little, Brown.

Helms, J. (1985). Cultural identity in the treatment process. In P. Pedersen (Ed.), *Handbook of cross-cultural counseling and therapy* (pp. 239–245). Westport, CT: Greenwood Press.

Ho, M. (1987). *Family therapy with ethnic minorities*. Newbury Park, CA: Sage.

Jones, R. (1983, September). Increasing staff sensitivity to the Black client. *Social Casework: The Journal of Contemporary Social Work*, 419–425.

Kavanagh, K., & Kennedy, P. (1992). *Promoting cultural diversity: Strategies for health care professionals*. Newbury Park, CA: Sage.

Lambert, M. (1981). The implications of psychotherapy. In A. Marsella and P. Pedersen (Eds.), *Cross-cultural counseling and psychotherapy* (pp. 126–158). New York: Pergamon Press.

Lappin, J. (1983). On becoming a culturally conscious family therapist. In L. Jones (Ed.), *Cultural perspectives in family therapy* (pp. 122–136). New York: Guilford Press.

Lee, C. (1991). Cultural dynamics: Their importance in multicultural counseling. In C. Lee & B. Richardson (Eds.), *Multicultural issues in counseling: New approaches to diversity* (pp. 11–16). New York: Wiley.

Lee, E. (1982). A social systems approach to assessment and treatment for Chinese-American families. In M. McGoldrick, J. Pearce, & J. Giordana (Eds.), *Ethnicity and family therapy* (pp. 527–551). New York: Guilford Press.

Lemoine, J. (1986). *Shamanism in the context of H'mong resettlement.* In G.L. Hendricks, B.T. Downing, & A.S. Deinhard (Eds.), *The H'mong in transition* (pp. 82–98). New York: Center for Migration Studies.

McGoldrick, M., Pearce, J., & Giordana, J. (1982). *Ethnicity and family therapy.* New York: Guilford Press.

Minnuchin, S. (1974). *Families and family therapy.* Cambridge, MA: Harvard University Press.

Minnuchin, S., & Fishman, C. (1981). *Family therapy techniques.* Cambridge, MA: Harvard University Press.

Parloff, M., Waskow, L., & Wolf, B. (1978). Research on therapist variables in relation to process and outcome. In S. Garfield & A. Bergin (Eds.), *Handbook of psychotherapy and development* (pp. 82–102). New York: Wiley.

Pedersen, P. (1987, January). Ten assumptions of cultural bias in counseling. *Journal of Multicultural Counseling and Development,* 16–23.

Pedersen, P. (1988). *A handbook for developing multicultural awareness.* Alexandria, VA: American Association for Counseling and Development.

Peoples, V., & Dell, D. (1975). Black and White student preferences for counselor roles. *Journal of Counseling Psychology, 22,* 234–259.

Robinson, J. (1989, July). Clinical treatment of Black families: Issues and strategies. *Social Work,* 323–328.

Sue, D.W., & Sue, D. (1990). *Counseling the culturally different: Theory and practice* (2nd ed.). New York: Wiley.

Sullivan, T., Thompson, K., Wright, R., Gross, G., & Spady, D. (1980). *Social problems.* New York: Wiley.

Tung, T. (1980). *Understanding the differences between Asian and Western concepts of mental health and illness.* Unpublished manuscript.

Vargas, L., & Koss-Chioino, L. (Eds.). (1992). *Working with culture.* San Francisco: Jossey-Bass.

Willis, D., Dobrec, A., & Sipes, D. (1992). Treating American Indian victims of abuse and molestation. In L. Vargas & L. Koss-Chioino (Eds.), *Working with culture* (pp. 276–299). San Francisco: Jossey-Bass.

Zastrow, C. (1993). *Introduction to social work and social welfare.* Pacific Grove, CA: Brooks/Cole.

# Part II
# Experiences and Approaches with Special Populations

# 3  Female Sexual Abusers: An Unrecognized Culture

*Gayane Minasian, M.A.*
*Alvin D. Lewis, Ed.D.*

Until 10 years ago, the literature contained virtually nothing about female sex offenders. Many clinicians and researchers thought that female sexual perpetrators were rare and probably had a history of mental problems. In recent years, the professional treatment and law-enforcement communities have come to realize that females act out sexually more often than is reported. This population is no longer overlooked; it is being discussed in the literature, and its members are being treated in clinical settings.

This chapter focuses on the prevalence of female sex offenders and the differences between male and female sex offenders. It also addresses adult and adolescent sex offenders and sexually reactive female children. Finally, areas for further research are suggested.

## Prevalence and Problems with Detection

Since the mid-1970s, the study of females who commit crimes has become a major intellectual and professional specialty. Within criminology, criminal justice, sociology, psychology, and economics, research on females who commit crimes has grown into a major area of interest (Simon & Landis, 1991). Despite this, the information on adult female sex offenders is limited. Even more limited is information concerning female adolescent sex offenders. Sexual abuse of children and adolescents by females was essentially ignored and thought to be rare until the early 1980s (Allen, 1991).

Many professionals have been biased and have overlooked sexual abuse by adult and adolescent females. They have chosen not to see a mother or female baby-sitter as a child molester (McCarty, 1986). Rape statistics were not kept on females because it was seen almost exclusively as a male offense (Simon & Landis, 1991). The public still finds it difficult to accept that females are perpetrators of child sexual abuse. Sexual abuse by females, both adults and adolescents, is still greatly underreported (Faller, 1995).

In the past 10 years, professionals have been seeing and documenting cases of females as child abusers. The number of known cases has increased significantly. Sexual abuse by females probably accounts for 5 percent of girls being abused, compared with 20 percent of boys (McCarty, 1986). Females are perpetrators in 1 to 24 percent of sexual abuse cases involving male victims and in 6 to 17 percent of cases involving female victims (American Humane Association, 1981; Finkelhor & Russell, 1984; Finkelhor, Williams, Burns, & Kalinoski, 1988).

Sexual abuse by females is difficult to detect for many reasons. According to Allen (1991), barriers to the recognition of female perpetration develop when feminist perspectives are presented as the only viable explanation for child sexual abuse, and female sexual abuse is consequently considered insignificant. The socialization of females in our society and their role as caretakers of children are barriers to the recognition of sexual abuse of children (Matthews, Matthews, & Speltz, 1991). Matthews, Matthews, and Speltz (1991) assert:

> Although social awareness of sexual abuse has greatly increased over the last decade, the female sexual offender has been virtually invisible. Viewing females as perpetrators of sexual abuse, perhaps parallel to viewing males as victims, challenges traditional cultural stereotypes. (p. 199)

Other reasons that detection is difficult are (1) the underreporting of incidents between male victims and female perpetrators, (2) the fact that males are less likely to report sexual abuse (Johnson, 1989), and (3) females' ability to mask sexually inappropriate contact with a guise of bathing or dressing the victim because childcare activities permit a certain amount of intimate contact.

Another area that allows sexual abuse by females to go unreported is the type of offense. Exhibitionism has generally been thought of as an exclusively male perversion (O'Conner, 1987). Even today, little information and research are available on females whose sexual misconduct includes frottage, exhibitionism, bestiality, and so forth (Faller, 1995).

Professionals must be trained to ask the right questions to aid in the detection of sexual abuse by females. Also, mental-health and law-enforcement professionals need to accept the fact that females, both adults and adolescents, commit many sexual offenses, as do their male counterparts.

## Salient Differences in Male and Female Sex Offenders

The etiology of sexual offenses by adult and adolescent females is not well understood. Some consensus exists in the literature about male sexual offenders (Kaufman, Wallace, Johnson, & Reeder, 1995). Theories about why males and females sexually act out differ. Canavan, Higg, and Meyers (1993) found that most females who become sexual perpetrators were also victims of sexual abuse. Frequently, they were in incestuous situations involving the father, the stepfather, or the older brother. Less often, the male perpetrator was a victim.

Females have ready access to children, whether as parents, neighbors, baby-sitters, or older siblings. A breach of the incest taboo by a female is viewed as a greater deviation than incest committed by males (Travin, Cullen, & Protter, 1990).

Allen (1991) noted that more female offenders than male offenders reported having negative family relations. Also, they experienced more physical or sexual abuse during childhood and adolescence.

Offering material gifts for participation in sexual acts is mostly a male phenomenon. However, exploitation of the victim (in which ejaculation took place) occurs more often with female perpetrators (Kaufman et al., 1995; Marvasti, 1986). Females also use foreign objects more frequently than males as part of the sexual offense.

Allen (1991) and Kaufman et al. (1995) suggest that the types of abuse perpetrated by males and females do not differ in many dimensions. The belief of Matthews et al. (1989), however, is that female sex offenders' motives for engaging in the abuse are quite different from males' motives. Females, unlike males, may act out sexually from a strong desire to establish intimacy. Although the definition of intimacy is distorted and confused, it may have developed due to the perpetrator's having been abused (Matthews et al., 1989).

Like their male counterparts, female offenders abuse children both within and outside the home. However, females are more likely to have greater unsupervised access to children (Faller, 1995). An offender in a day-care or preschool setting is more likely to be a female (Finkelhor et al., 1988; Allen, 1991), possibly because of the predominance of female caregivers.

Studies on emotionality suggest that female sex offenders may be more open in discussing their feelings than male sex offenders are. Also, female sex offenders are more likely to be in a dependent relationship and thus pressured into committing a sex offense due to dependence (Matthews et al., 1989). In that case, an adult co-offender may get the female to act out sexually with children in and outside the home (Finkelhor & Russell, 1984; McCarty, 1986).

## Adult Female Sexual Abusers

Child molesters are by far the largest subgroup of women sexual abusers (Wolf, 1985; Schwartz & Cellini, 1995). Very little information exists in the literature on females whose sexual perpetration includes frottage, exhibitionism, voyeurism, and bestiality.

Mothers and stepmothers have been found to abuse most frequently in the home, and teachers and baby-sitters outside the home. Many sexual offenses by women take place in institutional settings (Finkelhor et al., 1988). In a three-year study of reported sexual abuse in day-care settings in the United States, Finkelhor et al. (1988) found that women were 40 percent of the abusers. The incidence of women sex abusers in day-care settings is high because of the low percentage of men in day-care jobs.

Groth (1982) believes that some former incest victims may become offenders to resolve the sexual trauma experienced in childhood. Groth asserts that most child molesters he has worked with had themselves been sexually abused as children. He singles out this factor as contributing to the evolution of mother-child incest.

When the mother is a co-offender or accomplice, her dependency on her spouse or significant other is the major factor (McCarty, 1986). Finkelhor et al. (1988) found that nearly three-fourths of the female perpetrators acted with others, usually men, many of whom were their husbands. Cases involving female perpetrators as co-offenders were much less likely than those involving only male perpetrators to result in arrest or conviction of anyone involved (Bybee & Mowbray, 1993).

Differences in the legal response may stem in part from sex-role stereotyping. Investigators, prosecutors, judges, and juries find it difficult to consider females capable of abusing young children. In particular, they may struggle with this when the perpetrator is educated, married, and has no history of deviance (Bybee & Mowbray, 1993).

Culturally, women are permitted freer range of sexual contact with their children than are men. Mothers are perceived as nurturing and asexual with their children. Many people believe that women cannot be sexually abusive to their children, and at worst, their behavior is labeled as seductive and not helpful. The same behavior in a father is labeled child molestation (Banning, 1989).

Researchers and practitioners have much to learn about adult female sex offenders. Multifactor models developed from a variety of perspectives are the most effective strategies to explain child sexual abuse (Allen, 1991).

## Adolescent Female Sex Offenders

Adolescent female sex offenders present somewhat differently from adult females. One difference is the lack of a co-offender. Adolescents most frequently act independently and without coercion by co-offenders (Fehrenbach & Monastersky, 1988; Fehrenbach, Smith, Monastersky, & Deisher, 1986; Wolf, 1985).

More female than male adolescent sex offenders report having been sexually abused. In a study by Fehrenbach et al. (1986), a total of 46.4 percent of the adolescent females reported being abused, compared with 14.8 percent of the adolescent males. In a study by Hunter, Lexier, Goodwin, Browne, and Dennis (1993), all the teens reported being sexually abused.

Today, researchers know little about the role of fantasy in juvenile female perpetration. Also, the literature contains little information about whether teenage girls, like their male counterparts, have deviant sexual arousal and interest patterns. In a small study by Hunter et al. (1993), most of the youthful offenders reported sexual arousal during one or more of their sexual perpetrations.

Many female sex offenders, besides being victims of sexual abuse, were products of families with few boundaries around the parental dyad. Victims may begin to distort their view of the offender, and their roles become blurred (Canavan et al., 1993). Many of these young girls had experienced the need to go to any length to please a male. Often, they possessed low self-esteem and had incorporated promiscuity into their adult lives because of their childhood experiences (Allen, 1991). A study by McCarty (1986) revealed that between 40 and 50 percent of the subjects reported a history of sexual promiscuity.

Hunter et al. (1993) noted that the literature contains little research describing the developmental and clinical characteristics of adolescent females who sexually molest children. Also, much of what is written is based on data that often represent small samples (Cooper, Swaminath, Baxter, & Poulin, 1990).

## Assessment

The assessment of adolescent female sex offenders needs to be comprehensive. Clinicians need to be aware that deviant sexual behavior in juveniles often occurs in the context of other emotional and behavioral problems. Hunter et al. (1993) found a high incidence of depressive symptomatology, posttraumatic stress disorder, and histories of suicidal ideations and attempts in adolescent female perpetrators. Other common comorbidity conditions include attention deficit disorder, antisocial and narcissistic personality traits, conduct disorders, and chemical abuse.

When possible, the assessment should occur after adjudication and before sentencing of the youth. The court leverage is often essential to a female offender's compliance with treatment. Participation in treatment should be a condition of probation. Seavo (1989) notes that intervention is more effective during the early stages of aberrant behavior — before the behavior becomes chronic and while the abuser is still amenable to treatment. These arguments apply equally to the need for early intervention with male and female sexual abusers.

The evaluators need to recognize possible biases and stereotypes. Clearly, our society tolerates — and perhaps even encourages — more nudity among females than males. Exhibitionism in a female teenager might be labeled promiscuity rather than viewed as a sexual offense such as indecent exposure. The clinical interview is a very important aspect of the assessment process. Therefore, the evaluators need to conduct the interview with sensitivity and in a nonsexist manner.

If possible, the girl's parents or guardian should be part of a comprehensive interview. Often, the evaluator may want to interview the girl separately and again with the relatives present. The parents should also be interviewed separately from the girl. Frequently, the girl may find it difficult to discuss the nature of her sexual behavior in the presence of her family. However, the family has a right to know the extent of the problem after the assessment is completed.

Besides the clinical interview with the girl and the family, reviewing records is important. This might include, but is not limited to, court and social service records, hospital records, and any test results. Using police reports and victim statements is also helpful, according to Becker and Hunter (1992), who note that juvenile abusers often minimize the extent of their sexual perpetration.

For the adult and juvenile male sex offenders, specially designed questionnaires and scales aid the evaluator in the comprehensive assessment process. However, because few assessment tools for females exist, instruments designed to describe cognitions, beliefs, attitudes, and interests of females must be developed.

# Treatment

Treatment should include accountability, empathy, and behavioral management. Victimization issues must be addressed as well. Masturbatory satiation technique is not recommended. The use of photoplethysmography for female abusers is still controversial. It is not recommended for adolescent sex offenders (Cooper et al., 1990).

There needs to be a continuum of specialized treatment for the population of female adolescent sexual abusers. For the less invasive types of offenses, an outpatient program may be appropriate. A strong family component is necessary and should be an integral part of the program. Besides family therapy, the offender should receive individual and group therapy. Treatment should include a general psychotherapy group and specialized didactic groups.

Many outpatient and residential programs offer didactic groups to address the abuser's deficits. One of the current authors worked in an outpatient and residential program that offered groups over a 12-month period. Three groups were offered every four months, and there was a pretest and a posttest. The first phase consisted of sex education, social skills, and values clarification. During the second phase, group issues included cognitive distortions, covert sensitization, and living skills. In the final phase, the groups included empathy, relapse prevention, and relationship issues.

If the girl has perpetrated against a sibling, her removal from the home may be necessary. She may be placed with other relatives as long as no young children live in the relatives' home. When that is not feasible, she may have to be placed in a group home or with a foster family. Sometimes, reuniting the girl with her family may be contraindicated.

## The Victim's Needs

Factors that must be considered with respect to reintegration include the prognosis and the emotional needs of the victim (Becker & Hunter, 1992). The victim's therapist needs to play an active role regarding the appropriateness of a reintegration plan.

Once the girl has completed a residential placement, follow-up with outpatient or aftercare services is usually needed. This follow-up is also necessary if the offender was in an outpatient program. It is generally recommended that aftercare services run for at least a year. During that year, continued court involvement is considered a positive form of support. The girl needs as much support as possible during the first year.

## Sexually Reactive Female Children

Only during the past few years have professionals begun to address prepubescent children's sexual behavior. The perpetrators are children who molest other children. Today, child sexual behavior is frequently dismissed or denied (Johnson, 1989) because many people find it difficult to believe that a prepubescent child could perpetrate sexual aggression on another child. Friedrich and Luecke (1988) note that as the full spectrum of sexual abuse sequelae becomes known, some child victims exhibit sexually aggressive behavior. Their sexual behavior far exceeds the mutual exploratory behavior normally seen in young children and resembles more closely the behavior of older sexual abusers.

Sexual behavior problems in sexually abused children may be related to a child's age, the perpetrator, the number of perpetrators, the frequency and duration of the abuse, and the length of time since the last abuse (Friedrich, Urquiza, & Beilke, 1986). Additionally, Friedrich et al. (1986) found that younger children who were more recently abused by a parent or by multiple perpetrators, and whose abuse was frequent and long term, were more likely to behave in a sexualized manner. For example, in a case of incest between sisters, the older sister had been previously sexually abused. She admitted to abusing her younger sister to get her "sexual fix" (Fortenberry & Hill, 1986).

In the study by Friedrich et al. (1986), the sexual behavior problems noted in sexually reactive children included excessive masturbation, sexual preoccupation, and gender disturbance. Sexually aggressive behavior was not assessed. This study eventually resulted in the development of the Child Sexual Behavior Inventory (Purcell, Beilke, & Friedrich, 1986), a 42-item measurement taken from a review of a variety of sexual behavior problems in children, including sexually aggressive behaviors.

Practitioners need to learn more about sexually reactive children, especially females. They are underserved and understudied. This lack of attention is in part because most of our society wants to deny the existence of young girls acting out sexually and aggressively with other children.

Johnson (1988) was one of the first practitioners to acknowledge and address sexual misconduct between children under the age of 13. Since the early 1990s, sexually reactive children have been treated at The Pines Residential Treatment Program in Virginia, and treatment has been provided at the SPARK Program in California since the late 1980s. In recent years, several other programs have been developed or expanded to include treatment of younger preadolescent children.

Parents and professionals should understand that when children are naturally curious, they are not coercive. They do not use force and threat, and they respond to intervention. Children who are simply curious do not display adult behaviors. Usually when children are curious, they display development that is consistent with their age (Collins, 1992). Therefore, one aspect that must be considered in the assessment and treatment of sexually reactive children is the child's developmental level. This must be considered in terms of the age of the child at the time of onset of victimization, the duration of victimization, the age at which the child's own sexual misconduct began, and the age at which the child commenced counseling (Luecke & Friedrich, 1988).

Other criteria that are important in the assessment process include whether the behavior was persistent and involved coercion and genital contact, and whether the aggressor was at least two years older than the victim (Luecke & Friedrich, 1988). Clinicians must also assess for a psychiatric disorder, using DSM-IV criteria, and deficits in social skills. School-related problems and parent-child relations must be evaluated (Johnson, 1989).

The treatment needs of sexually reactive children are complex and present a therapeutic challenge for the treatment team. Once a thorough assessment has been done, comprehensive treatment should begin. This therapy should include individual, group, and family treatment. Court involvement in the treatment may be necessary. Johnson (1989) notes that criminal prosecution and involvement in the criminal justice and probation system are not necessary for many of these children. However, such measures should be considered for some young child perpetrators.

Frequently, justice-system intervention sends a clear message to girls of the seriousness of their sexually abusive behaviors. It also increases the likelihood that parents will take the child's behavior seriously. Without a firm mandate to treatment, according to Johnson (1989), the children's parents frequently do not follow through and bring them to treatment. The parents of these children also need to be mandated to participate in a parallel treatment process designed specifically for parents of sexually abusive girls.

# References

Allen, C. (1991). *Women and men who sexually abuse children: A comparative analysis.* Brandon, VT: Safer Society Press.

American Humane Association. (1981). *National study on child neglect and abuse reporting.* Englewood, CO: Author.

Banning, A. (1989). Mother-son incest: Confronting a prejudice. *Child Abuse and Neglect, 13,* 563–570.

Becker, J.V., & Hunter, J. (1992). Evaluation of treatment outcome for adult perpetrators of child sexual abuse. *Criminal Justice and Behavior, 19*(1), 74–92.

Bybee, D., & Mowbray, C.T. (1993). Community responses to child sexual abuse in day care settings. *Families in Society, 74*(5), 268–281.

Canavan, M., Higg, D., & Meyers, W. (1993). The development of an adolescent sex offender. *Journal of Sex Research, 29*(1), 131–139.

Collins, J. (1992). Kids hurting kids for sex. *Insight, 3,* 13–38.

Cooper, A., Swaminath, S., Baxter, D., & Poulin, C. (1990). A female sex offender with multiple paraphilias: A psychological, physiologic, and endocrine case study. *Canada Journal of Psychiatry, 36,* 334–337.

Faller, K. (1995). A clinical sample of women who have sexually abused children. *Journal of Child Abuse, 4*(3), 13–30.

Fehrenbach, P., & Monastersky, C. (1988). Characteristics of female adolescent sexual offenders. *American Orthopsychiatric Association, 58*(1), 148–151.

Fehrenbach, P., Smith, W., Monastersky, C., & Deisher, R. (1986). Adolescent sexual offenders: Offender and offense characteristics. *American Journal of Orthopsychiatry, 56,* 225–233.

Finkelhor, D., & Russell, D. (1984). Women as perpetrators. In D. Finkelhor (Ed.), *Child sexual abuse: New theory and research.* New York: Free Press.

Finkelhor, D., Williams, L., Burns, N., & Kalinoski, M. (1988). *Sexual abuse in day care: A national study.* Durham, NH: University of New Hampshire.

Fortenberry, J., & Hill, R. (1986). Sister-sister incest as a manifestation of multi-generational sexual abuse. *Journal of Adolescent Health Care, 7,* 202–204.

Friedrich, W.N., Luecke, W.J. (1988). Young school age sexually aggressive children. *Professional Psychology: Research and Practice, 19*(2), 155–164.

Friedrich, W., Urquiza, A., & Beilke, R. (1986). Behavior problems in sexually abused young children. *Journal of Pediatric Psychology, 11,* 47–57.

Groth, N. (1982). The incest offender. In Suzanne Sgroi (Ed.), *Handbook of clinical intervention in child sexual abuse.* Lexington, MA: DC Heath.

Hunter, J., Lexier, L., Goodwin, D., Browne, P., & Dennis, C. (1993). Psycho-sexual, attitudinal, and developmental characteristics of juvenile female sexual perpetrators in a residential treatment setting. *Journal of Child and Family Studies, 2*(4), 317–326.

Johnson, T. (1988). Child perpetrators: Children who molest other children: Preliminary findings. *Child Abuse and Neglect, 12,* 219–229.

Johnson, T. (1989). Female child perpetrators: Children who molest other children. *Child Abuse and Neglect, 13,* 571–585.

Kaufman, K., Wallace, A., Johnson, C., & Reeder, M. (1995). Comparing female and male perpetrators' modus operandi: Victims' reports of sexual abuse. *Journal of Interpersonal Violence, 10*(3), 322–333.

Luecke, W., & Friedrich, W. (1988). Young school age sexually aggressive children. *Professional Psychology: Research and Practice, 19*(2), 155–164.

Marvasti, J. (1986). Incestuous mothers. *American Journal of Forensic Psychiatry, 7*(4), 63–69.

Matthews, R., Matthews, J., & Speltz, K. (1989). *Female sex offenders: An exploratory study.* Brandon, VT: Safer Society Press.

Matthews, R., Matthews, J., & Speltz, K. (1991). Female sexual offenders: A topology. In M.Q. Patton (Ed.), *Family sexual abuse: Frontline research and evaluation* (pp. 199–219). Newbury Park, CA: Sage.

McCarty, L. (1986). Mother-child incest: Characteristics of the offender. *Child Welfare, 65,* 447–458.

O'Conner, A. (1987). Female sex offenders. *British Journal of Psychiatry, 150*, 615–620.

Purcell, J., Beilke, R., & Friedrich, W. (1986). *Assessing sexual behavior in children: The development of the child sexual behavior inventory.* Paper presented at the annual meeting of the American Psychological Association, Washington, DC.

Schwartz, B., & Cellini, H. (1995). Female sex offender. In B. Schwartz & H. Cellini (Eds.), *The sex offender: Corrections, treatment and legal practice* Vol. 1 (pp. 5.1–5.222). Kingston, NJ: Civic Research Institute.

Seavo, R. (1989). Female adolescent sex offenders: A neglected treatment group. *Social Casework: The Journal of Contemporary Social Work, 70*(2), 114–117.

Simon, R., & Landis, J. (1991). *The crimes women commit, the punishments they receive.* Lexington, MA: Lexington Books.

Travin, S., Cullen, K., & Protter, B. (1990). Female sex offenders: Severe victims and victimizers. *Journal of Forensic Sciences, 35*(1), 140–150.

Wolf, F. (1985, March). *Twelve female sexual offenders.* Presented at Next Steps in Research on the Assessment and Treatment of Sexually Aggressive Persons, St. Louis, MO.

# 4 A Perspective on Sex Offender Treatment for Native Americans

*Myrna Wyse, L.C.S.W.*
*Karen Thomasson, M.D.*

In this chapter on sexual offender treatment for Native Americans, we offer our insights and hope to show how we have come to understand them in our own experiences and healing journeys with Native American people who have sexually offended. We recognize that it does not and cannot represent a comprehensive treatise on the treatment of Native American sexual offenders, as they are a very diverse group (Schwartz, 1995). These offerings do not come from working exclusively with sex offenders but from a broader experience of treating children, youths, families, victims of sexual and physical abuse, victims of neglect and domestic violence, and substance abusers. This chapter is based on our experience with a broad range of psychological trauma and psychiatric conditions. It is a rare sex offender who comes to us with offending behavior as his or her first and only problem.

Advances are constantly being made in the understanding and treatment of sex offenders in psychodynamic and cognitive therapies. Yet a significant parallel exposition of theory that specifically encompasses culturally relevant and dynamic approaches to Native American people who sexually offend has not been made. Ethnic boundaries cannot be crossed, and methodology cannot be challenged, without countertherapeutic distortions arising, regardless of the skill and experience of the therapist (Dinges, Trimble, Manson, & Pasquale, 1981; Levly, 1986).

We set forth some considerations that we feel must be present to develop culturally intuitive and relevant healing stances and interventions for these populations. Nowhere is there less justification for psychological piety and rigidity, or holding closely to monistic conceptions of personality, psychological health, pathology, or treatment interventions, than there is in working with Native American people (Barter & Barter, 1974; Borunda & Shore, 1978). Theirs has been a complex and rich heritage of healing arts, holistic health, and interdependent and dynamic community functioning that worked well for them prior to European contact (Armstrong, 1971; Lockhart, 1981).

Western philosophy is based on what it considers to be a naturally occurring polarity and tension between individual self-fulfillment and social connectedness to the group or community. The "ideal" developmental progression favors movement toward more or less complete separation or individuation (rather than dependency) and full integration into the local community group (Watts, 1975). More closely related to Eastern philosophies, Native American epistemology conceives of "illness" as occurring when the gestalt or harmony among all elements, including community and nature itself, has somehow become unbalanced and nonsynchronous. Conceived of in this way, healing becomes a journey to reestablish harmony and balance within the continuum, not just within the individual. In this quest, entire social and animistic systems are called into play that encompass the involvement of entire clans and communities. It takes only a slight shift in understanding to realize the devastating — almost fatal — impact that community disintegration has had on Native peoples (Thornton, 1987).

Critical elements in working with Native American sex offenders are the understanding and appreciation of the fact that their cultural history is one of brutalization and dehumanization ("How to Use," 1975; Armstrong, 1971; Pearson, 1973). Just as one takes a careful developmental history of any patient, it is critical that therapists inform themselves of their patient's cultural history. Just as family history does, cultural and racial history informs diagnosis and treatment. Lateral abuse, that is, abuse occurring between and among Native Americans, can be linked to abuse at the hands of the dominant culture, that is, subjugation, displacement, dispersion, breakup, dislocation, identity erasure, and other assimilation efforts (Pearson, 1973; Thornton, 1986). We discuss the need to search for, validate, and make available extant cultural beliefs, practices, and healing metaphors in approaching a healing journey with a patient.

Whether one is a dominant-culture or Native therapist, ongoing and dynamic conflicts in spiritual, philosophical, personal, religious, sexual, political, legal, and professional belief systems will impede empathic and therapeutic responses to the sex offender. Although that can be taken as an obvious caveat to any therapy in any setting, it is even more relevant in the cross-cultural and sexual arena. An error in professional or cultural judgment may be compounded significantly and result in higher rates of treatment failure or dropout (Ryan & Spence, 1978). This cautionary note should not discourage therapists but is put forth to suggest one of the reasons why the treatment of this specific population has been notoriously unsuccessful.

Community lack of involvement with dominant-culture treatment and legal interventions (possibly perceived as continued abuse and subjugation) is another element contributing to lack of treatment or treatment failure (Sue & Zane, 1987). A culturally meaningful stance is just as important in mobilizing the family, clan, and community to invest and participate in treatment and assist in the perpetrator's healthy reintegration into the community. Thus, work with the individual perpetrator necessarily implies work with the traumatized community to restore its integrity, cohesion, and spiritual harmony and balance (Thornton, 1987).

# The Role of Historical Trauma

As immigration burgeoned and the birth of a nation spawned the need for a new homeland for European outcasts, adventurers, and persecuted groups, Natives came to represent a barrier to a new and desired life (Armstrong, 1971; Nabokov, 1991). Psychologically speaking, the newcomers needed to see Natives as less than rightful partners, less than equals (i.e., as "savages") in the process of merging two very different worldviews. The assumption that these "savages" must be brought into the fold or treated as unequal wards set into motion a complex series of events impacting the Native psyche. Those events foreshadowed the eventual loss of cultural identity and the internalization of intracultural violence as a way of life (Pearson, 1973). Clearly, no single event, person, or group is responsible for the destruction of the culture and psyche of any tribal group of people. Also, European immigration and land conquest initiated a complex set of interactions among many different tribal and immigrant groups, which led to the destructive interplay between them. Intrinsic factors of tribal life and extrinsic factors imported from outside the Americas combined to create a new gestalt for all groups concerned (Means, 1995). Sadly, the Native way of life interacted with the forces of European expansion and culture to render Natives the losers culturally, psychologically, and spiritually (Vioa, 1990).

Other relevant factors have lent their insidious contributions to the historical trauma suffered by Native Americans. Prime among them is the loss of Native identity as caretakers and protectors of the natural world. The view that settlers had the inalienable right to own and use the land and its resources in any way suitable to them was anathema to tribal people spiritually and politically. That view disrupted the natural order of their lives ("How to Use," 1975; Tedlock & Tedlock, 1975). Government acquisition of tribal lands through treaty, duplicity, outright seizure, land allotments, warfare, and the imposition of reservations led to the loss of sacred land and tribal self-sufficiency. The result: the concomitant loss of the Native identity as caretakers, protectors, and beings integral to the natural world (Hertzbert, 1971).

The psychological wound to the soul of Native people cannot be understated and exists in deep-rooted pain, unresolved grief, and a refugee mind-set (Hertzbert, 1971). The creation of reservations has never settled the core issues still extant for both Native Americans and immigrant descendants.

Schools further decimated the proud and rich Native heritage and effectively destroyed the family and tribal unit (Perry, 1994a, 1994b). Children were taken against their will, often without the consent of their parents, at very young ages. Some were transported to other states — lands unknown to them. They were often kept for years at a time without visits home. In those schools, they were absolutely forbidden to speak their own language, wear their own clothing, or practice their spiritual beliefs and customs (Jacobs, 1972). They were subjected to harsh corporal punishment. We now know that sexual abuse was a common practice (Peterson, Proust, & Schwarz, 1991).

Frightened, lonely, seemingly abandoned, denied their cultural coping rituals, and exposed to physical, emotional, and, in many cases, sexual abuse, the young people became emotionally traumatized, confused, and split in their loyalties. "They told us that Indian ways were bad. They said we must get civilized. I remember that word. It means 'be like the white man.' But I did not believe Indian ways were wrong. But they kept teaching. ... The books told how bad the Indians had been to the white man. We all wore white man's clothes and ate white man's food and went to white man's churches and spoke white man's talk. And so after awhile, we also began to say Indians were bad. We laughed at our own people and their blankets and their cooking pots" (Sun Elk, quoted in Colloway et al., 1995, pp. 236, 249). Sun Elk's statement highlights the move from resistance to acceptance and, most crucial, to the students' aggressive rejection of their own people and heritage.

The significance of the boarding-school experience in the dynamic link to abuse cannot be too strongly emphasized. Sun Elk's statement graphically depicts the tendency for a victim to internalize the abuse and take on the characteristics of the abuser, to become like the abuser. The "new" abuser, in turn, devalues the "new" victim and all that the victim stands for through the projection of the weak and despised self (Ochberg, 1988). The psychological key to survival for the victim of abuse necessitates internalizing the aggressor, thus producing an illusory sense of power and control over helplessness. Separations from tribal life and identity were temporal, geographic, and, eventually, psychological (Lockhart, 1981; Colloway et al., 1995).

Many children lost contact with their tribes, their families, their heritage, their selfhood. They were made to feel shame and guilt about their Native identities; many students eventually rejected their parents (whom they barely knew) because of their "Indianness" (Katz, 1979; Lockhart, 1981). In many instances, students who later returned to their tribes felt caught between two worlds, comfortable in neither; they were viewed by their clans and tribal communities with suspicion and treated as outsiders (Colloway et al., 1995). As a result of the abuse they suffered at school, the careful teachings of tribal elders concerning appropriate and meaningful social interactions and boundaries, sexual and otherwise, were discounted and, in many cases, forgotten (Pearson, 1973). Furthermore, children were exposed to a school culture in which parenting did not occur, so they were unable to internalize appropriate and loving parenting models that they could later incorporate into their own parenting.

Present-day boarding schools on and off the reservations are a far cry from earlier days. However, too many instances of abuse and neglect by non-Native and Native employees, as well as peers, still exist, indicating that this sad chapter in the history of the

United States is not over. This statement in no way casts aspersions on the many modern boarding schools that endeavor to provide excellent and loving education and caretaking for their young charges.

Many tribes were matrilineal, tracing descent on the female side, with female ownership of family resources (Armstrong, 1971; Beck, Walters, & Francisco, 1990). Long-established systems of teaching the oral histories, mores, and attitudes regarding sexuality and proscribed social behaviors among and between individuals (most often taught by mothers, aunts, grandmothers, or maternal male relatives through storytelling and lessons) were disrupted by intermarriage outside the Native community (Armstrong, 1971; Mankiller, 1993; Nabokov, 1991). Native women in interracial unions were often expected to leave the tribal community and move to the homes of their European husbands, thereby cutting the links in the communal teaching of gender respect, roles, and responsibilities. Native women frequently became subservient to their European husbands, in many instances were the victims of sexual and domestic violence, and were treated as slaves or property (Jacobs, 1972; Thornton, 1987). Those shifts rendered women and children bereft of rights and respect and contributed to a change in intertribal relationships from democratic and egalitarian to gender- and age-related oppression, control, and devaluation (Thornton, 1987). A more obvious consequence was the attenuation of childbearing potential and the loss of children as the repositories of their Native ethos.

The eradication of (and changes to) deeply held Native spiritual beliefs of oneness with the universe was espoused and supported by the Christian missionary movement through conversion ("How to Use," 1975; Deloria, 1992). The goal was to impose Judeo-Christian subjectivity on indigenous forms of spirituality. Tribal spiritual practices and beliefs were rejected outright. Evangelistic missionaries were unable to see, interpret, or even acknowledge the meaningfulness or validity of Native cosmology, including sexual beliefs and practices, and attempted to eradicate the Natives' non-Christian worldview and the behaviors associated with it (Armstrong, 1971). The fragmentation and compartmentalization of holistic social orders and belief systems reconstructed spirituality into religion and spiritual imbalance in the continuum (oneness and balance with all life) into individual psychopathology. The resulting hybrid robbed the effectiveness of spiritual healing rituals and ceremonies designed to restore balance in the community and in the individual (Beck et al., 1990; Mooney, 1982). Many healing ceremonies were irrevocably lost.

## Psychotherapeutic Approaches

We emphasize the importance of studying the cultural beliefs and practices of tribal groups in their particularity, because no generic Native American philosophy exists. In addition, we caution against the exclusive use of Western-based psychotherapies that can be irrelevant and traumatize the patient seeking help. We now move to more direct considerations of the therapeutic role and stance of both non-Native and Native therapists.

The non-Native therapist must not only know about but also fully accept and respect a different paradigm or worldview, although the therapist may not, or cannot, fully comprehend the less obvious and more complex components of that paradigm. Shrouded in their own worldview, time and place in history, and gender and personality, therapists can be expected to struggle to understand; however, their awareness of that circumstance is the sine qua non of thoughtful cross-cultural therapeutic contact (LaFromboise & Rowe, 1983). At the same time, therapists must be grounded in their own traditions without arrogance or deification of them. Those non-Native therapists comfortable with uncertainty, who maintain an openness to philosophical expansion and are able to build an empathic stance in the face of personal doubt, will probably be able to survive the painful realization that despite previous successes in the application of Western-oriented psychology, they often cannot produce effective treatment outcomes when working with Native Americans (Shweder, 1991; Sue & Zane, 1987). As in all caveats directed at therapists working with diversity (even within their own culture), this one enjoins the therapist to "accept patients where they are" and to respect diversity. But moreover, it is very difficult to avoid psychological hegemony when the two worldviews are so vastly different. It is equally difficult to take into account the pervasive cultural posttraumatic stress syndrome now endemic to Native Americans (Ochberg, 1988). Western academic institutions have taught therapists to view dysfunction myopically and outside its context, thus fostering the belief that pathology

resides solely within the patient (Robbins, 1996; Shweder &
Bourne, 1982).

Compounding these barriers to an empathic stance is the fact
that non-Native therapists are often regarded by Native clients as
representatives and members of the oppressing culture. Therapists
may even view themselves that way and come to the therapy with
unresolved guilt or with a defensive stance that seeks to distance
them from their own dominant culture: "Those events occurred long
ago and were not perpetrated by me," or, "I don't think that way,
though members of my culture do." Other defensive stances may
project anger, shame, or guilt onto the patient in an attempt to
counter those feelings (Brachette, 1990; Deloria, 1992). There are
no easy answers to these dilemmas. Unless therapists validate and
acknowledge that they are members of the perpetrating culture and
understand the role that sociohistorical factors leading to violence
and oppression have played in the problems that the client is experiencing, the therapy at best is doomed and, at worst, may even be
destructive to the client (Lockhart, 1981). Supervision by a therapist experienced in working with both worldviews and cultures is
highly recommended.

Many Native Americans mistrust non-Native mental-health
practitioners and researchers, a distrust that must be accepted non-
defensively and without reprisal (Lockhart, 1981; Pearson, 1973).
In this vein, therapists who attempt to become caricatures of
shamans or medicine men in an attempt to do good fail to realize
that they will frequently be perceived as stealing and wresting
away from Natives yet another sacred sense of themselves (Dippe,
1982; Shoshan, 1989). Therapists need not abandon Western psychologies to be effective. A systemic approach can be employed
whereby traditional Native psychologies are practiced in conjunction with Western models but not made subservient to them
(Attneave, 1974; Borunda & Shore, 1978).

Native therapists are also presented with enormous challenges
as they formulate a therapeutic stance. Both therapists and patients
may have been exposed to intergenerational violence, have had differing responses to it, and be in varying stages of healing. Both
have incorporated, to varying degrees, aspects of the dominant culture, giving the appearance of one party in the therapist-client dyad
as more "traditional" or "Western" (Morgan, 1931; Whitaker &
Malone, 1953). A dynamic dance exists between having an understanding of a patient and overidentifying with him or her. Also

important are the distinctions that therapists must make between understanding the sociohistorical context of sexual offending and prescribing the therapeutic steps that must be taken by perpetrators in fully acknowledging and changing their offending behaviors. (This difficulty is also encountered by non-Native therapists whose horror at, and perhaps, guilt over, the plight of a Native patient may blur their psychotherapeutic judgment.)

As with non-Native therapists, Native therapists must not do violence to their own belief systems, as ambivalent and evolving as they may be (Borunda & Shore, 1978). This seems self-evident. However, many Native therapists are trained in Western universities, hired by Western-oriented institutions and agencies, and work alongside dominant-culture therapists who may be critical of traditional practices. In this climate it is most difficult to maintain a sense of one's culture and its long tradition of healing, especially since so many of these traditions and rituals cannot be reinstated in their original and unaltered forms. This quandary may be made more difficult if, in the therapists' need to defend against these criticisms, unintentional or intentional distortions around their use are made (Ryan & Spence, 1978).

A discussion about whether and to what degree any Native American ever becomes totally acculturated or, conversely, whether the patient can ever return to a purely Native worldview would be lengthy and fruitless. The most relevant consideration for our purposes is to point out that Native therapists face the enormous subjective task of juggling their own personal, dynamic, and evolving belief systems and resolving their own issues and, at the same time, avoiding the pitfall of pseudocompliance with or adulation of Western psychological systems. Such deference can contribute to a conscious or unconscious devaluation of self, Native culture, and patient, thus replicating the original trauma in yet another sphere (Colloway et al., 1995).

Natives seeking help from agencies and clinics staffed by both Native and non-Native therapists may request that they be seen by a non-Native therapist. The reasons for this request are not always immediately apparent. A patient may fear that his or her disclosures and difficulties will not be held in confidence by a Native therapist who might be a member of the community, whether or not this fear is valid. This is often the case when the help sought is sexual in nature. Those seeking help may feel a great deal of discomfort, shame, and humiliation. If patients believe the discussion of certain sexual topics to be taboo among their own people, they may deal with such concerns by turning to a non-Native therapist (Sandner, 1979). A clinician should not automatically conclude that the choice has to do with a preference for a non-Native therapist and should take the opportunity to explore with the patient the more relevant concerns and resistances associated with seeking and receiving help.

The role, function, and stance that medicine men, diagnosticians, shamans, or other traditional healers assume with their patients are fundamentally different from those taken by Western therapists or Native therapists schooled in Western models. In general, their practices are less client centered, less temporally based (Adair, 1963; Bergman, 1971; Locke, 1989). They are predicated on prescribed ritual and are community oriented. Native healers assume boundary dimensions and protocol between healer and patient prescribed by that tradition and ritual (Erdoes & Ortiz, 1984). Rarely, if ever, is there a melding of traditional and Western modalities in these Native healing practices. When the ceremonies and counsel of Native healers are sought, profound and stable changes can occur (Albaugh & Anderson, 1974; Borunda & Shore, 1978). They are mentioned here because they are effective and, just as with Western therapists, those who practice their healing methods with competence can be considered therapists of high skill and potency. The inclusion of Native healers in any setting offering therapy to offenders is highly recommended.

## Treatment Considerations

Just as a Native worldview must be taken into account in working with Native Americans, so must the meaning of psychopathology be construed as occurring within the culture and as being shaped and defined by it. The way in which dysfunction is conceived and the efforts taken to ameliorate it — even the way in which the process of change is thought to occur — may be fundamentally different from that conceived by Western models and treatment providers who use them (Barter & Barter, 1974; Harmon 1989). This difference raises some important questions about whether we can ever truly understand, much less fully comprehend, the factors, forces, beliefs, and practices that allow healing in any individual within the culture in which they were born and raised. In the most ideal sense, the process of therapy and healing is a mutual discovery of what the healing potential is within the individual and within the culture itself (Morgan, 1931; Colloway et al., 1995). We contend that what is known about the causes and treatment of sexual offending in Western paradigms will be largely ineffective when applied in Native communities. The power inherent in Native concepts of wellness; the interconnectedness of community, clan, and universe; and the practice of powerful healing ritual should be tapped and employed. Viewed from this perspective, Whitaker and Malone's (1953) observations are germane:

> Clients ... who leave psychotherapy must enter a community of cultural values and function adequately in a real sense. Therefore, psychotherapy must be based on some of the given values around which the culture is patterned. There must be some unity of purpose between psychotherapy and the culture. (p. 63)

There is no such thing as a collective Native American personality, and a thorough understanding of each community in its unique social and historical context is critical. What follows comes largely from our understanding of the Navajo, and although there are similarities to other Native tribes, no attempt is made to conduct a comparative analysis with them.

For the Navajo, mind, body, spirit, and nature are perceived as one, and in traditional belief and practice there is no sense of separation between religion, medicine, philosophy, law, and activities of everyday life (Morgan, 1931). Illness is evidence that there has been a disruption in the harmony of these elements. Emphasis is placed more on the cause of the disruption than on symptoms that arise from it, and in traditional healing practices, the patient is relatively passive, while diagnostic and curative power resides within the practitioner (Kunitz & Levy, 1981; Watts, 1975). It is the patient's stance to assume a hopeful and receptive attitude toward the practitioner. The goal of ceremony is to restabilize, restructure, and restore harmony among all elements. Traditional Navajo belief holds that one of the causes of illness and psychic pain is the violation of moral, social, and ceremonial rules (Beck et al., 1990; Morgan, 1931). Another cause is supernatural or natural events or a person's accidental contact with these events (lightning, for example) (Locke, 1989). Moreover, thinking thoughts about disease may induce its presence, maintenance, and negative outcome. Improper and negative thinking may presage disease.

Compare these beliefs with the Western psychiatric paradigm that asserts that the origins of psychic pain lie within the individual (psychodynamic or learning theory) and/or within the group and society of which the individual is part (social cause theory). In this schema, patients are expected to be active partners in the treatment, with the locus of control regarding change ultimately residing within themselves (Barter & Barter, 1974; Morgan, 1931). This therapeutic process can be described as patient centered as distinct from therapist centered, which is the traditional method of intervention for the Native patient (Atkinson, Morton, & Sue, 1979; Morgan, 1931). A passive stance on the part of a Native patient toward the therapist or treatment may not necessarily signify lack of motivation. When Native patients discuss their behavior or attribute causes to it, they may be misconstrued as employing defense mechanisms, such as denial or other defenses as conceived in Western psychodynamic theory (Bergman, 1973; Dinges et al., 1981).

What, then, are some foundations in Native culture? What are the beliefs regarding the causes of psychic disturbance and the healing methods that can be employed when treating the sex offender? We start on a cautionary note. Psychometric testing validated only for dominant-culture populations should be viewed with skepticism and carefully reviewed before application (Dinges et al., 1981; Ryan & Spence, 1978). The pitfalls and inaccuracies should be apparent to all sophisticated therapists and evaluators. One of us recently attended a national conference on the treatment of sexual offenders and noticed that there was not one plethysmograph or sexual thematic test using pictures of Native subjects or themes in its protocol, although there were pictures of Hispanics and Blacks. When she asked about this, every exhibitor responded that it had not occurred to them or that there would be no market for them. To assess the nature and content of sexual fantasies, proclivities, and preferences from this Western-weighted testing may result in grave misunderstandings about the nature of the offending and the role it plays for the patient (Schwartz, 1995). At the present time it is recommended that this information be obtained from the face-to-face interview and from continuing discussion in treatment about the nature of the sexual life of the offender, despite the obvious disadvantages implicit in self-reporting. This is a challenging area of exploration and research as treatment programs proliferate on reservations and as the legal system increasingly calls on "experts" to assess culpability and dangerousness of offenders.

## The Power of the Group to Induce Change

In the Native American world, a powerful healing mechanism is belief in the power of the group to induce change (Forsyth, 1990). Although there may be a present-day tendency to shun or turn aside the plight of the offender, historically it has been viewed as an investment by the community at large in the eradication of any "disease" or maladjustment (Erdoes & Ortiz, 1984; Hertzbert, 1971). This philosophy is no longer fully intact, given the install-ment of Western mental-health, social-service, and legal systems in which individual culpability is assigned and adjudicated. Yet, tra-ditionally, the clan or community at large assumed collective responsibility for the aberrant behavior of any one of its individual members and would make restitution to the aggrieved party in an appropriate manner (Brachette, 1990; Erdoes & Ortiz, 1984). The concept of social relatedness and collective harmony is embedded in the Navajo term *K'e nsdzin*, or "I am at peace with all; I am related to all; I am respectful to all" (Locke, 1989; Skynner, 1975). Socially, the Navajo relate to one another as kin, and it is within the clan system that physical and emotional needs are identified and taken care of. *K'e* encompasses principles and procedures to establish and maintain relationships of goodwill and solidarity (Locke, 1989; Morgan, 1931). In such enduring systems, related-ness and collective oneness are derived. From a psychological per-spective, the concept of identity is contained within the social group, which provides a sense of security and cohesion. There is no sense of polarization or opposition between self and group, as in Western societies. Meaningful identity and purpose in life for any one individual are derived from maintaining harmony among all elements, not from becoming separate and distinct from them (Locke, 1989).

Some implications for the treatment of Native sex offenders based on *K'e* can be considered. The Peacemaker Court is an indige-nous system based on traditional principles of justice and social relatedness, used when one party or clan feels aggrieved by another. Peacemaker Courts can be used when devising interventions, social sanctions, monitoring, and control of an offender and keeping the community's safety in mind (Locke, 1989; Wilber, 1990). There is precedent for those courts to intervene in each of these areas, although the prosecution of sex offenses is currently the jurisdiction of the federal court system. Because the Native court is an indigenous form of community intervention and justice, and because it directly and explicitly sanctions the principle that the power and wisdom to effect change lie in the community itself, it can be an effective agent in dealing with sex offenders (Locke, 1989).

The Western legal system has not been fully accepted in Native communities, and some Native jurists themselves perceive tremendous flaws in it when it comes to dispensing justice and promoting healing in Indian country (Lockhart, 1981). At the present time, the FBI is called in to investigate sexual crimes committed on the reservation, another "outside" agency associated with the dominant culture. Western courts are viewed as dispensers of punishment, thereby creating more disharmony, not less. We must recall that law, spirituality, and living within $K'e$ are viewed as one and are not reducible to their constituent elements; to leave any party involved unhealed and out of balance is to create imbalance in the entire system (Locke, 1989). The present investigative and legal system is flawed from this point of view, resulting in limited cooperation by families and victims. One way to look at this phenomenon is to see the lack of cooperation and underutilization of services vital to victims and offenders as a cultural boundary-maintenance function in which noncooperation represents an attempt to avoid further erosion of the personal identity with the culture (Bergman, 1974; Lockhart, 1981). Viewed in this way, it is vital that the community or group becomes the foundation of intervention, with individual treatment formulations flowing from it.

The concept that groups contain the power to heal is not merely superficial but a real and profound component of the Native worldview that should be used in present-day treatment interventions. Elders no longer hold the time-honored position of containing and maintaining the teaching of sexual and relational mores and practices within their social group (Attneave, 1974; Beck et al., 1990; Janis, 1972). This situation makes it imperative that all group programs afford an opportunity for group members to discuss, grapple with, and fully explore with one another why there is so much confusion around their own sexual identities and practices. The inclusion of tribal elders in this process is very useful. Such discussion should include information from a knowledgeable source about the "soul wound" suffered by Native peoples, which has been eloquently and persuasively described by Duran and Duran in their book *Native American Postcolonial Psychology* (1975). Intergenerational sexual abuse (many offenders in Indian country have been abused themselves) can be explored through the documentation of rampant sexual abuse in boarding schools and by discussing the effects on individual and collective self-esteem through the erosion of cultural mores by the dominant culture (Armstrong, 1971; Terr, 1990).

Although this group approach may appear to be merely an intellectual exercise, it is rarely experienced that way by offenders, who are eager to understand and explore the historical roots and precursors to their own sexually abusive behavior. It is this acknowledgment, first from outside sources, then from internal "knowing," that Duran and Duran (1975) cite as a necessary precursor to healing; it in no way impedes the progress of the abuser in taking personal responsibility for his or her own sex abuse in the present. In the group setting, these principles can be most effectively underscored and reinforced, with offenders further along in their treatment becoming excellent mentors to those just entering treatment. Western therapists, trained in sex offender treatment, are strongly cautioned by their teachers against enabling patients to project blame and responsibility onto any outside agent to rationalize away, minimize, or avoid responsibility for their offenses; however, we strongly believe that the "soul wound" inflicted upon Natives through generations of cultural genocide perpetrated against them must be dealt with before the offender can change his or her own personal sex-offending behavior. The offender can then be directed, with the help of other group members, to examine and explore concepts of *K'e* in developing a relapse-prevention plan. This aspect is considered to be an important individual component of sex offender treatment protocols and directly relates to the sense of social relatedness critical in Native thinking (Barter & Barter, 1974).

## Group Expectations of Healing and Support

Throughout the history of the Navajo, group expectations of healing and support have been in place (Barter & Barter, 1974; Locke, 1989). This might be a concept that Anglos or those brought up in a primarily Western philosophical paradigm "dream" about or experience only periodically. In the 1960s, young people attempted to enact such principles in their own groups, though it was never incorporated into Western society at large (Janis, 1972). Therapists and patients who have used group treatment report powerful experiences within the group in its collective expectation that change and growth will occur for its individual members (Forsyth, 1990). There is a wealth of material, especially in the fields of sociology, political science, mental health, and anthropology, about group phenomena (Forsyth, 1990). No doubt Americans, who worship at the altar of separation-individuation and individual accountability, would shudder at the amount of change occurring in themselves that can be laid at the door of group expectation and interface. One important difference between Whites and Natives is that Native daily life and practice reflect this belief: it has been the norm, and variations from the norm have come about since "first contact."

In traditional healing ceremonies, the patient's friends, relatives, and extended clan members, as well as interested community members, gather outside the hogan (the traditional dwelling). Bergman (1973) points out an important element in this participation that may well have eluded the Western eye. Participation is community based but nonanalytic; that is, the community of well-wishers is not there to analyze, treat, or attempt to explore the role they may play in the patient's problem or to actively involve themselves in its amelioration (Locke, 1989). This distinction is important and may account for the fact that, although the community, clan, and immediate family members are intensely related to and concerned about the patient's suffering, their participation in the treatment occurs at a completely different level from that expected by Western-oriented helpers (Attneave, 1974). These helpers may understand participation to mean something quite different and inaccurately conclude that the patient's support system is flawed or even absent — although this may well be the case in the presence of alcoholism, family disruption, and physical and sexual abuse. Again, personal regulation and the power of the group in healing are sociocentric and interpersonal, not intrapsychic, egocentric, and lineally construed (Forsyth, 1990; Morgan, 1931). Those close to the patient will be involved, but not in a way that suggests that there is a direct, causal (linear) link in etiology between patient and family, mother and child, and so forth. The association is more systemic, and the disharmony created by the problem is partially, if not fully, ameliorated by the *presence of those involved in the life of the patient who is suffering.*

These considerations suggest that offender treatment should occur in a group setting through which offenders become used to dealing with others during treatment and where the dynamics of cultural and personal posttraumatic stress disorder will have been experienced by all group members. It also suggests that, whenever the social system is sought (family, clan, friendship) to give support and input to the treatment, there should be no attempts to squeeze participants into active soul-searching about their role in the offending; rather, participation should be reframed into searching for ways to be supportive to the patient. This stance has been helpful to us in our work with children and families, although some families involve themselves in ways more in line with a Western worldview of causation, conflict, personality disturbance, and intrapsychic distress. Even when that happens, it is within a milieu of a sociocentric relatedness that healing may ultimately and most effectively occur for the Native sex offender (Barter & Barter, 1974; Borunda & Shore, 1978).

*Resistance, Taboo, and Social Behavior*

The technical term for resistance in Western psychodynamic theory and practice involves both conscious and, more frequently, unconscious processes of conflict, motivation, and intentionality. These processes work to protect individuals from experiencing crosscurrents of emotional conflict in their own consciousness (Atkinson et al., 1979; Barter & Barter, 1974). Likewise, taboos can be both unconscious and explicitly taught and learned through individual or group experiences. Taboos are prohibitions against certain behaviors or expressions that might bring harm to the individual and/or other members of the group. In the Navajo worldview, violation of taboo is often at the heart of what is believed to cause illness (Locke, 1989).

Unfortunately, Western healers, though they understand the concept of resistance, all too often regard taboos as mere "superstition" and evidence of primitive and magical thinking (Lockhart, 1981). According to the Westerner, such beliefs add more misery than enlightenment to those believing in them. They then fail to treat taboo respectfully, or psychotherapeutically, and summarily dismiss it in diagnosis and treatment.

Furthermore, taboo can be naively and inaccurately attributed to resistance on the patient's part. Education regarding the "real truth," and subtle or not-so-subtle pressure on the patient to eschew and reframe Native taboo as a causative agent in illness, is all too often practiced by misinformed therapists. The effect of taboo on the patient, or a violation of taboo, is often dismissed by the therapist as a meaningless, if not vexing, hurdle to overcome in the treatment process for the patient. Viewing it that way, the therapist loses out, and a significant, perhaps vital, dynamic is bypassed.

Therapists treating Navajo sex offenders often encounter patients' beliefs about taboo. Incest and improper sexual behavior and contact both inside and outside clan groups are taboo and are directly referred to in the creation stories (Locke, 1989; Wyman, 1936). There are discrete principles and procedures to follow to maintain the balance of a peaceful, harmonious coexistence in nature and in social groups, the violation of which causes irreparable harm unless prescribed rituals and ceremonies are undertaken to ameliorate their impact (Attneave, 1974; Locke, 1989). Although incest and sex offending are also taboo in Western society, violation neither calls for a concept of healing in a spiritual context nor is necessarily thought of in a holistic paradigm of health and illness (Barter & Barter, 1974). It could be argued that treatment should be thought of in this light, and several Western religious groups have sought to do precisely that. Frequently, the latter employ guilt- or shame-enhancing mechanisms to induce control of deviant thoughts and fantasies, an approach very different from Native healing practices, which arise from an entirely different cosmology.

Patients who subscribe to Native or other organized religious beliefs should be offered an opportunity to consult with a traditional healer or religious guide and to have their beliefs included in their relapse-prevention plan (Adair, 1963; Beck et al., 1990; Borunda & Shore, 1978). Consultation with Native healers or other Native therapists is critical (Adair, 1963; Bergman, 1974; Wyman, 1936).

The question has been asked whether, by consulting a Native healer, the offender is capitalizing on a dualistic model of intervention to avoid treatment in either domain. Discussion of this problem should occur on a case-by-case basis within the treatment team; however, more often than not, therapists err in the direction of excluding Native healing practices in the treatment and relapse-prevention plan of the offender. Another complex issue calling for careful and sensitive consideration arises when patients have undergone a traditional healing ceremony (Adair, 1963; Erdoes & Ortiz, 1984). They may be instructed not to discuss their illness after such ceremonies in order not to undo the curative effects of the ceremony. Such instructions, if followed, make it next to impossible for offenders to undergo treatment elsewhere. Some treatment teams suggest that, when an offender requests traditional healing that disallows subsequent disclosure and talk about the offense, the request be respected and that a Western-oriented approach not be combined with it concurrently (Adair, 1963; Dinges et al., 1981). The supervising agent (usually the court and/or social-service agency) will then require proof that a ceremony has occurred and will continue to monitor the offender after treatment. In other words, either mode can be elected, but it must be adhered to, and the offender must be monitored. Obviously we are referring to outpatient therapy here and not incarceration or inpatient therapy when the court orders a specific treatment facility or program. Efficacy studies regarding this approach are not available and may never be; however, we caution against any treatment program that does not include Native beliefs and treatment modalities, most notably in the identification and attenuation of the sex-offending cycle itself.

Social behavior is also culturally construed and derives from collective beliefs and attitudes deeply embedded in the psyche (Dinges et al., 1981). Again, we cannot stress strongly enough that social convention must not be mistaken for resistance. Soft, gentle speech, avoidance of direct eye contact, gentle or absent handshaking upon meeting, long pauses between sentences or between two conversing parties, or hesitation in speaking of sexual matters are culturally modal behaviors, although not uniform among all Native populations. Natives consider these behaviors to be respectful, and such behaviors are not meant to convey avoidance, discomfort, or off-putting attitudes during conversation (Barter & Barter, 1974; Borunda & Shore, 1978). Furthermore, any offender program incorporating social skills learning should include socially normative behavior of the client's culture in its curriculum.

## The Role of Cognitive, Time-limited, Problem-focused Therapy

The field of sex offender therapy is in a constant state of flux and change. Both clinical and research data point to several treatment methods that are considered necessary to effectively treat the sexual offender. *The ATSA Practitioner's Handbook* (Association for the Treatment of Sexual Abusers, 1993) lists these as (1) arousal control, (2) cognitive therapy, (3) relapse prevention, (4) improvement in primary relationships, (5) couples or family therapy, (6) increase in social competence, (7) support systems, (8) victim empathy, (9) biomedical approaches, and (10) follow-up treatment (pp. 7–9). Note that this is a cognitive, problem-focused model targeted specifically at the sexual offending behavior of the perpetrator. Cognitive therapy addresses distortions in thought and attitude that eventually enable the offender to minimize, justify, and rationalize deviant behavior, which break down standard constraints and allow the offender to move from fantasy to behavior.

There is reason to believe that these components of treatment can be effectively applied to the treatment of Native American offenders in a contextually relevant manner. In the above model, the locus of control lies more with the therapist than with the patient and is similar to traditional treatment methodology in which the medicine man teaches and admonishes the patient to engage or not to engage in specific thoughts and behavior. The approach is problem centered and emphasizes family and community support systems. It pays particular attention to the antecedent thought processes leading to the offending behavior itself, not unlike the Native emphasis on thought as central to illness and health. Healing in the Native sense is more spatially than linearly conceived and does not involve the passage of time so much as it does the intensity of the psychotherapeutic experience (Duran & Duran, 1975). A therapy should be designed that is more need and result oriented than time oriented. To summarize, an offender treatment program can be designed that is cognitive, problem focused, and used in a time frame that addresses the needs of the offender and the safety of the community.

# Developing a Treatment Program

At the present time, not much is known about the efficacy of cross-cultural treatment models designed specifically for Native American sex offenders. It is very tempting to resort to Western treatment models, still in their infancy, and to construct research designs based on them. We are aware of several training projects for therapists working with Native Americans who offend and know of several programs in operation in Indian country that are community based and report positive results. Among these, the Fort Peck Youth Treatment Program is notable, as is a program developed with the Hopi tribe under the direction of Anita Schacht, who also developed the Special Child Sexual Abuse Project. Dewey Ertz, Ed.D., a Cheyenne River Sioux from the Manlove Psychiatric Group in Rapid City, South Dakota, trains therapists to work with Native juvenile offenders.

If the power of the group and the interrelatedness of the offenders and their social group are to be utilized and not denigrated, sex offending should be conceived of and treated as a public-health problem. It is critical that the larger society of which the offender is a part devises treatment programs and strategies to examine what is known about the treatment of those who sexually offend. Home visits, availability of treatment providers 24 hours a day and 7 days a week in cases of crisis (sexual offenses often occur at times of great stress), community commitment to treatment of alcohol abuse (a problem interwoven with sexual abuse), and the understanding that employment and economic considerations may contribute to the problem — all these approaches and factors are a part of the public-health approach.

Studies of combat-related posttraumatic stress disorder among second-generation Holocaust survivors suggest that the Holocaust trauma has been transmitted from survivors to their children in ways not yet fully understood (Solomon, Kotler, & Mikulincer, 1988; Krell, 1990; Moskovitz & Krell, 1990). Duran and Duran (1975) refer time and again to the "soul wound" sustained by Native people cross-generationally in their book *Native American Postcolonial Psychology*. In her article "Every Time History Repeats Itself, the Price Goes Up: The Social Reenactment of Trauma," Sandra Bloom (1996) suggests that whole nations become organized around traumatic experiences. Until the deleterious influences of alcoholism, unemployment, poverty, and sociocultural disintegration loosen their hold, it cannot be known whether the dynamics of sexual offending in the Native population are similar to the ones documented in the dominant culture. In the meantime, working, collaborative, community-based task forces can be formed that include as many sectors of the community as possible. Public-health and community organizations may be as helpful as a mental-health treatment team. In this intervention model, assessments would be formulated and services linked, thus ensuring offenders and their families access to agencies and caretakers that will be most effective in meeting their needs. Whole communities and clans are welcomed in this process that seeks to tap the wisdom of all who participate.

The Alkali Lake band of the Shuswap in British Columbia, using a grassroots public-health model to eradicate alcoholism within the community, produced amazing results. The design can be adjusted and implemented in any community seeking help for sexual offenders. The most important lesson documented by the success of the Alkali Lake project was the affirmation of the culture (and the community embedded in that culture) that consensually created its own formal and informal sanctions (i.e., social control) regarding modal, acceptable, and deviant behavior (Duran & Duran, 1975). Through awareness and control mechanisms, Native communities have the ability to recover their former strength and communal power when informed by current realities and evolving knowledge.

# References and Bibliography

Adair, J. (1963). Physicians, medicine men, and their patients. In I. Gladston (Ed.), *Man's image in medicine and anthropology* (pp. 237–257). New York: International Universities Press.

Albaugh, B.J., & Anderson, P.O. (1974). Peyote in the treatment of alcoholism among American Native Americans. *American Journal of Psychiatry, 131*(11), 1247–1250.

Armstrong, V. (1971). *I have spoken: American history through the voices of Indians.* Chicago: Sage.

Association for the Treatment of Sexual Abusers. (1993). *The ATSA Practitioner's Handbook.* Lake Oswego, OR: Author.

Atkinson, D.R., Morton, G., & Sue, D.W. (1979). *Counseling American minorities: A cross-cultural perspective.* Dubuque, IA: Brown.

Attneave, C. (1974). Medicine men and psychiatrists in the Indian Health Service. *Psychiatric Annals, 4*(1), 49–55.

Barter, E.R., & Barter, J.T. (1974). Urban Native Americans and mental health problems. *Psychiatric Annals, 4*(11), 37–43.

Beck, P., Walters, A., & Francisco, N. (1990). *The sacred: Ways of knowledge, sources of life.* Flagstaff, AZ: Northland.

Bergman, R. (1971). The importance of psychic medicine: Training Navajo medicine men. *National Institute of Mental Health Program Reports, 5,* 20–43.

Bergman, R. (1973). Navajo medicine and psychoanalysis. *Human Behavior, 2,* 8–15b.

Bergman, R. (1974). Paraprofessionals in Indian mental health programs. *Psychiatric Annals, 4,* 76–84.

Bloom, S.L. (1996). Every time history repeats itself, the price goes up: The social reenactment of trauma. *Sexual Addiction and Compulsivity, 4*(3) 161–191.

Borunda, Z., & Shore, J. (1978). Neglected minority: Urban Native Americans and mental health. *Journal of Social Psychiatry, 24*(3), 220–224.

Brachette, W. (1990). Traditionalism and the problem of cultural authenticity. In R. Fox (Ed.), *Nationalist ideologies and the production of national culture* (pp. 112–129). American Ethnological Society, Monograph No. 2. Washington, DC: American Ethnological Society.

Colloway, C., Hurtato, A.L., Iverson, P., Jonaitis, A., Kopper, P., Miller, J., Nabakov, P., Sando, J.S., Silber, T., Tanner, H.H., & Wilson, T.P. (1995). *Through Indian eyes: The untold story of Native American peoples.* Pleasantville, NY: Reader's Digest Association, Inc.

Deloria, V., Jr. (1992). *God is red: A native view of religion.* Golden, CO: North American Press.

Dinges, N.G., Trimble, J.E., Manson, S.M., & Pasquale, F.L. (1981). Counseling Native Americans. In A.J. Marcella & P. Pederson (Eds.), *Cross-cultural counseling and psychotherapy* (pp. 71–86). New York: Pergamon.

Dippe, D. (1982). *The vanishing American: White attitudes and U.S. Indian policy.* Lawrence, KS: University Press of Kansas.

Duran, E., & Duran, B. (1975). *Native American postcolonial psychology.* Albany, NY: State University of New York Press.

Erdoes, R., & Ortiz, A. (Eds.). (1984). *American Indian myths and legends.* New York: Pantheon.

Forsyth, D.R. (1990). *Group dynamics* (2nd ed.). Pacific Grove, CA: Brooks/Cole.

Fox, R. (1990). *National ideologies and the production of national cultures.* American Ethnological Society, Monograph No. 2. Washington, DC: American Ethnological Society.

Freire, P. (1990). *Pedagogy of the oppressed.* New York: Continuum Press.

Harmon, A. (1989). When is an Indian not an Indian? *Journal of Ethnic Studies, 18*(2), 95–123.

Hertzbert, H.W. (1971). *The search for an American Indian identity.* New York: Syracuse University Press.

How to use the Bible to justify Manifest Destiny and genocide. (1975). *Akwesasne Notes, 7*(5), 20–31.

Jacobs, W.R. (1972). *Dispossessing the American Indian.* New York: Scribners.

Janis, I.L. (1972). *Victims of groupthink.* Boston: Houghton Mifflin.

Katz, P. (1979). Saulteauz-Ojibway adolescents: The adolescent process amidst a clash of cultures. *Psychiatric Journal of the University of Ottawa, 4*(4), 315–321.

Krell, R. (1990). Holocaust survivors: A clinical perspective. *Psychiatric Journal of the University of Ottawa, 15*(1), 18–21.

Kunitz, S.J., & Levy, J.E. (1981). Navajos. In A. Harwood (Ed.), *Ethnicity and medical care* (pp. 337–396). Cambridge, MA: Harvard University Press.

LaFromboise, T.D., & Rowe, W. (1983). Skills training for bicultural competence: Rationale and application. *Journal of Counseling Psychology 30, 589–595.*

Levly, H. (1986). Why cross-cultural training? In H. Lefley & P. Pederson (Eds.), *Cross-cultural training for mental health professionals* (p. 90). Springfield, IL: Charles C. Thomas.

Locke, R. (1989). *The book of the Navajo.* Los Angeles: Mankind.

Lockhart, B. (1981). Historic distrust and the counseling of American Indians and Alaska natives. *White Cloud Journal, 2,* 31–34.

Mankiller, W. (1993). *Mankiller: A chief and her people.* New York: St. Martin's Press.

Means, R. (1995). *Where white men fear to tread.* New York: St. Martin's Press.

Mooney, J. (1982). Myths of the Cherokee and sacred formulas of the Cherokees. In *Nineteenth* and *Seventh annual reports,* Bureau of American Ethnology. Reprint. Nashville, TN: Elder Booksellers.

Morgan, W. (1931). Navajo treatment of sickness: Diagnosticians. *American Anthropologist, 33,* 390–402.

Moses, R. (1995). The pitfalls and promises of group psychotherapists addressing the political process. In M.F. Ettin, J.W. Fidler, & B.D. Cohen (Eds.), *Group process and political dynamics* (pp. 109–126). Madison, CT: International Universities Press.

Moskovitz, S., & Krell, R. (1990). Child survivors of the Holocaust: Psychological adaptations to survival. *Israel Journal of Psychiatry and Related Sciences,* 27(2), 81–91.

Nabokov, P. (Ed.). (1991). *Native American testimony.* New York: Viking Penguin.

Ochberg, F.M. (1988). *Post-traumatic therapy and victims of violence.* New York: Brunner/Mazel.

Pearson, K.L. (1973). *The Indian in American history.* New York: Harcourt Brace Jovanovich.

Perry, B.D. (1994a). Neurobiological sequelae of childhood trauma: PTSD in children. In M.M. Murburg (Ed.), *Catecholamine function in posttraumatic stress disorder: Emerging concepts* (pp. 233–255). Washington, DC: American Psychiatric Press.

Perry, B.D. (1994b). Neurodevelopment and the psychobiological roots of post-traumatic stress disorder. In L.F. Koziol & C.E. Stout (Eds.), *The neuropsychology of mental disorders: A practical guide* (pp. 81–98). Springfield, IL: Charles C. Thomas.

Peterson, K.C., Proust, M.F., & Schwarz, R.A. (1991). *Post-traumatic stress disorder: A clinician's guide.* New York: Plenum Press.

Robbins, M. (1996). *Conceiving of personality.* New Haven, CT: Yale University Press.

Ryan, R.A., & Spence, J.D. (1978). American Native American mental health research: Local control and cultural sensitivity. *White Cloud Journal, 1,* 15–18.

Sandner, D.F. (1979). *Navajo symbols of healing.* New York: Harcourt Brace Jovanovich.

Schwartz, M.F. (1995). In my opinion: Victim to victimizer. *Sexual Addiction and Compulsivity, 2,* 81–88.

Shoshan, T. (1989). Mourning and longing from generation to generation. *American Journal of Psychotherapy, 43*(2), 193–207.

Shweder, R. (1991). *Thinking through cultures.* Cambridge, MA: Harvard University Press.

Shweder, R., & Bourne, E. (1982). Does the concept of the person vary cross-culturally? In A. Marcella & G. White (Eds.), *Cultural concepts of mental health and therapy*. Boston: Reidel.

Skynner, A.C.R. (1975). The large group in training. In L. Kreeger (Ed.), *The large group: Dynamics and therapy*. London: Karnac.

Solomon, Z., Kotler, M., & Mikulincer, M. (1988). Combat-related post-traumatic stress disorder among second-generation Holocaust survivors: Preliminary findings. *American Journal of Psychiatry, 145*(7), 865–868.

Sue, S., & Zane, N. (1987). The role of culture and cultural teachings in psychotherapy: A critique and reformation. *American Psychologist, 42*, 37–45.

Tedlock, B., & Tedlock, D. (1975). *Teachings from the American earth*. New York: Livewright.

Terr, L. (1990). *Too scared to cry*. New York: Harper & Row.

Thornton, R. (1986). *We shall live again: The 1870 and 1890 Ghost Dance movements as demographic revitalization*. ASA Rose Monograph Series. Minneapolis, MN: University of Minnesota.

Thornton, R. (1987). *American Indian holocaust and survival: A population history since 1492*. Norman, OK: University of Oklahoma Press.

Van der Kolk, B.A. (1989). The compulsion to repeat trauma: Reenactment, revictimization, and masochism. *Psychiatric Clinics of North America, 12*, 389–411.

Vioa, H. (1990). *After Columbus: The Smithsonian chronicle of the North American Indians*. Washington, DC: Smithsonian Institution.

Watts, A. (1975). *Psychology East and West*. New York: Vintage.

Whitaker, C.A., & Malone, T.B. (1953). *The roots of psychotherapy*. New York: Blakiston.

Wilber, K. (1990). *Eye to eye: The quest for a new paradigm*. Boston: Shambala.

Wyman, L.C. (1936). Navajo diagnosticians. *American Anthropologist, 38*, 216–246.

# 5  Sexual Offending Behavior in the African-American Family

Charles S. Broadfield, Ph.D.
Mary H.S. Welch, Ed.D.

*E*ven today, the literature contains little on sexual offending behavior in the African-American community. Historically, much has been written about the adjustment problems of young African-American males and of teen pregnancy rates among African-American females. Yet issues of sexual deviancy within the African-American community remain unexplored.

For many years, however, powerful stereotypes that the African-American male is oversexed and that he particularly lusts after White women have existed. Only since the 1960s (Billingsley, 1968) has research on African Americans gained greater prominence among social scientists, thus creating the possibility for dispelling these especially harmful and misleading stereotypes. Yet even now, many people believe that African Americans of both genders are sexually permissive, with few moral strictures about sexual conduct, either inside or outside marriage (Williams, 1986).

The best way to understand the true nature of sexual attitudes and sexual misconduct among African Americans is to examine those issues within their historical and cultural contexts.

## Historical and Cultural Contexts

Although the roots of African-American culture are embedded in slavery, African Americans have survived as a distinct culture within the U.S. population. Slavery was, however, a major disruption in the formation and sustenance of close kinship ties within the African-American community.

Throughout their years of enslavement, neither African-American men nor African-American women were permitted by slave

108

masters to legitimize marriages among themselves. Frequent changes of partners thus became the rule. Slave women were expected to produce as many children as possible to supply the greatest number of future slaves to work in the master's fields and household.

The male African-American was used as a breeder (Pinkney, 1975). Also, slave owners frequently coerced their female slaves into having sex with them, producing mixed-race offspring. A slave husband and wife were expected not to discuss this practice, however, and to pretend (despite abundant evidence to the contrary) that it did not happen (White, 1972).

Historically and culturally, then, African-American males have had to endure much racism, oppression, humiliation, and emotional abuse. These societal forces have undermined the male as husband and father (Hill, 1972). As a result, many African-American women have come to empathize with African-American men and thus have difficulty holding them responsible for any sexually offending behavior they may be guilty of, either within or outside the family or community.

Traditionally, the church has also played a key role in the lives of African Americans. During times of crisis or stress, the church has served to provide help. An African-American family's minister is held in very high esteem but is also expected to hold a family's pain or secrets in confidence as part of his or her relationship with that family.

# The Family

The condition of the African-American family has undergone much positive change since the 1960s. Between 1960 and 1975, many constructive social, economic, and educational measures were taken to improve the lives of average African Americans. However, many gains made during those years have been eroded in the past 15 years (Gibbs, 1991). As a result, many African-American families still live in poverty and still experience the effects of racism and family discord (Gibbs, 1991).

In fact, approximately 48 percent of African-American families still live in poverty (Wilson, 1992). Many of these are single-parent families headed by females. The mother is usually employed outside the household, which allows for (and requires) much role flexibility within the family (Boyd-Franklin, 1989).

Additionally, within the African-American community itself, much diversity exists. This truth contrasts sharply, however, with many still commonly held, overgeneralized beliefs about African-American individuals and communities. Many middle-income families, for example, resemble their White counterparts. Conversely, in low-income African-American families, values may be quite different from those held in the dominant culture (Boyd-Franklin, 1989).

Some adaptive strengths appear to exist, though, that transcend all differences among African-American families. These include (1) kinship bonds, (2) role flexibility, (3) religion, (4) work and industry, (5) the importance of education, and (6) extended kinship networks (Boyd-Franklin, 1989).

### Kinship Bonds and Role Flexibility

Within traditional African society (from which African-American culture derives), a strong emphasis on unity has always existed. The well-known adage "It takes a whole village to raise a child" is rooted in African culture. In Africa, then, the extended family asserted significant influence over its members, providing the basis for economic and political life (Franklin, 1969). From this rich background of shared loyalty and strong kinship bonds African Americans are descended.

Role flexibility, derived from a strong historical tradition of interdependence, is another strength of the contemporary African-American family. Less sex-role stereotyping occurs than in other communities; therefore, African-American children learn to share sex roles. Similarly, in tasks including child rearing and household chores, responsibility is often shared. As a result, African-American children may not learn a rigid distinction between male and female roles (McAdoo, 1978).

### Religion

Today, a strong religious or spiritual orientation continues to be a strength of African-American families. When the family can turn to no one else, the church and its members are there to lend emotional, nutritional, and financial support. Therefore, understanding the importance of the church in this community is important for a therapist or helper of a sexually abusing African American. The church is traditionally an institution in which African-American men and women can show their leadership skills and abilities. It is also a place to see friends regularly and to socialize. According to Ho (1992), the strong humanistic orientation of African-American families, evidenced by a concern for others and by spontaneous and natural interactions, is related to a strong sense of spirituality.

Wedded to religion and spirituality is the perceived value of the endurance of suffering. The key belief is that through prayer one may endure any hardships life presents. Many religious songs capture the essence of this cornerstone belief (McAdoo, 1978).

### Work and Industry

Even today, a belief persists that African Americans are lazy, shiftless, ignorant about world affairs, and poor managers of money. Also, it remains a commonly held perception that most people on public assistance are African American (Zastrow, 1996). The reality is, however, that a very strong work ethic prevails in the African-American community (Hill, 1972). Education and industry are seen by the African-American community as ways to improve lifestyles. Many families therefore make extreme sacrifices to see their children succeed. Achievement is highly valued in African-American families (Boyd-Franklin, 1989).

In one of the authors' families, going to college was expected and was discussed in the family circle regularly. Many African-American churches today hold fund-raising activities to help their members raise money for college expenses. Some churches even award scholarships to all members who are college bound.

### Extended Kinship Network

Most African-American households consist of a complex kinship network of blood-related and non-blood-related persons (Hill, 1972). Three generations living in one home is common (Frazier, 1957). Various people exchange roles, family functions, and jobs. Many relatives live close to one another. In times of need or crisis, relatives expect and accept help from one another (Willa, 1989).

In many families, children are not always blood related but have been informally adopted. Alternatively, a family may include a blood relative of a prospective adoptee who has already lived in the adoptive home for years. The practice of informal adoptions continues to be common in today's African-American community. In recent years, the church has become even more directly involved with the adoption process. The notion of "one child, one church" has grown increasingly prevalent in the past two decades. The church also tries to have at least one African-American child formally adopted by members every year.

## Attitudes Toward Sexuality

The degree to which different cultures permit or encourage sexual activity varies greatly (Miller & Dreger, 1973). Different sociocultural groups interpret, express, and incorporate standards of appropriate sexuality in varying ways. Many African-American families promote sexual behavior only in marriage. This is especially true in deeply religious families (Hill, 1972). Yet many young males receive very little in the way of formal sex education, especially in single-parent families.

Today, myriad myths and stereotypes still exist about African-American sexuality. During slavery, the African-American male was regarded primarily as a breeder who could help produce more field and household help for the master (Hill, 1972). The female was often sexually abused by the slave owner but made to feel that she was a seductive woman (Williams, 1986). In many respects, the sexual abuse of the African-American female was legitimized by society. Also, African-American males were viewed as hypersexual rapists or studs who lusted after White women (Boyd-Franklin, 1989).

Today there still exists the need to correct many myths about the sexuality of African Americans. Early in their lives, African-American children, especially males, hear of these lingering stereotypes and must sort out on their own what society expects of them (Willa, 1989). The response to sexual abuse of and by African Americans is related to these myths (Wyatt, 1990).

In reality, African Americans and Whites may differ in their approaches to sexuality, but not in their morals (Pierce & Pierce, 1984). As stated earlier, African-American children are raised with fewer rigid sex roles than are many other cultural groups. According to Lewis (1978), African Americans' sexual identity is more relational and less rigidly scripted by society.

Despite more flexibility in roles in African-American families, homophobia may be a salient issue. Although homosexuality may not be openly discussed, the gay male or female is ridiculed and called names (Breer, 1992; Hunter, 1990). Therefore, for a male who was abused by a male, it may seem next to impossible to reveal the abuse (Thornton & Carter, 1986).

## Sexual Abuse and Misconduct

Sexual abuse in the African-American family is less prevalent than in other racial and ethnic groups, but the incidence is increasing (Abney & Priest, 1995; Fontaise, 1993; Pierce & Pierce, 1984). However, in the literature, little attention has been given to incest among African Americans and the attendant treatment issues (Eliata, 1980; Gabarino & Eliata, 1983). Incest reflects complex sociocultural and emotional problems. The absence of analysis of incest and other sexual deviancies in the African-American family in the literature may be related to the many myths and misconceptions about the interactions among African-American family members (Thornton & Carter, 1986).

According to McAdoo (1989), single-parent families headed by females are particularly common among African Americans. Additionally, African-American women who marry and then divorce may remarry several years later, on average, than their White counterparts. Their children may thus be at greater risk of being sexually abused by the mother's boyfriend or live-in partner (McAdoo, 1989).

Typically, African-American families are extremely reluctant to reveal family secrets (Ho, 1992). The church itself may unfortunately serve as a major deterrent to the disclosure of incest within a family. A factor often overlooked in attempting to understand attitudes about sexually offending behavior in the African-American community is the influence of the church and of religious practices on African-American families (Willa, 1989).

After sexual abuse begins to occur in an African-American household, the victim may elect to endure rather than report the abuse. He or she may fear that the perpetrator will be mistreated by the police, the courts, and the prison system. If a child or adolescent has had direct experience with racism, memories of that experience may further reinforce the impulse to protect the abuser (Pierce & Pierce, 1984). Pierce and Pierce, however, also found that African-American mothers tended to accept the disclosure of sexual abuse in the household more readily, and to reject the victim less frequently, than would White mothers in comparable situations.

The mother of a sexually abused African-American child might typically force her boyfriend or partner to move out of the house, yet she would not report him to the authorities. She would usually be wary of how the perpetrator might be treated by a racist judicial system.

Wilson (1994) asserts, however, that the choice not to involve the criminal justice system is a disservice both to the abused child and to the African-American community as a whole; the abuser should be held fully accountable for his actions.

CASE EXAMPLE:

Robert was a 10-year-old African-American male who resided with his mother and two sisters, ages 14 and 17. The mother's boyfriend, John, had his own apartment but often spent nights with Robert's mother in the family home. John took a particular interest in Robert after he began to date the boy's mother. After about six months, Robert began spending one to two nights per week alone with John at his apartment. The mother encouraged this practice, because Robert had no contact with his own father. She believed that Robert's visits to John would promote "male bonding" with a father figure, of which she thought her son had been deprived, and that John would be an excellent role model.

Instead, however, John began to abuse Robert sexually four months later. He also gave Robert alcohol and showed him adult magazines and movies. Eventually, John began to fondle Robert, progressing then to fellatio and anal sex. John threatened that if Robert refused to participate in sex or told his mother about John's behavior, he would tell Robert's mother that the boy had approached him for sex. Those threats intimidated Robert into silence about the sexual abuse he was enduring.

The mother eventually learned of John's sexual abuse when Robert had to be taken to an emergency room for rectal bleeding.

Robert then admitted to his mother what had been happening for the past 18 months. The mother spoke with her minister about John's abuse of her son but decided not to pursue legal action. Instead, she continued to date John but would not let him spend nights at her house or let Robert stay at his apartment.

A few months later, Robert attempted suicide. Apparently, children in the neighborhood had somehow learned of John's sexual abuse and began calling Robert a "fag" because Robert had had anal intercourse with John. Reluctantly, Robert's mother took him for counseling following his suicide attempt. As a result of Robert's injury, suicide attempt, and subsequent counseling, John was arrested and charged.

## Assessment

Like other sexual abusers, African-American sexual abusers are often in denial about their behavior. Also, minimization of and cognitive distortions about their actual offenses commonly occur among this group. However, consideration of and sensitivity to the distinct cultural factors in the African-American community during the evaluative process are necessary.

Historically, African Americans have lower rates of use of mental-health services than do Whites. They rely much more heavily on prayer, the advice of ministers, their own spirituality, and families and friends (Martin & Martin, 1985). Especially among low-income families, distrust of the White community occurs (McAdoo, 1989; Boyd-Franklin, 1989). Consequently, fewer social services operate in the African-American community (Russell, Schurman, & Trocki, 1988).

The therapist who evaluates an African-American perpetrator should be aware that even today, submitting to counseling may be viewed as a sign of weakness, both in the African-American community and by the perpetrator. Some clients believe that by going to counseling they will be "brainwashed" by the White establishment (Ho, 1992). It is therefore extremely important for the therapist to be sensitive to these sorts of statements and viewpoints about the counseling process.

Frequently, African Americans have had only negative contact, if any, with the crisis network in the community. The therapist must be sensitive to this fact as an integral part of his or her comprehensive assessment. These systems include, but are not limited to, law enforcement, criminal justice, and court agencies. Other organizations are social services, hospitals, and emergency care centers (Ho, 1992).

Regarding sexual attitudes, the evaluator needs to understand how homosexual behavior is viewed in the African-American community. The most frequently held belief is that homosexuality is a sin. Issues of sexual deviancy and "alternative lifestyles" remain uncomfortable areas of discussion in the African-American community. A person believed to be gay or lesbian will be ostracized and ridiculed. The African-American community is thought to be homophobic (Mindel & Habenstein, 1976).

Unfortunately, the strong taboos against any form of homosexual contact in the African-American community make it difficult for a victim of same-gender abuse to discuss his or her victimization. Community attitudes about homosexuality make it even more difficult for a male victim to admit his trauma or to seek treatment for fear of how he will be viewed in the community (Breer, 1992; Hunter, 1990).

If any standardized tests are administered by the therapist as part of the evaluation process, such tests should be culturally sensitive. The therapist needs to explain the use of the instrument and make clear how the results will be used. If paper-and-pencil tests that are not designed to be culturally sensitive are used, the therapist needs to interpret the results of the tests cautiously.

With both adult and older-adolescent offenders, the polygraph examination and/or psychophysiologic measurement of sexual arousal may be important (Abel, Becker, & Cunningham-Rathner, 1988). The realities of being a person of color (Thornton & Carter, 1986; Courtois, 1988) require that part of the focus of treatment consist of the offender's being guided toward a greater understanding of how his or her behavior affects the African-American community as a whole. Strong emphasis should be placed on the political, psychological, and sociological impacts of the offender's behavior on the community.

According to Courtois (1988), spirituality often needs to be part of the treatment and recovery processes for perpetrator, victim, and family. In addition, Courtois suggests that a strong sense of spirituality may enhance the African-American victim's recovery from sexual abuse. The therapist's approach must respect the perpetrator's and family's spiritual and religious beliefs, whether Judeo-Christian, Muslim, Vodoun, or other.

The cognitive-behavioral approach developed by Abel, Becker, and Cunningham-Rathner (1984) has utility with the African-American offender. It focuses on a task-oriented ideology to correct cognitive distortions, to reduce deviant arousal, and to increase social and living skills. Also, the offender must develop an individualized relapse-prevention plan.

This approach, along with knowledge of and sensitivity to the culture, offers the best therapeutic approach to treating both the perpetrator and the family (Bowman, 1992).

Other important areas of awareness for the therapist include:

1. Acknowledging cultural diversity.
2. Recognizing diversity in the African-American culture.
3. Finding ways to incorporate African-American cultural dimensions into the therapeutic process.
4. Delivering therapeutic services based on an Afrocentric worldview.
5. Focusing therapy toward goals of a proactive nature.
6. Using a group approach to counseling African-American males.
7. Employing active therapy techniques.
8. Recognizing and, where appropriate, refraining from using Eurocentric aspects of therapy.
9. Using affirmation techniques.
10. Respecting resistance and understanding its meaning.

CASE EXAMPLE:

Mr. Jones had a military career. He was convicted of the sexual abuse of his stepdaughter, age eight, three years ago. His wife went to her minister after her daughter revealed that she had been being abused by Mr. Jones for two years. The minister was supportive of Mrs. Jones and helped her make telephone calls to Child Protective Services (CPS) and to the police.

The minister also knew Mr. Jones. Though supportive of him, he also held him fully accountable for his sexually abusive behavior. Therefore, he did not permit him to use religion to justify the behavior. The minister made himself available to CPS for the Jones family's sake and attended a few counseling sessions at the family's request.

Mr. Jones entered an outpatient sex offender program in which he received individual, group, and family therapy. His Anglo therapist was knowledgeable about the African-American culture but also consulted with African-American colleagues and the minister.

The Jones family remained in therapy for more than two years. After a year, Mr. Jones moved back into the family home. He completed his individual and group therapy. The focus of his therapy then shifted to marital and family issues. At the end of two years, Mr. Jones continued in an aftercare group once a month. Also, as part of his probation, he took a polygraph exam periodically.

The family believed that having a culturally sensitive and knowledgeable therapist was the key to its success in therapy. They also believed that their minister played a major role in helping them cope with the reality of the abuse, enabling them to begin becoming a functional family again.

The African-American family, like all other families, has been strongly and negatively affected by incest and sexual abuse. However, little empirical research has been done on either the perpetrator or the victim.

We do know that using the strengths of the African-American culture is key to successfully treating this population of sexual offenders. Also, the cognitive-behavioral approach to treatment seems to have utility. The combination of these approaches may be the best treatment regimen. African-American sexual offenders can best benefit from treatment models that are both problem focused and culturally sensitive.

Obviously, much more research on African-American sexual offenders, victims, and families is needed. The role of religion in the lives and mental health of African Americans also merits study in greater depth. Clearly, we have much to learn about sexually offending behavior among African Americans. However, we hope to see within the next decade a fully integrated approach to treating this seriously underserved population of sexual offenders, victims, and families.

# References

Abel, G.G., Becker, J.V., & Cunningham-Rathner, J. (1984). Complications, consent and cognition in sex between children and adults. *International Journal of Law and Psychiatry, 7,* 89–103.

Abel, G., Becker, J., & Cunningham-Rathner, J. (1988). Multiple paraphiliac diagnoses among sex offenders. *Bulletin of the American Academy of Psychiatry, 17,* 223–232.

Abney, E., & Priest, R. (1995). Sexual abuse of Afro-American children. In R.A. Bass, G.E. Wyatt, & G.J. Powell (Eds.), *The Afro-American family: Assessment, treatment, and research issues* (pp. 333–346). New York: Grune & Grune.

Billingsley, A. (1968). *Black families in White America.* Englewood Cliffs, NJ: Prentice-Hall.

Bowman, B. (1992). Culturally sensitive inquiry. In J. Gabarino, F. Scott, & Faculty of the Erickson Institute (Eds.), *What children can tell us* (pp. 92–107). San Francisco: Jossey-Bass.

Boyd-Franklin, N. (1989). *Black families in therapy: A multisystems approach.* New York: Guilford.

Breer, W. (1992). *Diagnosis and treatment of the young male victim of sexual abuse.* Springfield, IL: Charles C. Thomas.

Courtois, C. (1988). *Healing the incest wound: Adult survivors in therapy.* New York: Norton.

Eliata, F. (1980). *Incest and culture.* New York: Free Press.

Fontaise, H. (1993). *Minorities and sexual abuse.* New York: Random House.

Franklin, J. (1969). *From slavery to freedom: A history of Negro Americans* (3rd ed.). New York: Vintage Books.

Frazier, E. (1957). *Black bourgeoisie.* New York: Free Press.

Gabarino, D., & Eliata, F. (1983). *Treatment of sexually abused children.* Palo Alto, CA: Counseling Psychological Press.

Gibbs, J. (1991). Black American adolescents. In J.T. Gibbs, L.N. Huana, & Associates (Eds.), *Children of color: Psychological interventions with minority youths* (pp. 179–223). San Francisco: Jossey-Bass.

Hill, R. (1972). *The strengths of Black families.* New York: Emerson Hall.

Ho, M. (1992). *Minority children and adolescents in therapy.* Newbury Park, CA: Sage.

Hunter, M. (1990). *Abused boys: The neglected victims of sexual abuse.* Lexington, MA: Lexington Books.

Lewis, D. (1978). The Black family: Socialization and sex roles. In R. Staples (Ed.), *The Black family: Essays and studies* (pp. 215–225). Belmont, CA: Wadsworth.

Martin, J., & Martin, E. (1985). *The helping tradition in the Black family and community.* Silver Spring, MD: National Association of Social Workers.

McAdoo, H. (1978). The impact of upward mobility of kin: Help patterns and the reciprocal obligations in Black families. *Journal of Marriage and the Family, 4*(4), 761–776.

McAdoo, H. (1989, March). *African-American family patterns.* Paper presented at the Black Family Summit, University of South Carolina, Columbia.

Miller, K.S., & Dreger, R.M. (1973). *Comparative studies of Blacks and Whites in the United States.* New York: Seminar Press.

Mindel, C.Y., & Habenstein, R. (Eds.). (1976). *Ethnic families in America: Patterns.* New York: Elsevier Scientific Publishing.

Pierce, L.H., & Pierce, R.L. (1984). Race as a factor in the sexual abuse of children. *Social Work Abstracts, 20,* 9–14.

Pinkney, A. (1975). *Black Americans.* Englewood Cliffs, NJ: Prentice-Hall.

Russell, D., Schurman, R., & Trocki, K. (1988). The long-term effects of incestuous abuse: A comparison of Afro-American and White American victims. In G. Elizabeth & G.P. Powell (Eds.), *Lasting effects of child sexual abuse* (pp. 119–134). Newbury Park, CA: Sage.

Thornton, C.I., & Carter, J.H. (1986). Treatment considerations with Black incestuous families. *Journal of the National Medical Association, 78*(1), 49–53.

White, J. (1972). Toward a Black psychology. In R. Jones (Ed.), *Black psychology*. New York: Harper & Row.

Willa, M. (1989). The Black family: A unique social system in transition. In A.W. Edwards (Ed.), *The state of Black Cleveland*. Cleveland: Urban League of Greater Cleveland.

Williams, L. (1986). Race and rape: The Black woman as legitimate victim. Research Rep. No. MH15161. Durham, NH: University of New Hampshire, Family Violence Research Laboratory.

Wilson, M. (1992). Perceived parental activity of mothers, fathers, and grandmothers in three-generational Black families. In A. Burlew, W. Banks, H. McAdoo, & D. Azibo (Eds.), *African-American psychology* (pp. 87–104). Newbury Park, CA: Sage.

Wilson, M. (1994). *Crossing the boundary: Black women survive incest*. Seattle: Seal Press.

Wyatt, G. (1990). Sexual abuse of ethnic minority children: Identifying dimensions of victimization. *Professional Psychology: Research and Practice, 21*(5), 338–343.

Zastrow, C. (1996). *Introduction to social work and social welfare* (6th ed.). New York: Brooks/Cole.

# 6    Intervention with Hispanic Sexual Abusers

*Carlos M. Loredo, Ph.D.*

This chapter focuses on psychocultural perspectives that facilitate understanding of Hispanic values and cultures. It discusses salient variables that are crucial in assessment and intervention with Hispanic individuals and their extended families. Because my professional experience with Hispanics has largely been with Mexican-American families, the counseling literature reviewed focuses primarily on this population. The findings of the National Task Force on Juvenile Sex Offending subcommittee on "minority issues" are discussed. The scarce literature on treatment of Hispanic sex offenders is reviewed. Finally, specific issues relevant to the treatment of Hispanic sex offenders are presented. This chapter is also derived from my Cuban heritage; my experience as a refugee in the United States; and my assessment and treatment of Hispanic families, Hispanic sexual abuse victims, and Hispanic juvenile sex offenders.

## Establishing a Framework for Culture

In discussing multicultural sexual education, Irvine (1995) points out:

> No one ... can become expert in the sex/gender systems of every culture ... [but] through deepened awareness of our own sexual culture, and a commitment to learning about some other cultures, educators can develop the skills for working with difference. (p. xiv)

Although her work addresses sexual education across cultures, her commentary is directly relevant to the treatment of Hispanic sex offenders.

Irvine (1995) notes that becoming an interculturally competent sex educator involves accepting the following assertions:

1. Our skills, motivation, and attitude are the most important didactic tools we possess.

2. Readiness to accept and confront our discomfort and uneasiness regarding difference is essential. We should not be unduly concerned with doing or saying the wrong thing, or of being "error-free" before addressing these issues.

3. Knowledge of our own culture's sex/gender system is essential.

4. Some knowledge of other cultures' sex/gender system is crucial.

5. Educators, particularly those from "dominant" cultures, must acknowledge the history of discrimination and power inequities.

6. Intercultural competence must cross all cultures. All of us, including those from less dominant cultures, must enhance our awareness and respect for other cultures.

7. Personal commitment is imperative. We must challenge individuals, agencies, and institutions that promote cultural ignorance and social inequality.

In discussing Rubin's (1975) sex/gender system, Irvine (1995) writes that understanding individualized sexual behavior requires an awareness of how a particular society or culture "organizes and regulates sexuality in a specific period ... [T]here is no sexual behavior, identity, or belief system that is universally normal or natural. Cultures may differ considerably" (p. 13). She adds that dramatic and often significant changes occur in the sex/gender system of a particular culture over time.

Irvine (1995) provides a helpful perspective to address the issue of sexuality across cultures. She discusses the assumptions and differences between *essentialism* (the notion that sexuality is a "deep and natural individual expression" [p. 2]) and *social construction* theory (the notion that sexuality is a product of the meanings, beliefs, values, and practices of our culture and can often vary in different times and cultures [p. 12]). Irvine further outlines the assumptions inherent in each approach.

Essentialism encompasses the following assumptions (Irvine, 1995, p. 3):

1. There is an internal, and likely biological, sexual drive.

2. Sexuality is commonly expressed throughout different historical periods.

3. Sexuality is universally expressed across different cultures.

Social construction theory, which she espouses, consists of the following assumptions (Irvine, 1995, p. 14):

1. Sexuality is not universal across cultures or time.

2. The existence of an internal, essential sexual drive is doubtful.

3. Biology plays a minimal role in our sexuality.

4. Sexuality is greatly affected by social, political, economic, and cultural factors.

5. The values and meanings ascribed to sexuality in different historical periods and within particular cultures must be examined.

Culture, as defined by Irvine (1995), is a "set of historically created world views, rules, and practices by which a group organizes itself" (p. 25). As perceived by Irvine, culture shapes and constructs sexual behavior, determines what we believe is sexual, and prescribes rules for being sexual (what, where, when, how, and with whom).

Irvine (1995) also provides some useful constructs in providing effective, culturally specific sexual education, which are relevant to interventions with culturally different populations. These constructs are as follows:

1. *Cultures construct but do not determine our behavior* (p. 27): We learn, are taught, and are shaped by our culture, but we are not bound by cultural proscriptions.

2. *Cultures are not static but dynamic* (p. 27): Cultural rules and expectations evolve and change over time and respond to historical and social changes.

3. *Cultures are not monolithic and homogeneous, but internally contradictory* (p. 28): Contradictions exist within cultures. Individuals and particular groups may resist their own cultural values and expectations.

4. *Cultures are fractured in many dimensions* (p. 29): There are differences within cultures when one considers factors of race, ethnicity, gender, social class, level of assimilation, and age. Assimilation is defined as the degree to which a cultural group absorbs and takes on the beliefs and practices of another. Acculturation refers to the process by which the immigrant and "host" culture impinge on and effect change in each other.

5. *Individuals have multiple cultural identities* (p. 30): Individuals within cultures identify with a variety of groups and factors in differing ways. An individual may occupy both dominant and nondominant positions in his or her culture, depending on the various groups and/or factions with whom he or she identifies. At times, individuals are forced to chose between groups, or identities, within their own culture.

6. *Everyone has a culture, even those in dominant groups* (p. 31): Culture, often reflected by such terms as *multicultural* or *cultural diversity*, typically refers to the nondominant group, which is then considered "different" from the dominant or majority group. The danger in such terminology and conceptualization is that the dominant group is then perceived as being universal, thereby defining what is "normal" or typical.

7. *Culture is not biological or essential but socially constructed* (p. 32): Identification with one's culture is an ongoing (not biological) process. Patterns in cultures are determined by social, political, and historical precedents. Specific cultures are not inherently "better" or "worse" but are accorded value through social factors, not biological ones.

## Understanding Traditional Hispanic Values

Hispanics, in the context of this chapter, are defined as individuals residing in the United States whose cultural origins are in Mexico, Puerto Rico, Cuba, and other Spanish-speaking countries, such as those located in Central and South America. It should be understood that Hispanic cultures (and some groups within those cultures) use differing terms to identify their heritage and culture (such as Mexicano, Chicano, Mexican American, Latino, Hispanic, Spanish, Spanish American).

Although the following discussion addresses Hispanic ideals and values, significant historical, geographic, regional, political, and socioeconomic differences abound among Hispanic individuals and subgroups. The common thread is that of Spanish colonization. Apart from that, we are a diverse group. Those of us living in the United States have learned to acculturate (to varying degrees) to the regional and dominant cultures. Our differences, along with our acculturation experiences, help determine the relative significance of our traditional cultural values (Simoni & Pérez, 1995).

## Hispanics in the United States

Hispanics are the fastest growing ethnic group in the United States (Ho, 1992; U.S. Department of Commerce, 1989). Hispanics are the second largest minority group in the United States (Ho, 1992). If this trend continues, Hispanics will be the largest ethnic minority group in the United States by the early 21st century (*Household and Family Characteristics*, 1990).

The 1990 U.S. census estimates that about 22 million Hispanics live in the mainland United States, which constitutes about 9 percent of the total population (Spencer, 1986). The major subgroups are Mexican Americans (13.5 million, living primarily in the West and Southwest), Puerto Ricans (2.7 million, with the largest concentration living in the Northeast), Cubans (1.0 million, living primarily in the Southeast), and other Hispanics (5.1 million, including those from Central and South America). The greatest concentration of Hispanics lives in California, Texas, New York, and Florida; lesser concentrations are found in New Jersey, New Mexico, Arizona, and Colorado (Rosado & Elias, 1993).

About 85 percent of Hispanics live in large urban centers and have unskilled and semiskilled occupations (Padilla & DeSnyder, 1987). In some counties in Texas, the poverty level of some Hispanic communities is as high as 70 percent. (D. García, director, Bi-National and Demonstration Initiative — Migrants Clinicians Network, personal communication, 1996). Approximately 50 percent of Hispanic families are headed by a single female parent; unemployment rates are estimated at about 25 percent, more than four times the current national average (*Household and Family Characteristics*, 1990). Others have found that between 25 and 40 percent of Hispanics drop out of high school, with a median of 10 years of education. Family size is larger than that of other American families (three to four children on the average, not including extended family members), and the median household income is lower than that of other American families (Padilla & DeSnyder, 1987).

Hispanics in the United States are relatively young: the median age is 23.2, compared with 30 for all U.S. residents and 31.3 for Anglos. Almost 33 percent of all Hispanics are under the age of 15 (Casas & Vasquez, 1989). Nearly 50 percent of the population is under 18 years of age, and one-third live in poverty, 2.5 times the national average (Rosado & Elias, 1993).

## Language

Citing a 1976 U.S. Census Bureau report, Ho (1992) indicated that 80 percent of Hispanics lived in homes where Spanish was spoken. He added that among Hispanics who immigrated to the United States, about two-thirds used Spanish as their primary language; among Hispanics who were born in the United States, about one-fifth spoke Spanish.

## The "Traditional" Culture

Again, much of the information reported and discussed pertains to "traditional Mexican-American" culture. However, I do not believe that any one set of inscribed assumptions or values accurately portrays the "typical" Mexican American or Hispanic person residing in the United States. I do believe that knowledge of traditional Hispanic values will assist in accurately assessing and effectively treating the Hispanic individual and his or her family.

The Texas Migrant Council's National Resource Center on the Mexican American Family has produced an excellent training manual (1985) that I highly recommend to anyone working with Mexican-American clients. The manual contains four articles (Gibson, 1985a, 1985b; Sotomayor, 1985; Tello, 1985) and formulates the following goals:

[to] familiarize the reader with the cultural influences affecting Mexican American families, the cultural issues in service delivery, the four basic levels of cultural competence: awareness, sensitivity, integration, and competent intervention, and with culturally relevant models of service delivery to Mexican Americans. (p. iii)

Gibson (1985b) notes that the Mexican-American family has been stereotyped over the years and has been characterized as follows:

> poor, large, extended, patriarchate, disinterested in the education of their children, superstitious and dependent on *curanderos* (faith healers) for health care, traditionally Catholics, living in rural areas or poor urban barrios, and "alingual" and essentially "pathological and maladaptive." (p. II-1)

Gibson (1985b) adds that many researchers have attributed the problems of Mexican Americans to their culture and to their families' values and approach to life. Gibson asserts that current authors are depicting Mexican-American families as heterogeneous (ranging from traditional to contemporary), flexible, and demonstrating strength through their ability to cope with considerable stress.

Investigators have recognized certain values and beliefs that are significant to a traditional Hispanic individual (Gutiérrez, Ortega, & Suarez, 1990; Marín & VanOss-Marín, 1991). For Hispanics, the family is considered most important. An integral concept in understanding Hispanic families is the value of *familismo* (familism). It includes extended relationships beyond the nuclear family and stresses that the needs of the family supersede individual needs. Loyalty to the family is taught and encouraged by fostering cooperation, affiliation, and interdependence (Ramos-McKay, Comas-Díaz, & Rivera, 1988). The individual is expected to be committed to the family, to subordinate his or her needs to those of the family, and to accept the responsibilities and obligations that that entails (García-Preto, 1982).

Integral to familism are the concepts of *su dignidad, personalismo,* and *carnalismo. Dignidad* is literally translated as "dignity," but for Hispanics, this term also reflects one's self-respect. *Personalismo* (personalism) is a value that emphasizes the internal qualities and character that make an individual unique and constitute one's self-worth. This value contrasts with Anglo values of individuality, which stress individual accomplishments for social and economic goals. *Carnalismo* (blood relationship) can be characterized by the feelings that one extends to others, encompassing many of the loyalties and obligations one might have to blood kin. The individual is expected to accept some commitment for caring for and supporting others, particularly relatives, extended family, and friends.

A related concept is that of *respeto* (respect). Within the family, the individual is expected to obey elders. *Respeto* also dictates how one responds in interpersonal relationships and provides the template for interactions with others on the basis of age, gender, socioeconomic status, status in the family, and relation to authority figures.

Closely associated with *respeto* is *verguenza* (shame). In traditional Hispanic culture, one's deeds, values, and actions reflect not only on oneself but also on one's family. Personal shame can be perceived as the family's dishonor. *Verguenza* is a critical concept and an issue that must be addressed in all sex-abuse interventions with Hispanics.

The system of *compadrazgo* (co-parenthood) is also an integral part of familism and the extended family. This system derives from Spanish influence: at baptism, sponsors became *padrinos* (godparents) of the child and *compadres* (co-parents) with the child's parents. That system assumes that the godparents will be responsible for the child's spiritual and religious development if the parents die. The system also assumes that the godparents will raise the child as their own if necessary.

One often-used term associated with Hispanic males is *machismo*. The term literally means "maleness" but is often misunderstood outside of the cultural context. Within the culture, *machismo* reflects the value that man is the provider, protector, and leader and is responsible for the honor and well-being of his family. Of utmost importance for the Hispanic male is self-respect. The term is often used negatively and stereotypically to reflect an innate capacity for violence and an oversensitivity to insult. Inherent in the negative concept is a tendency toward male dominance through sexual conquest and through domination of wife, children, and others who may be perceived as weak or submissive. This negative stereotype, however, ignores the fact that it is a positive value within the culture, if understood correctly.

*Hembrismo* (femaleness) is the corollary of *machismo*. This concept "connotes strength, perseverance, flexibility, and an ability to survive ... [it] can translate into [a woman's] attempt to fulfill her multiple role expectations as a mother, wife, worker, daughter, and member of the community" (Comas-Díaz, 1995, p. 41). As with *machismo*, *hembrismo* has sometimes been used out of context — incorrectly — to describe why a Hispanic woman may be submissive and dependent on her husband, without addressing the ethnocultural reality.

A related concept is that of *marianismo*. This concept is based on the Catholic worship of the Virgin Mary, who is considered virginal, pure, and long-suffering. This concept assumes that women are spiritually superior to men. Unmarried women, therefore, are expected to remain "pure" and virginal until they marry; once they are married, Hispanic women become "Madonnas and are expected to sacrifice for their children and husbands" (Comas-Díaz, 1995, p. 41).

In the traditional Hispanic family, gender roles and sexual expectations are clearly defined. Boys and girls are taught two very different codes of sexual attitudes and behaviors (Ho, 1992). Boys are expected to be assured, independent, brave, and available for sexual interactions with anyone outside their extended family. Conversely, girls are expected to be demure, submissive, dependent, and virginal until marriage. This particular view was expressed to me many times during childhood by various adult males, who told stories of girls "returned" after the wedding night for being "impure." Sexual matters are not typically discussed in a family setting or across genders. If sexual issues are discussed, males typically speak with other males, and females speak with their sisters, mothers, aunts, or grandmothers.

Most Hispanics are Catholics, although many are involved with various other religions. The Catholic Church is important in shaping the sexual values and sexual expression of many Hispanics. The traditional Catholic theology prizes self-denial, endurance of suffering, and asexuality (until marriage). The traditional catechism classes I attended did not provide any sex education. The prevailing attitude at that time was that sexual intercourse was conducted for the primary purpose of procreation. Any form of sexual expression, especially before marriage, was considered a "sin." Birth control and masturbation were also considered "sins." Although the Catholic Church currently provides sex education, the issues discussed and the manner in which the issues are discussed vary greatly. Some researchers have suggested that the "traditional" religious virtues and cultural values may prevent Hispanics from seeking psychological intervention (Acosta, Yamamoto, & Evans, 1982).

Some Hispanics attribute many everyday events to spiritual intervention. Various cultures and groups may practice differing types of "folk healing," often in conjunction with their Catholic beliefs: Mexican Americans practice *curanderismo*; Puerto Ricans, *espiritismo*; and Cubans, *santería*. One might surmise that folk healing is inversely related to the degree of acculturation: that is, the more one acculturates to the more "scientific" or "rational" mainstream U.S. culture, the more likely one is to discard the old remedies. I and others (Castro, Furth, & Karlow, 1984; Comas-Díaz, 1995) recognize that for many Hispanics, assimilation to the dominant culture may coexist with reliance on traditional folk remedies and beliefs.

A related concept is that of cultural fatalism. This concept implies that events are fated to occur despite any attempt to intervene for change: things happen. Events take place, and we are powerless to control the outcome. In sex-abuse cases, this worldview can take the expression of *así es* ("that's how it is"). Some theorists suggest that this orientation assuages guilt, removes accountability, and leads to an acceptance that all is inevitable (Fitzpatrick, 1971). Again, these values and concepts did not materialize in a vacuum. A look at the colonization of Hispanic peoples in Mexico, Central and South America, and the Caribbean reveals that this attitude may have been a realistic response to the conquering hordes who dictated every aspect of their subjugated lives. One group of researchers reported that although Hispanics have a fatalistic outlook, this tendency was more evident among those of lower socioeconomic classes (Ross, Mirowsky, & Cockerham, 1983).

## Counseling Hispanics

A growing body of literature in the past 15 years has examined mental-health issues of Hispanic clients (Black, Paz, & DeBlassie, 1991; Casas, 1984; Casas & Vasquez, 1989; Cervantes & Ramírez, 1992; Chavez & Roney, 1990; Herrerías, 1988; Hines, García-Preto, McGoldrick, Almeida, & Weltman, 1992; Ho, 1992; Mendoza, Smith, Poland, Lin, & Strickland, 1991; Morales, 1992; Padilla & DeSnyder, 1987; Rodriguez & Zayas, 1990; Rosado & Elias, 1993; Sciarra & Ponterotto, 1991; Simoni & Pérez, 1995; Solomon, 1992; Zuniga, 1991). Many studies have concluded that mental-health service delivery for urban, economically limited Hispanic clients has been lacking (Casas & Vasquez, 1989; Chavez & Roney, 1990; Malgady, Rogler, & Costantino, 1987; Rosado & Elias, 1993; Sue & Zane, 1987). Some investigators (Padilla, Ruiz,

& Alvarez, 1975; Snowden & Cheung, 1990; Sutton & Kessler, 1986) noted that low-income Hispanics, when compared with middle-class Anglos, were perceived as being more pathological, were less preferred, were more likely to be treated pharmacologically, were given poorer prognoses, and were more likely to be institutionalized. Although numerous authors have stressed the need for counselors to be culturally sensitive (Casas & Vasquez, 1989; Parker, Bingham, & Fukuyama, 1985; Rosado & Elias, 1993), the literature is replete with studies demonstrating that the mental-health service delivery system does not recognize and/or implement an ethnocultural approach in the planning, evaluation, and delivery of programs for Hispanics (Kleinman, 1978; Mio & Morris, 1990; Sue, 1990).

Therapists and program designers must address the counseling of Hispanic clients with a coherent and pragmatic theoretical framework. LeVine and Padilla (1980) introduced the concept of *pluralistic counseling*, which stresses an understanding and awareness of the client's cultural values, beliefs, and behaviors.

Casas and Vasquez (1989) proposed an excellent and culturally relevant clinical intervention model that encompasses the issues promoted by pluralistic counseling. Their model presents a continuum of categorical variables across three areas: counselor variables, client variables, and therapeutic process variables. In that model, counselor variables are divided into professional and personal issues. The authors indicate that the profession has a basic set of assumptions and beliefs that support and reflect the majority culture: "rugged individualism, competition, action orientation, the Protestant work ethic, progress and future orientation, the scientific method of inquiry, the nuclear family structure, and rigid timetables" (p. 156).

The authors stress that these values are not inherently good or bad, but note that those basic assumptions and values may be problematic in intervening with Hispanic clients who adhere to the more traditional values of their own culture. They add that interpretation of behavior based on the counselor's own value system and assumptions can lead to erroneous interpretations and assessments and may result in inappropriate, ineffective, and at times destructive interventions.

In their article, Casas and Vasquez (1989) cite Pedersen (1987), who identified several culturally based and biased assumptions frequently observed in multicultural counseling:

1. *The issue of "normalcy"*: What is considered "normal" or "natural" must be considered within an ethnocultural perspective.

2. *Individualism*: Counselors who assume that the goal of therapy is to actualize the individual, as opposed to units of individuals or groups (such as family and/or society), may run into difficulties with Hispanic individuals and/or families who value the family and/or the social unit above the individual.

3. *Interdependence*: Individualism and independence must be understood in the context of the Hispanic experience. These are not inherently positive or negative traits but must be viewed within the Hispanic experience of *familism*.

4. *Cooperation and resistance*: A basic premise is that cooperation is based on the client's desire to be open and direct. For Hispanics with traditional values, problems of an intimate or familial nature are handled quietly, privately, and within the family or extended support system.

5. *Assimilation*: A basic goal of counseling is that the individual learn how to adapt and cope with the environment, so that he or she can function more effectively within the social milieu. A critical factor that must be considered, however, is that the environment may be a significant part of the problem.

6. *"Here and now" orientation*: Therapists must understand and recognize clients' sociohistorical experience, particularly for refugees, immigrants, and first-generation Americans.

7. *Counselor bias*: Many well-meaning therapists assume that they are cognizant of the assumptions and values inherent in their profession. The difficulty, however, is that many of these assumptions and values are unchallenged by us and by our profession. Counselors and intervenors must recognize that their values and attitudes also arise out of their own culture and professional experience.

A critical issue, often overlooked or ignored in many studies of Hispanics, is that of acculturation. Olmedo (1979) identified three major variables that influence acculturation: (1) language preference, use, and ability; (2) socioeconomic experience; and (3) values, beliefs, and attitudes specific to the culture. Studies of Hispanics must address acculturation issues so that the research, findings, and interpretations of the investigations can provide meaningful, accurate, and relevant data. To understand sexuality and the dynamics of sexual abuse among Hispanic individuals (and their families), one must understand the ethnocultural context (Fontes, 1993a, 1993b).

Of particular concern to many investigators, particularly those of Hispanic origin, are methodological flaws contained in many investigations (Casas, 1984; Okazaki & Sue, 1995; Sundberg, 1981). The problems include the varying and often confusing definitions of race, ethnicity, and culture (Betancourt & Lopez, 1993); ethnic comparisons using demographics (Cervantes & Castro, 1985); identification of participants, such as those with mixed racial or ethnic backgrounds (Hall, 1992); equivalence of measures (Brislin, 1993); assessment methods (Brink, 1994; Draguns, 1990); and data interpretation (Rogler, Malgady, & Rodriguez, 1989). A common and critically erroneous assumption made by many is that individuals who identify themselves with a particular culture, race, or ethnicity are the same as or similar to others who characterize themselves as belonging to the same group (Sasao & Sue, 1993)

## Sexual Abuse Counseling of Hispanics

Numerous articles have addressed ethnic and cultural difference in response to sexual abuse and sexuality (Mennen, 1994, 1995; Sanders-Phillips, Moisan, Wadlington, & English, 1995). Although many of the studies I reviewed cited "significant" differences, the results, in my opinion, were not very meaningful. Many of the articles cited limitations in their studies, particularly in the way ethnicity or race was defined, and suggested caution in generalizing findings to racial and/or cultural differences when many possibly significant factors had not been measured. The critical significance is that many findings may be attributed to ethnicity or culture, when other variables such as education; economic, political, and social realities; and acculturation may provide more accurate and meaningful results. Many practitioners share the perception that future studies should investigate the effect of family functioning and values in response to migration and acculturation and related social and cultural experiences (Fischer, 1987; Levy, 1988; Sanders-Phillips et al., 1995; Wyatt, 1990).

# National Task Force on Juvenile Sex Offending Subcommittee on "Minority Issues"

I previously reviewed the issue of "minority status" and its implications in juvenile sex offender treatment. My work originated through membership in the National Adolescent Perpetrator Network (the Network). The Network was made up of a group of individuals from over 800 programs (at the time) who intervened with sexually abusive juveniles. A survey of the Network in 1986 supported the creation of a task force to suggest standards for the assessment and treatment of juvenile sex offenders. Task-force members reviewed pertinent documents and literature, created various working drafts, solicited and obtained feedback, and completed the *Preliminary Report from the National Task Force on Juvenile Sexual Offending* in January 1988.

To facilitate more detailed analyses of specific issues in the report, task-force members joined subcommittees with other network members to address topical areas. I chaired the subcommittee on minority issues, a topic that had not been addressed in the preliminary report.

I reviewed the juvenile sex offender literature concerning cultural issues and could not find any relevant articles. Using "Minority Youth in the Juvenile Justice System: A Judicial Response" (National Council of Juvenile and Family Court Judges, 1990) as a guide, I reviewed the publication and presented relevant information to the task force in December 1991. Other members with experience in this area were asked to attend this discussion, including Saundra Johnson, Ted Pillow, and Howard C. Stephenson. Following that active discussion, the four of us compiled the information obtained in the December 1991 task-force discussion, reviewed additional literature, and presented our synopsis to the task force.

## Synopsis

The following was derived from the National Council of Juvenile and Family Court Judges (1990):

1. Minority youth are overrepresented at all stages of the juvenile system, compared with their percentage within the general popu-

lation. The council's primary recommendation was that strategies should be developed and implemented so that minority youth not be overrepresented by the practices and philosophies of the various components of the juvenile justice system.

2. Juvenile justice practitioners should receive periodic minority and ethnic sensitivity training.

3. Minority persons should be represented in the intervention and decision-making levels of the juvenile justice system.

4. Familial, cultural, and community factors are important considerations in making dispositions for these youth.

5. Evaluation and research components are lacking and often methodologically flawed when minority issues are addressed. More qualitative (process) research was suggested.

The following ideas, issues, and assumptions were raised at the National Task Force on Juvenile Sexual Offending discussions regarding minority issues:

1. Professionals intervening at all levels of the juvenile justice system need to be aware of their own ethnic, cultural, and/or racial myths.

2. It is our responsibility to educate ourselves about ethnic and cultural issues.

3. We should participate in cultural and ethnic sensitivity training.

4. We must educate, treat, and communicate from a cultural worldview.

5. Discussions about racism are likely to evoke tension. Tension can be a constructive and positive change agent.

6. Racism is trauma.

7. Racism affects systemic and clinical issues.

8. Racial discrimination is influenced by socioeconomic factors.

9. Treatment is education (for ourselves and for our clients). We need cross-cultural treatment, not knowledge of how to treat different cultures.

10. Treatment issues are similar for minority and nonminority juvenile sex offenders.

11. We need to determine whether there are specific systemic treatment factors that predispose minority juvenile sex offenders to fail.

12. We need to identify programming interventions that may be particularly helpful to minority youth.

13. Ethnic and cultural issues need to be integrated into existing treatment programs.

14. Juvenile sex offenders need appropriate ethnic role models, particularly in treatment programs.

15. Relapse prevention and aftercare are imperative in helping the minority youth reintegrate back into the family and/or community.

16. In working with families of minority youth, we must be aware of cultural, ethnic, and attitudinal issues to heighten our sensitivity and efficacy.

17. Despite our ignorance about culture, we need to determine how minority youth are sexual within their own culture and subgroup.

18. We need to be aware of sexual myths within the various cultures and subgroups.

19. Some of our minority youth have little identity with their own culture.

20. We need to acknowledge the institutionalized discrimination inherent at all levels of the juvenile system, as demonstrated by unwarranted overrepresentation of minority youth. We must develop strategies and help implement policy decisions to address this problem.

21. It is important to support culture and ethnicity as positive factors.

Much of this synopsis was included in the task force's revised report (National Council of Juvenile and Family Court Judges, 1993), specifically, the section entitled "Systems Response to Minority Youth" (pp. 13–14). As with many sensitive discussions confronting our ignorance and biases, the task-force process related to cultural diversity and minority issues was fraught with many challenges, much frustration, and great excitement for many.

## Treatment of Hispanic Sex Offenders

Although a few articles discuss Hispanic sex offenders (Becker, Kaplan, Tenke, & Tartaglini, 1991; Carrasco, Louis, & King, 1996; Velasquez, Collahan, & Carrillo, 1989), little if any information is available to aid practitioners in the assessment and treatment of Hispanic sex offenders (Cullen & Travin, 1990). Cullen and Travin (1990) note that apart from the obvious language barriers, a number of transcultural barriers affect the assessment, engagement, and treatment of Hispanic clients. They add that language and cultural factors specific to certain groups of individuals may negatively affect treatment productivity. The authors cite several cultural factors that affect the efficacy of group therapy: language; relationship to authority figures; attitudes toward sexuality; and *dignidad, respeto*, and *honor*.

Cullen and Travin (1990) cite Delgado and Humm-Delgado's (1984) review of the literature on group therapy of Hispanics, noting the importance of language and bilingualism as a positive and significant influence on developing group identity and cohesion. They also cite Martinez (1977), who notes that bilingualism affords the client flexibility to clarify, expound, and discuss emotions and experiences (in their language) through *dichos* (sayings), stories, and idiomatic expressions. The authors also note Marcos and Alpert (1976), who indicate that language can be a deterrent when clients attempt to express themselves in a second language (English) in which they are less fluent or proficient.

Cullen and Travin (1990) indicate that a cognitive-behavioral approach is consistent with Hispanics' attitude toward authority figures and thereby facilitates engagement with Hispanic clients. They affirm the traditional values of deference to parents and adult members of the extended family as beliefs that support the directive factors in cognitive behavior therapy. The reader must be aware, however, that other traditional cultural values of the young toward authority figures (such as little direct eye contact, *respeto*, and no direct expression of anger and/or negative feelings) may hamper the interaction between the group member and the therapist.

The authors also discuss various gender-specific traditional values (such as *respeto* and *verguenza*) that offer additional difficulties for the offender discussing sexually "deviant" material. Significantly, though the authors recognize the role of traditional cultural factors, they also emphasize that these factors should not be the primary focus of treatment to the exclusion of individual personality differences.

*Implications for Interventions with*
*Hispanic Sex Offenders*

As indicated previously, little information in the literature assists the practitioner in engaging, assessing, and treating the Hispanic sex offender. Evidently, the first objective is to engage the offender and his or her family in the clinical process.

## LANGUAGE

The first practical barrier is that of language. It is patently unethical to conduct an interview or an assessment if one of the parties cannot understand what the therapist is saying or if, conversely, the interviewer cannot respond to queries by the non-English speaker. At a minimum, a competent translator should be present when one of the parties cannot speak English. The difficulty with translators, however, is that there are numerous Spanish dialects and great regional and geographic differences in how Spanish is spoken. If the translator is unsure about a particular phrase or idiomatic expression, the translator should clarify the meaning to convey to the examiner the true nature of the expression. If the translator is not fluent in the dialect, the interview process can become a rather stilted and frustrating experience for all participants. A Spanish-speaking interviewer, however, can address that issue during the course of the intervention and minimize the communication difficulties.

Tello (1985) offered the following excellent suggestions in addressing the issue of language and culture:

1. Linguistic (Spanish) translation of materials does not ensure that the information is culturally relevant or appropriate.
2. A bilingual and bicultural individual may not necessarily be culturally competent.
3. One must avoid the trap of "clinical/cultural extremeness": either that a person or family's behavior is based on culture alone, or at the opposite end of the continuum, that all is based on psychodynamics, with no consideration given to culture. (p. III-13)

The translation issue has cropped up in all stages of treatment and throughout the legal process. Recently, in a commitment hearing, one immigrant parent (who spoke only Spanish) told the judge that her son was *un mal educado* (literally translated as "poorly educated"). The translator informed the judge that the parent was concerned about the child's academic education. The parent in fact was attempting to tell the judge that the child had no respect for parental authority or that of the court. In that and similar instances, it is imperative that the language be translated in its cultural context, so that the proper meaning is clearly expressed. If the translator does not do so, someone in that particular setting must convey the actual meaning of the term (even if it means intervening in the proceeding, as was done in the situation cited here).

Most offenders I assess or treat can read, understand, and speak English. Although the offenders have varied proficiencies in reading, understanding, and speaking Spanish, many of them rely on Spanish *dichos* (or sayings) when they are emphasizing a significant point or issue. At times, when they become nervous or excited, they may speak only in Spanish. What is critical (in the context of this article) is that Hispanics often "use their native language to describe personal, intimate, or gut-level issues" (Ho, 1992, p. 107).

Alternating between English and Spanish has been frequently observed in individual, group, and family therapy. In one program, clients were more likely to do so in the presence of the two Hispanic therapists, even though all three staff members spoke Spanish fluently. When asked about this phenomenon, they typically stated that they did not want to be disrespectful to the "non-native Spanish speaker." It is important to realize, however, that this "non-native speaker" (therapist) was adept at understanding and responding (in Spanish) to the *dichos*. It is also important to realize that although the Hispanic offenders could show tremendous sensitivity about the language issue, they could also be rude and crass with all the therapists about other matters.

Language is critical during the assessment phase, particularly during the interviews of parents, spouses, and the extended family. One linguistic issue that often surfaces is the use of double negatives. Many Hispanics find the use of double negatives confusing. This was particularly evident to me when reviewing test items on protocols such as the Minnesota Multiphasic Personality Inventory (MMPI; old versions). Review of individual test items often revealed that test takers found the sentences using double negatives difficult to understand. Hispanics sometimes responded to these items without truly understanding the questions. They rarely voiced their confusion, until I addressed the apparent inconsistencies in their responses. At times, their confusion and frustration were so great that they stopped reading the questions and began using a stylized response set. When using standardized protocols, it is beneficial to ask the test takers whether they had any difficulty with the examination or with any test items. That intervention is helpful, even if the tests have been translated to Spanish, because the dialect or terminology of the norm group (and the nuances of the particular culture) may be quite dissimilar from those of the client.

At times, therapists and other intervenors have used children or other family members as Spanish translators. This practice is strongly discouraged because it often places the children or family members in conflicting roles. The translator should be an impartial and unrelated individual who can translate the information objectively and accurately, without fear of repercussions.

As documented previously, families and extended kinship are very important to most Hispanics. In incest cases and in cases in which the offense involved extended kin, intervention with family members is necessary. Invariably these interventions will include some elderly family members or immigrants who speak only Spanish. Because these interventions and discussions are likely to be emotional and intense and directly controvert many traditional values, the use of a translator in such sessions will probably be frustrating, inefficient, and often counterproductive.

I believe that the exclusive use of a translator in families who speak only Spanish is inappropriate. Surprisingly, the situation is frequent and has produced many disastrous results.

ENGAGEMENT

As noted previously, many traditional values emphasize deference to elders and to persons in positions of authority. Traditionally, this means that one does not directly question or confront those individuals with status. Such deference may be demonstrated toward attorneys, therapists, and others (such as judges and probation officers) if clients perceive them as respected individuals or people of status.

The most significant manifestation of that value is typically seen during court pleadings and interactions with court personnel and therapists. Frequently, many Hispanic clients (and their parents) have little or no understanding of the legal process. Many Hispanic clients have their parents or elder family members raise their questions and concerns. Some Hispanic adults (and juveniles) may not ask questions for fear of appearing ignorant and showing disrespect (by asking questions). Also, it is not sufficient to ask them if they "understand," because they may often say yes out of courtesy to their attorney or therapist. It is important that the party intervening ask the client and/or family to repeat the information discussed to ensure that they have given informed consent, that they understand documents and information presented to them, and that they understand the implications of what they are being asked to do and the consequences of their decisions.

## TREATMENT ISSUES

Knowledge about traditional Hispanic culture is essential. Specific awareness about Hispanic culture is invaluable. To begin with, we must all be aware of our own cultural issues and values and be able to compare our images of Hispanics with the Hispanics we are treating. We must be aware of our stereotypes and our myths with respect to this population, or we will commit grievous errors that may have significant effects on our clients. This is a recurrent theme that often emerges in assessments and disposition hearings. My most recent experience with it arose during consultation with a foster placement agency, dealing with a young Hispanic female who had seriously neglected her two infants. The report to the court documented the fact that the girl had been sexually abused by her stepfather on numerous occasions, producing her two children. The report to the court stated that the stepfather's sexual "experiences" with his daughter were culturally accepted and should therefore not be a cause for concern or investigation. What is particularly appalling is that neither the judge nor the Child Protective Services (CPS) worker nor some of the therapists brought up the issue of sexual abuse of a child, because the psychologist stated that this was an "accepted and normal" occurrence in this particular culture.

The most difficult interventions frequently arise when discussing sexuality, sex offending, and the need for supervision and monitoring. As with many families, these issues often evoke intense emotional reactions. The critical issue in treating Hispanic families is determining the interplay of traditional values, acculturation, and responses and values that are unique to those individuals and their families. By understanding this interplay, the intervenor will be better able to serve clients and their families.

No firm rules about specific types of interventions with Hispanic clients exist. Therapists must recognize several important factors, however, including these:

1. Offenders and their families are sometimes reticent to admit that sexual abuse has occurred, because they will be "shamed" by their own family and extended kin, as well as by their community. This is true for "stranger rapes," after which girls may be perceived as no longer virgins, and for boys who have been sexually abused by males and may be called *maricones* (a derogatory term for homosexuals). For many families, incest is the ultimate sign of personal and familial dishonor (parents are seen as unprotective, and family members as disgracing one another).

   The practitioner must understand the concepts of *respeto* and *verguenza* within the Hispanic culture specifically as they apply to the offender and his or her family. How to best intervene is determined by an understanding of the client and the family. Sometimes, educational sessions with the family or with particular family members about sexuality and the effects of sexual abuse are sufficient. Often, it is useful to incorporate priests, supportive elders in the family, and other Hispanic families (who have dealt with similar issues) when confronting sensitive issues (such as sex education, sexual development, and sexual expression) with the family. At times, priests have been very helpful in giving the family "permission" to discuss matters that are typically not discussed with their children or with anyone outside of the extended kinship.

2. Although Hispanic offenders may willingly speak about their sexual offenses, at times they may have difficulty discussing what they perceive as "deviant" sexual attitudes and behavior. For males, these "deviant" sexual thoughts and acts may include oral sex, masturbation, and sexual arousal and/or interaction with other males. Discussion of what is perceived as "deviant" typically produces concerns about *verguenza*, *respeto*, and *machismo*.

   In our program, some male Hispanic offenders agree to address this issue with the female staff initially, attempting to determine an adult woman's (and status figure's) perspective. Once they feel reassured that they will not be demeaned or humiliated for discussing the "deviant" acts or thoughts, they discuss the issues with me and other staff members in more graphic detail. As with all offenders, these discussions are addressed in a personal, communal, and cultural context and focus on the perceived and/or actual instances of inappropriate sexual acts or thoughts raised. With Hispanic offenders, the topics of discussion include the concepts of "Madonna and whore," sexual arousal and "sin," *maricón* ("queerness"), personal and family honor (*respeto*), and shame (*verguenza*).

3. During various portions of the treatment process, the offenders and their families (at times including extended family members)

discuss issues of sexuality, sex education, and sex-offending dynamics. These conferences can be especially sensitive for those families who do not believe that sexuality should be discussed openly, especially with minor children. *Respeto* becomes a crucial variable in sexual abuse cases in which the abuser is a "respected" figure, because an outcry can be perceived as a betrayal of the "honor" accorded to the valued adult. In all cases, the therapist must acknowledge (but not necessarily agree with) the family's value system and also advocate for direct and appropriate communication that addresses supervision, safety, and protection issues.

The most frequently voiced concern is that the minor children are "innocent" and that discussions about physical and sexual contact, sexual victimization, and sex offending would impair their emotional and spiritual development. To ease this concern, therapists initially consult with parents and elders about the topics of discussion and review specific treatment expectations and recommendations. These issues are also routinely discussed in the monthly parents' educational groups, where other Hispanic members can recognize individual and familial conflicts, support the person with the difficulty, and validate the cultural issues.

Another type of difficulty often arises when discussing males offending against other males or younger boys. For some traditional Hispanic families, a male offending against another male, particularly if the victim is a brother or son, is the ultimate in disrespect and dishonor. It can become a collective shame that often includes the extended family. This is often a difficult and shameful experience for the elder male members of the family. It can be a highly sensitive and explosive issue for some and must be treated with caution and prudence.

Often, one of the most difficult aspects of dealing with sexual victimization within the family is the issue of retribution. Male siblings or relatives of the victim often feel compelled to exact punishment or vengeance against the perpetrator, out of a feeling of restoring respect and honor for the victim and the family.

4. Apparent from this discussion is the need for family therapy that may include the extended family. Although specific circumstances may preclude family therapy, the significance of the family and the associated cultural values cannot be ignored in treating Hispanic sex offenders. It is my contention that true healing will not be achieved unless the offender and his or her family are treated.

At times, our program has attempted to include parents who speak Spanish only (along with an interpreter) in the parent education group, where only English is spoken. These interventions were not productive, because the Spanish translations disrupted the flow of the group process. As might be expected, the Hispanic Spanish speakers would not ask questions or volunteer information unless they were directly asked to respond. The "mixed" group was somewhat frustrating for all involved. We have opted to deal with this issue by providing educational intervention with the Spanish speakers separate from the larger English-speaking group. In the Spanish-only meetings, the discussions were conducted entirely in Spanish. When there were two or more Spanish-speaking families, or when other Spanish speakers attended the Spanish-only groups, the intra- and interpersonal dynamics of the group members radically changed. We found that those who spoke only Spanish engaged much more quickly and were more open when they participated with other Spanish speakers in a group setting.

It is important to remember that Hispanics are heterogeneous and adaptive, whether "traditional" or not. Generalizations about Hispanic individuals and families must be carefully made, based on sound research that addresses ethnocultural variables. It is imperative that generalizations about traditional versus nontraditional families not lead to assumptions about what is "better." The characteristics, values, and traits ascribed to Hispanic families and individuals are influenced by the ethnocultural context.

We all have a culture, and we all have our biases. As intervenors, we must strive to be aware of our personal and professional biases and assumptions, particularly when we interact with those we perceive as different from us. There is no one "type" of Hispanic or one kind of value or ideal that all Hispanics believe in. By understanding the interaction of traditional Hispanic values and idiosyncratic beliefs, however, the practitioner is in a much better position to provide an accurate assessment and afford more culturally relevant and effective treatment planning. This awareness will help us understand how certain cultural values may influence the implementation of particular intervention strategies. Without this awareness, some interventions will be doomed from the start.

It is clear that we do not need to learn Spanish to treat all Hispanic offenders. We must, however, recognize the importance of language and its nuances while conducting assessments and interventions and should be aware when our linguistic limitations do not serve our clients and our interventions. Programs and interventions designed to intervene with Hispanic offenders must have clinical staff (and not simply a support staff or administrative person who sits in on "special" cases) who are bilingual and culturally competent to address these needs.

Traditional Hispanic values, including *verguenza*, *respeto*, and *machismo*, must be understood when dealing with sexual abuse issues with Hispanics, particularly in cases of incest. Although children are considered sacrosanct within Hispanic families, other concepts come into play that affect the clinical picture. For girls who have been sexually abused, they may no longer be perceived as sexually "pure," as is expected within their culture, because they "had sex" outside of a marriage relationship. Hispanic boys who have been sexually abused may experience various levels of shame. Disclosure of sexual abuse by a male would require that he admit to being victimized, the antithesis of what is considered "male." If the perpetrator is a male, issues of homosexuality and manhood are sure to arise. If the perpetrator is a female, boys are likely not to report the abuse because they may be expected to be sexually available to girls or women at all times. All these scenarios can lead to blaming the victim.

Often, with me, clinical intervention is conducted with families and individuals who are conjointly speaking with folk healers and/or priests, elder members of their family, or *compadres* about the sexual abuse issue. It is imperative that the practitioner determine who these crucial players are, so that services can be provided in a cooperative fashion (if possible) to maximize effectiveness.

Again, it is imperative to recognize that Hispanics are a very diverse group whose level of acculturation varies along a broad continuum of values, attitudes, and expectations. As important is the fact that Hispanics are impacted by factors outside of their culture. To be effective, one must address not only how the Hispanic may fit into the traditional mode but also how he or she is affected by a variety of other factors. It has been my experience that with sensitivity, awareness, and training, Hispanic sex offenders can be assisted in their healing process.

# References

Acosta, F.X., Yamamoto, J., & Evans, L.A. (1982). *Effective psychotherapy for low income and minority patients*. New York: Plenum.

Becker, J.V., Kaplan, M.S., Tenke, C., & Tartaglini, A.T. (1991). The incidence of depressive symptomatology in juvenile sex offenders with a history of abuse. *Child Abuse and Neglect, 15*, 531–536.

Betancourt, H., & Lopez, S.R. (1993). The study of culture, ethnicity, and race in American psychology. *American Psychologist, 48*, 629–637.

Black, C., Paz, H., & DeBlassie, R.R. (1991). Counseling the Hispanic male adolescent. *Adolescence, 26*(101), 223–232.

Brink, T.L. (1994). The need for qualitative research on mental health of elderly Hispanics. *International Journal of Aging and Human Development, 38*, 279–291.

Brislin, R.W. (1993). *Understanding culture's influence on behavior*. New York: Harcourt.

Carrasco, N., Louis, D.G., & King, R. (1996). The Hispanic sex offender: Machismo and cultural values. *The Forum (Association for the Treatment of Sexual Abusers), 8*(1), 4–5.

Casas, J.M. (1984). Policy, training, and research in counseling psychology: The racial/ethnic minority perspective. In S.D. Brown & R.W. Lent (Eds.), *Handbook of counseling psychology* (pp. 785–831). New York: Wiley.

Casas, J.M., & Vasquez, M.J.T. (1989). Counseling the Hispanic client: A theoretical and applied perspective. In P.B. Pederson, J.G. Draguns, W.J. Lonner, & J.E.Trimble (Eds.), *Counseling across cultures* (pp. 153–175). Honolulu: University of Hawaii Press.

Castro, F.G., Furth, P., & Karlow, H. (1984). The health beliefs of Mexican, Mexican American, and Anglo American women. *Hispanic Journal of Behavioral Sciences, 6*, 365–383.

Cervantes, J.M., & Ramírez, O. (1992). Spirituality and family dynamics in psychotherapy with Latino children. In L.Vargas & J. Koss-Chioino (Eds.), *Working with culture: Psychotherapeutic interventions with ethnic minority children and adolescents* (pp. 103–128). San Francisco: Jossey-Bass.

Cervantes, R.C., & Castro, F.G. (1985). Stress, coping, and Mexican American mental health: A systematic review. *Hispanic Journal of Behavioral Sciences, 7*, 1–73.

Chavez, J.M., & Roney, C.E. (1990). Psychocultural factors affecting the mental health status of Mexican American adolescents. In A.R. Stiffman & L.E. Davis (Eds.), *Ethnic issues in adolescent mental health* (pp. 73–91). Newbury Park, CA: Sage.

Comas-Díaz, L. (1995). Puerto Ricans and sexual child abuse. In L.A. Fontes (Ed.), *Sexual abuse in nine North American cultures: Treatment and prevention* (pp. 31–66). Thousand Oaks, CA: Sage.

Cullen, K., & Travin, S. (1990). Assessment and treatment of Spanish-speaking sex offenders: Special considerations. *Psychiatric Quarterly, 61*(4), 223–236.

Delgado, M., & Humm-Delgado, D. (1984). Hispanics and group work: A review of the literature. *Social Work with Groups, 7*, 85–92.

Draguns, J.G. (1990). Application of cross-cultural psychology in the field of mental health. In R.W. Brislin (Ed.), *Applied cross-cultural psychology*. Newbury Park, CA: Sage.

Fischer, G. (1987). Hispanic and majority student attitudes toward forcible rape as a function of differences in attitudes toward women. *Sex Roles, 17*, 93–101.

Fitzpatrick, J.P. (1971). *Puerto Rican Americans: The meaning of migration to the mainland*. Englewood Cliffs, NJ: Prentice-Hall.

Fontes, L. (1993a). Considering culture and oppression: Steps toward an ecology of sexual child abuse. *Journal of Feminist Family Therapy, 5*(1), 25–54.

Fontes, L. (1993b). Disclosures of sexual abuse by Puerto Rican children: Oppression and cultural barriers. *Journal of Child Sexual Abuse, 2*(1), 21–35.

García-Preto, N. (1982). Puerto Rican families. In M. McGoldrick, J.K. Pearce,

& J. Giordano (Eds.), *Ethnicity and family therapy* (pp. 164–186). New York: Guilford Press.

Gibson, G. (1985a). Methods of preventing child abuse among Mexican American families. In Texas Migrant Council's National Resource Center on the Mexican American Family (Laredo, TX), *Developing cultural competence: Awareness, sensitivity, integration, competence. A training manual for improving the efficiency and effectiveness of social services delivered to Mexican American families* (pp. IV-1–IV-47). Washington, DC: National Clearinghouse on Child Abuse and Neglect Information.

Gibson, G. (1985b). The Mexican American family. In Texas Migrant Council's National Resource Center on the Mexican American Family (Laredo, TX), *Developing cultural competence: Awareness, sensitivity, integration, competence. A training manual for improving the efficiency and effectiveness of social services delivered to Mexican American families* (pp. II-1–II-12). Washington, DC: National Clearinghouse on Child Abuse and Neglect Information.

Gutiérrez, L., Ortega, R.M., & Suarez, Z.E. (1990). Self help and the Latino community. In T.J. Powell (Ed.), *Working with self-help* (pp. 219–236). Silver Spring, MD: National Association of Social Workers.

Hall, C.C.I. (1992). Please choose one: Ethnic identity choices for biracial individuals. In M.P.P. Root (Ed.), *Racially mixed people in America* (pp. 250–264). Newbury Park, CA: Sage.

Herrerías, C. (1988, Fall/Winter). Prevention of child abuse and neglect in the Hispanic community: The MADRE parent education program. *Journal of Primary Prevention, 1&2*, 104–119.

Hines, P.M, García-Preto, N., McGoldrick, M., Almeida, R., & Weltman, S. (1992, June). Intergenerational relationships across cultures. *Families in Society: The Journal of Contemporary Human Services, 23*, 323–338.

Ho, M.K. (1992). Hispanic American children and adolescents. In *Minority children and adolescents in therapy* (pp. 94–115). Newbury Park, CA: Sage.

*Household and family characteristics.* (1990, March). Series P-20, No. 477. Washington, DC: U.S. Government Printing Office.

Irvine, J.M. (1995). *Sexuality education across cultures: Working with differences.* San Francisco: Jossey-Bass.

Kleinman, A. (1978). Clinical relevance of anthropological and cross-cultural research: Concepts and strategies. *American Journal of Psychiatry, 139*, 427–431.

LeVine, E.S., & Padilla, A.M. (1980). *Crossing cultures in therapy: Pluralistic counseling for the Hispanic.* Monterey, CA: Brooks/Cole.

Levy, B. (1988). Taking care of me: Preventing child sexual abuse in the Hispanic community. In L.E. Walker (Ed.), *Handbook on sexual abuse of children* (pp. 387–401). New York: Springer.

Malgady, R.G., Rogler, L.H., & Costantino, G. (1987). Ethnocultural and linguistic bias in mental evaluation of Hispanics. *American Psychologist, 42*, 228–234.

Marcos, L.R., & Alpert, M. (1976). Strategies and risks in psychotherapy with bilingual patients: The phenomenon of language independence. *American Journal of Psychiatry, 133*, 1275–1278.

Marín, G., & VanOss-Marín, B. (1991). *Research with Hispanic populations. Applied social research methods series.* Vol. 23. Newbury Park, CA: Sage.

Martinez, C. (1977). Group process and the Chicano: Clinical issues. *International Journal of Group Psychotherapy, 28*, 225–231.

Mendoza, R., Smith, M.W., Poland, R.E., Lin, K., & Strickland, L. (1991). Ethnic psychopharmacology: The Hispanic and Native American perspective. *Psychopharmacology Bulletin, 27*(4), 449–461.

Mennen, F.E. (1994). Sexual abuse in Latina girls: Their functioning and a comparison with White and African American girls. *Hispanic Journal of Behavioral Sciences, 16*(4), 475–486.

Mennen, F.E. (1995). The relationship of race/ethnicity to symptoms in childhood sexual abuse. *Child Abuse and Neglect, 19*(1), 115–124.

Mio, J.S., & Morris, D.R. (1990). Cross-cultural issues in psychology training program: An invitation for discussion. *Professional Psychology: Research and Practice, 21*, 434–441.

Morales, A.T. (1992). Therapy with Latino gang members. In K.A. Vargas & J.D. Koss-Chioino (Eds.), *Working with culture: Psychotherapeutic interventions with ethnic minority children and adolescents* (pp. 129–154). San Francisco: Jossey-Bass.

National Council of Juvenile and Family Court Judges. (1990). Minority youth in the juvenile justice system: A judicial response. *Juvenile and Family Court Journal, 41*(3A).

National Council of Juvenile and Family Court Judges. (1993). The revised report from the National Task Force on Juvenile Sexual Offending, 1993, of the National Adolescent Perpetrator Network. *Juvenile and Family Court Journal, 44*(4).

Okazaki, S., & Sue, S. (1995). Methodological issues in assessment research with ethnic minorities. *Psychological Assessment, 7*(3), 367–375.

Olmedo, E.L. (1979). Acculturation: A psychometric perspective. *American Psychologist, 34*, 1061–1070.

Padilla, A.M., & DeSnyder, N.S. (1987). Counseling Hispanics: Strategies for effective intervention. In P. B. Pederson (Ed.), *Handbook of cross-cultural counseling and therapy* (pp. 157–164). Westport, CT: Greenwood Press.

Padilla, A.M., Ruiz, R.A., & Alvarez, R. (1975). Community mental health services for the Spanish speaking/surnamed population. *American Psychologist, 30*, 892–905.

Parker, W.M., Bingham, R.P., & Fukuyama, M. (1985). Improving cross-cultural effectiveness of counselor trainees. *Counselor Education and Supervision, 24*(4), 349–352.

Pedersen, P.B. (1987). Ten frequent assumptions of cultural bias in counseling. *Journal of Multicultural Counseling and Development, 15*, 16–24.

Ramos-McKay, J., Comas-Díaz, L., & Rivera, L. (1988). Puerto Ricans. In L. Comas-Díaz & E.H. Griffith (Eds.), *Clinical guidelines in cross cultural mental health* (pp. 204–232). New York: Wiley.

Rodriguez, O., & Zayas, L.H. (1990). Hispanic adolescents and antisocial behavior: Sociocultural factors and treatment implications. In A.R. Stiffman & L.E. Davis, (Eds.), *Ethnic issues in adolescent mental health* (pp. 147–171). Newbury Park, CA: Sage.

Rogler, L.H., Malgady, R.G., & Rodriquez, O. (1989). *Hispanics and mental health: A framework for research*. Malabalar, FL: Kreiger.

Rosado, J.W., & Elias, M.J. (1993). Ecological and psychocultural mediators in the delivery of services for urban, culturally diverse Hispanic clients. *Professional Psychology: Research and Practice, 24*(4), 450–459.

Ross, C.E., Mirowsky, J., & Cockerham, W.C. (1983). Social class, Mexican culture, and fatalism: Their effects on psychological distress. *American Journal of Community Psychology, 11*, 383–399.

Rubin, G. (1975). The traffic in women: Notes on the political economy of sex. In R. Reiter (Ed.), *Toward an anthropology of women* (pp. 157–210). New York: Monthly Review Press.

Sanders-Phillips, K., Moisan, P.A., Wadlington, S.M., & English, K. (1995). Ethnic differences in psychological functioning among Black and Latino sexually abused girls. *Child Abuse and Neglect, 19*(6), 691–706.

Sasao, T., & Sue, S. (1993). Toward a culturally anchored ecological framework of research in ethnic-cultural communities. *American Journal of Community Psychology, 21,* 705–727.

Sciarra, D.T., & Ponterotto, J.G. (1991). Counseling the Hispanic bilingual family: Challenges to the therapeutic process. *Psychotherapy, 28*(3), 473–480.

Simoni, J.M., & Pérez, L. (1995). Latinos and mutual support groups: A case for considering culture. *American Journal of Orthopsychiatry, 65*(3), 440–445.

Snowden, L.R., & Cheung, F.K. (1990). Use of inpatient mental health services by members of ethnic minority groups. *American Psychologist, 45,* 347–355.

Solomon, A. (1992, June). Clinical diagnosis among diverse populations: A multicultural perspective. *Families in Society: Journal of Contemporary Human Services,* 371–377.

Sotomayor, M. (1985). The Mexican American family: Coping with stress. In Texas Migrant Council's National Resource Center on the Mexican American Family (Laredo, TX), *Developing cultural competence: Awareness, sensitivity, integration, competence. A training manual for improving the efficiency and effectiveness of social services delivered to Mexican American families* (pp. V-1–V-16). Washington, DC: National Clearinghouse on Child Abuse and Neglect Information.

Spencer, G. (1986). *Projections of the Hispanic population: 1983–2082.* United States Bureau of the Census current population reports, series P-25: Population estimates and projections (No. 995). Washington, DC: U.S. Government Printing Office.

Sue, D.W. (1990). Culture-specific strategies in counseling: A conceptual framework. *Professional Psychology: Research and Practice, 21,* 424–433.

Sue, S., & Zane, N. (1987). The role of culture and cultural techniques in psychotherapy: A critique and reformulation. *American Psychologist, 42*(1), 37–45.

Sundberg, N.D. (1981). Cross-cultural counseling and psychotherapy: A research overview. In A.J. Marsella and P.B. Pedersen (Eds.), *Cross-cultural counseling and psychotherapy: Foundations, evaluation, and cultural considerations* (pp. 28–62). New York: Pergamon.

Sutton, R.G., & Kessler, M. (1986). National study of the effects of clients' socioeconomic status on clinical psychologists' professional judgments. *Journal of Consulting and Clinical Psychologist, 54,* 275–276.

Tello, J. (1985). Developing cultural competence: Awareness, sensitivity, integration, competence. In Texas Migrant Council's National Resource Center on the Mexican American Family (Laredo, TX), *Developing cultural competence: Awareness, sensitivity, integration, competence. A training manual for improving the efficiency and effectiveness of social services delivered to Mexican American families* (pp. III-1–III-14). Washington, DC: National Clearinghouse on Child Abuse and Neglect Information.

Texas Migrant Council's National Resource Center on the Mexican American Family (Laredo, TX). (1985). *Developing cultural competence: Awareness, sensitivity, integration, competence. A training manual for improving the efficiency and effectiveness of social services delivered to Mexican American families.* Washington, DC: National Clearinghouse on Child Abuse and Neglect Information.

Velasquez, R.J., Collahan, W.J., & Carrillo, R. (1989). MMPI profiles of Hispanic-American inpatient and outpatient sex offenders. *Psychological Reports, 65,* 1055–1058.

Wyatt, G. (1990). Sexual abuse of ethnic minority children: Identifying dimension of victimization. *Professional Psychology: Research and Practice, 21,* 338–343.

Zuniga, M.E. (1991). "Dichos" as metaphorical tools for resistant Latino clients. *Psychotherapy, 28*(3), 480–483.

# 7 Assessment and Treatment of Spanish-speaking Sexual Abusers: Special Considerations

*Ken Cullen, M.S.W.*
*Sheldon Travin, M.D.*

Although an expanding body of literature pertains to the special considerations related to the treatment of Hispanic patients with a variety of psychiatric disorders whose primary language is Spanish (Delgado & Humm-Delgado, 1984), virtually no information exists to aid in the assessment and treatment of Hispanic sex offenders. Beyond the obvious problems posed by differences in language, many transcultural factors affect the evaluation and engagement of Hispanic patients in treatment when, as noted by Arce and Torres-Matrullo (1982), they are also "relatively unacculturated, of poor socioeconomic background and psychologically unsophisticated" (p. 231).

These factors compound the difficulty generally encountered when attempting to engage sex offenders in therapy, whatever their primary language or ethnic background. In describing primarily English-speaking sex offenders mandated for treatment evaluation, clinicians often note that the initial interviews are characterized by denial, minimization, and cognitive distortions of the abusive act (Cullen, 1983; Travin, Cullen, & Melella, 1988). The individual's reluctance to acknowledge the deviancy of his or her behavior must eventually give way during treatment to the acceptance of responsibility and the need to change. Obviously, these same considerations apply to all ethnic groups. However, failure to be sensitive to certain language and cultural factors unique to a specific ethnic group can negatively affect treatment effectiveness.

Our experiences in modifying and carrying out a special program to satisfy the needs of Spanish-speaking patients are presented in this chapter. Reticence to discuss sexuality in a group

150

setting, the relationship between therapists and patients as affected by rules of social etiquette, and the reluctance to criticize other members in the group were prominent features attributed to religious and cultural factors. We consider it necessary to be sensitive to these subtle nuances to provide adequate treatment.

# Engaging Patients in Coerced Treatment

The first obstacle to engaging sex offenders stems from the dual nature of the disorder as both a deviant psychological process and unlawful behavior (Melella, Travin, & Cullen, 1989). Often, the sex offender is referred for treatment only after detection of his or her criminal activity by an agency of the legal system. Therefore, the sex offender frequently experiences the initial contact with the therapist as a potential form of continued punishment. Fear of continued punishment may understandably lead to avoidance of any involvement in a therapeutic alliance. This avoidance is further bolstered by the offender's cognitive distortions of the deviancy of his or her sexual behavior (Abel, 1976). Although the mandatory nature of the referral for treatment may be initially viewed as excessively coercive, it is the necessary means by which the offender overcomes his or her reluctance to enter therapy. During successful treatment, the locus of motivation for compliance changes from a predominantly external to a predominantly internal focus. The therapist must ease this transition from external to internal motivation by helping the patient acknowledge the deviant nature of his or her acts and learn more socially acceptable behavior.

The initial avoidance of treatment by involuntary patients, as noted by Rooney (1988), is most often labeled by therapists as resistance. Rooney points out that this phenomenon can more correctly be described by Brehm's (1972) reactance theory of the individual's response to the threat of loss of freedom. As defined by Brehm, individuals are likely to react by attempting to restore their freedom, displaying hostility, complying only minimally, subverting the compliance of others to the mandate, or evidencing interest in other restricted behaviors. According to Brehm (1976), this initial reluctance by the involuntary patient may be best addressed by using a variety of engagement strategies. These include eliciting some degree of agreement from the patient that the mandate is valid, that the patient may benefit from involvement despite feelings of ambiguity, that compliance will result in relief from the original mandate, and that refusal to comply will lead to adverse consequences. Specifically, Brehm suggests emphasizing choices available to the patient whenever possible, exploring all sides of an argument, noting the particular behaviors that need to be changed and those behaviors that can be maintained, and pointing out that compliance ultimately will lead to the restoration of freedom.

The setting in which treatment is offered may exacerbate the responses of the involuntary patient described by the reactance theory. A forensic setting such as a court clinic may initially alienate the individual, who may view it as an extension of the court procedure. The setting may become less threatening as the patient develops a therapeutic liaison with the therapist in the clinical milieu. The treatment setting may have particular importance to Hispanic patients. Delgado (1983) notes that therapists in mental-health settings have generally found it difficult to engage Hispanics in treatment and cites Boulette's (1975) assertion that Hispanics eschew the notion of mental illness as the possible cause of interpersonal conflicts. Similarly, Mizio (1979) observes that Puerto Ricans are more likely to avail themselves of mental-health services offered in a multipurpose facility, thereby avoiding the stigmatization of mental disease.

Once the patient has overcome his or her avoidance of therapeutic contact, including the potential negative response induced by the setting during the assessment phase of treatment, the patient may exhibit renewed reluctance to continue contact, depending on the treatment modality. In our integrated treatment program for sex offenders in a court clinic, the core modality of assessment and treatment follows a cognitive-behavioral paradigm (Travin, Bluestone, & Coleman, 1985). Treatment is provided primarily in a group format of 8 to 12 patients seen for weekly 90-minute sessions over a period of approximately one year. Upon completion of the assessment, the patient is seen individually to explain the nature of the group treatment approach. This pregroup contact addresses the possible fears the patient may have regarding participation in group therapy (Devore & Schlesinger, 1987). It informs the patient of the rationale underlying the choice of specific cognitive-behavioral treatment components and the benefits to the patient of the group therapy format. When working with a subgroup of Hispanic patients who are primarily Spanish speaking, relatively psychologically unsophisticated, and from a low socioeconomic group, the therapist must recognize the role of language, the patients' relationship to authority figures, their attitude toward sexuality, and certain other factors unique to this ethnic background that may increase their reluctance to participate in treatment in a group therapy context.

## Cultural Factors and Group Therapy

*Language*

In a review of the literature on group therapy with Hispanics, Delgado and Humm-Delgado (1984) note that 9 out of 28 articles cite the role of language in helping group identity and cohesion. Additionally, the acceptance of bilingualism as part of the group process provides flexibility and greater precision in the patients' expression of their feelings. This precision, according to Martinez (1977), can be observed by the patient's shift from English to Spanish "in order to clarify a feeling, share an experience, use an analogy, or recall and apply a Mexican proverb." In contrast, Marcos (1976) points out that language may serve as an emotional barrier in psychotherapy when patients choose to express themselves in the second language in which they lack proficiency. Such patients, termed "subordinate bilinguals" by Marcos, may prefer the second language over the mother tongue because it provides sufficient emotional detachment to reveal highly charged material. Kolers's (1968) concept of information processing in bilingual learning suggests that certain information the patient experienced or learned in one language may be unavailable to the patient in the alternative language. If one language is used to the exclusion of the other, Marcos and Alpert (1976) emphasize that important psychic material may be omitted and therefore go untreated. Although the exact role of a second language, foreign to patients, continues to be a subject of discussion, the nature of the bilingual shifts by the individual patient should be noted by the therapist because of their likely clinical significance.

*Relationship to Authority Figures*

Although a variety of therapeutic modalities have been employed
in the treatment of sex offenders (Lockhart, Saunders, & Cleveland,
1988), the group therapy approach is the most widely used treatment format. In group therapy using a cognitive-behavioral protocol, the group leader takes on the active, directive role of the
teacher, helping group members unlearn aberrant sexual behavior
and learn more socially appropriate behavior.

The cognitive-behavioral approach is conducive to the engagement of Hispanic sex offenders in treatment, as the nature of this
group process is culturally syntonic with Hispanics' attitude
toward authority figures (Arce & Torres-Matrullo, 1982; Comas-
Díaz, 1985). As McKinley (1987) notes, in Hispanic cultures, children are raised to show great deference to parents and other adult
members of the extended family. Similarly, children are admon-
ished from an early age not to make direct eye contact or to display anger, disagreement, or other negative emotional responses to
adults in positions of authority. This culturally entrained noncriti-
cal, reverential attitude toward authority figures enhances Hispanic
patients' acceptance of the directive aspects of cognitive-behavior
therapy. However, this reverential relationship to the group leader
(Tylim, 1982) may markedly inhibit the patient's verbal participation in the therapy sessions.

*Attitudes toward Sexuality*

The individual's capacity to discuss sexual material openly in a
group setting is largely determined by the patient's general attitudes
toward sexuality. Although such attitudes are derived from a variety of sources, the influence of the ethnic culture cannot be minimized. Lister (1986) presents a conceptual framework of the impact
of ethnic culture on the development of human sexuality. Lister
stresses the need to view the individual's sexual behavior in the
context of his or her relationship within the ethnic group.

Burgos and Perez (1986) note that the socialization process that
occurs within the Puerto Rican family unit engenders a double
standard regarding acceptable sexual behavior for males and

females. Female children are taught to accept "dependency, obedience, virginity, responsibility and submission" as appropriate role behavior. Male children are expected to be "independent, strong, and aggressive," and "they should identify with machismo and virility." Consequently, *machismo* and *marianismo* relegate the role of a sex object to the female and impose on the male extreme pressure for constant sexual readiness and heightened expectations of sexual performance. Due to this sex-role stereotyping, homosexual behavior by either male or female is considered a cultural anathema, as it is a display of *poca verguenza* ("lack of shame").

Discussion of sexuality is usually eschewed by Hispanic patients in the group context because it may be culturally viewed as a display of disrespect for the group therapist. This aversion to revealing sexual information is exacerbated when the sexual material to be discussed is of a deviant nature.

## Dignity, Respect, Honor, and Personalism

Despite the differences among group members that may be attributed partly to their own unique personality characteristics, four major cultural values emerge as significant factors in the success of the group process (Olarte & Masnik, 1985). These values are dignity (*dignidad*), respect (*respeto*), honor (*honor*), and personalism (*personalismo*). They refer to the tendency in Hispanic culture to derive self-worth not primarily from one's position in society, level of education, or material possessions but rather from dignity of the individual; the respect of others is gained through the accomplishment of cultural role expectations. Thus, a man who provides for the security and well-being of his family, although financially poor, may be treated with greater dignity and respect in the community than a wealthy professional who does not act honorably. *Personalismo* stresses the preference of many Hispanics to relate personally and informally in all forms of interpersonal transactions rather than to deal formally through an institutional process. These deeply ingrained cultural factors underlie and influence the ways in which individual group members relate to one another and to the group leader and thus profoundly determine the ongoing group dynamic.

## Assessment and Treatment Protocol

The Sex Offender Treatment Program is a clinical research component of the multiservice Forensic Psychiatry Clinic in the Bronx Criminal Court Building. The treatment approach is a modification of the cognitive-behavioral paradigm established by Drs. Abel and Becker (Abel, Becker, & Cunningham-Rathner, 1984) at the New York State Psychiatric Institute. The program comprises two components: the assessment phase and the treatment phase. The assessment phase consists of psychiatric interviews, psychometric testing, and psychophysiologic measurement of sexual arousal conducted on an individual basis. The treatment phase involves a task-oriented treatment regimen to reduce deviant arousal, increase social and assertiveness skills, and correct cognitive distortions that support involvement in deviant sexual behavior.

### Assessment Phase

In the developmental stage of the program, due to the nonexistence of testing material in Spanish, we were unable to evaluate 11 males who were exclusively Spanish speaking. To address the needs of this patient population, we recruited a specially trained bilingual technician who would also serve as an interpreter in the assessment and treatment process. This individual translated the original psychometric and audiotaped physiological testing material following the principle of back-translation of Brislin (1970, 1981).

Since the addition of the translated material and the specially trained staff member, we have evaluated 20 Hispanic patients who were primarily Spanish speaking, relatively psychologically unsophisticated, and from a low socioeconomic group. It should be noted that this group of patients is a small percentage of the 750 individuals referred for assessment of paraphiliac disorder since the inception of the program in January 1984 and that other patients of Hispanic origin were not included in this group, as they were primarily English speaking and integrated into the host culture.

In this study, we tested the validity of making generalizations about the physiologic assessment protocol with this Spanish-speaking group. Similarly, Earls and Proulx (1986) investigated this issue with a French-speaking population. We also compared these 20 offenders with 287 primarily English-speaking sex offenders on such parameters as demographic variables, history of psychiatric intervention, alcohol and substance abuse, history of personal victimization, and criminal arrests. Although such a comparison may not be statistically reliable, this preliminary study suggests several interesting trends.

Erection measurement results, including responses to both visual and audiotaped cues, revealed that 100 percent of the 20 Spanish-speaking subjects evidenced arousal to deviant stimuli of the primary presenting problem (see Table 7.1). In an earlier study of 185 primarily English-speaking subjects, 167, or 90.3 percent, evidenced arousal to deviant stimuli of the primary presenting problem (Cullen, 1983). Physiologic results for these Spanish-speaking subjects also showed that 22 percent evidenced arousal to cues depicting or describing aggression and sadomasochism. Further, 33.3 percent of the Spanish-speaking sample showed arousal to other paraphilia cues, in contrast to the more than 60 percent of subjects studied by Abel, Becker, and Cunningham-Rathner (1988) who showed arousal to multiple paraphilias. Thus, these initial results support the validity of using the physiologic assessment instrument to generalize about this Spanish-speaking group.

When comparing the Spanish-speaking group with the larger group, we found notable differences in demographic characteristics, abuse and victimization history, deviant behavior history, and arrest history. For demographic variables, when contrasting the Spanish-speaking group with the English-speaking group, we found that the mean age was 39.2 versus 33 years, the marital status was 75 percent versus 26 percent currently married, and 100 percent versus 67 percent had full-time employment (see Table 7.2). The Spanish-speaking group reported a much lower incidence of personal sexual victimization (5 percent versus 60 percent),

**Table 7.1** Spanish-speaking Patients Who Evidenced Positive Physiologic Assessment Results

| *Stimulus* | *Percentage* |
|---|---|
| Presenting problem | 100 |
| Aggression | 22 |
| Sadomasochism (slides) | 22 |
| Other paraphilia | 33.3 |

**Table 7.2**   Demographic Characteristics

| Variable | Spanish Speaking (n=20) | English Speaking (n=287) |
|---|---|---|
| Age (years) | | |
| Mean | 39.2 | 33 |
| Range | 21–59 | 17–75 |
| Marital status | | |
| Single | 2 (10%) | 121 (48%) |
| Married | 15 (75%) | 66 (26%) |
| Divorced | 3 (15%) | 66 (26%) |
| Children | | |
| Mean | 1.9 | 0.6 |
| Range | 0–5 | 0–9 |
| Employed | 100% | 67% |

**Table 7.3**   Abuse and Victimization History

| Variable | Spanish Speaking (n=20) | English Speaking (n=287) |
|---|---|---|
| Sexual victimization | 3 (15%) | 172 (60%) |
| Prior psychiatric history | 1 (5%) | 89 (31%) |
| Previous sex therapy | 1 (5%) | 57 (20%) |
| Alcohol/substance abuse | 10 (50%) | 52 (18%) |
| Drinking at time of commission | 12 (60%) | 80 (28%) |

prior psychiatric history (5 percent versus 31 percent), and previous involvement in sex therapy (5 percent versus 20 percent) and a greater involvement in alcohol or substance abuse (50 percent versus 18 percent) (see Table 7.3). Spanish-speaking subjects had a markedly higher mean age of the onset of deviant behavior (30.2 versus 23.4 years) and a lower mean number of victims per offender (7.6 versus 15.8) (see Table 7.4). The Spanish-speaking group also had fewer nonsexual arrests (10 percent versus 26 percent) and fewer prior sexual arrests (5 percent versus 61 percent) than did their English-speaking counterparts (see Table 7.5).

**Table 7.4**   History of Deviant Behavior

|  | Spanish Speaking (n=20) | English Speaking (n=287) |
|---|---|---|
| Age of onset (years) |  |  |
| Mean | 30.2 | 23.4 |
| Range | 16–50 | 12–60 |
| Number <18 | 1 (5%) | 52 (18%) |
| Mean number of victims per offender | 7.6 | 15.8 |

**Table 7.5**   Arrest History

|  | Spanish Speaking (n=20) | English Speaking (n=287) |
|---|---|---|
| Nonsexual arrests | 2 (10%) | 52 (26%) |
| Prior sexual arrests | 1 (5%) | 175 (61%) |
| Incarceration | 1 (5%) | 101 (35%) |

*Treatment Phase*

Of the 20 Spanish-speaking sex offenders who underwent assessment, 5 refused treatment, 5 are awaiting placement into a group (at the time of this writing), and 10 have completed our modified treatment paradigm. As certain alterations had to be made in the assessment protocol, similar modifications were required in the treatment phase.

Group treatment was conducted by an English-speaking therapist with simultaneous translation by a bilingual technician. This essentially doubled the length of treatment. The number of sessions devoted to discussing therapy components outlined in the treatment consent form was significantly expanded for pregroup contracting.

Despite these considerable attempts to engage these patients in treatment, the group members remained reserved and reticent, avoided eye contact with the group leader, and did not participate in any verbal exchange unless directly questioned. Although primarily silent, they showed respect and deference to the group leaders.

To overcome this initial reluctance to participate in the group process, we introduced a socialization period at the beginning of each session. The patients were served coffee and cake and were encouraged to discuss recent personal and family events. The therapist began to relate more informally and to reveal some germane personal life experiences. These modifications were culturally syntonic and greatly enhanced the formation of group identity and the beginning of the group process.

As the group process evolved, the patients showed greater ease in using both English and Spanish phrases less formally to express their personal feelings and experiences. At times, when discussing emotionally charged material, such as the impact of sexually deviant behavior on their families, these shifts in language took on greater clinical significance. These shifts gave the therapist important insights into the individual dynamics and behavioral response patterns of the group members.

Most significant, the cultural prohibition against discussing sexual practices posed a major obstacle to involving these patients in meaningful therapy for their sexual deviancy. We overcame this obstacle by stressing that to regain the respect of their families and communities and to restore their personal sense of dignity, frank discussion of their sexual problems was essential. Indeed, we emphasized that this type of difficult discussion of sexuality required great courage, and this reframing appealed to their sense of machismo.

# Case Illustrations

The following cases are profiles of two patients disguised to preserve anonymity. They represent the major paraphiliac behaviors presented by this group — namely, pedophilia and exhibitionism. They also illustrate the kinds of problems that occurred most frequently in the assessment and treatment process.

CASE EXAMPLE NO. 1:
A 39-year-old factory worker was referred by the Department of Probation for assessment and treatment stemming from his incestuous abuse of his 12-year-old stepdaughter. This patient initially minimized the extent of the sexual abuse and the negative impact it had

on his stepdaughter. During assessment, he insisted that the issue of sexual abuse had ended with disclosure and the ensuing court proceedings. When interviewed regarding the nature of the abuse, he often became very angry and stated that he felt insulted by the interviewer's focus on his sexual life. During treatment, the patient gradually increased disclosure of the true nature of the incest. At first he attributed the incest to marital conflict and distance from his wife, coinciding with her increasing independence since migration to New York City. He also claimed that his stepdaughter seduced him by the provocative nature of her newly acquired American dress and speech. Cognitive restructuring informed by cultural sensitivity enabled the patient to correct his faulty thinking and to begin to acknowledge his remorse for the trauma he had caused the victim.

CASE EXAMPLE NO. 2:

A 43-year-old married automobile mechanic was referred by the court for treatment following his third arrest for exhibitionism. He denied that he had exposed himself, insisting that he had merely urinated in a public place while intoxicated. Following confrontation with positive assessment findings of arousal to exhibitionistic stimuli, the patient admitted exposing himself several times. He described feeling not respected by women because of his low social status and inability to speak English. He recounted a pattern of anticipating rejection by attractive women, becoming angry, drinking alcohol, and then exposing himself. The patient believed that by exposing himself he would attract these women by his potency and power. Treatment focused on the interplay of alcohol abuse, anger control, and sex-role stereotyping. Therapeutic alliance was strengthened by the patient's belief that by addressing these issues he would regain his sense of dignity and self-respect.

In summary, awareness of the common ethnocultural factors that emerge from a review of the literature on treatment issues concerning work with Hispanic patients takes on a new importance when dealing with primarily Spanish-speaking and unacculturated sex offenders, as it may give the ethnically sensitive clinician a powerful tool to conquer the denial and treatment avoidance that typifies this patient population. Further, respect for the nuances of cultural differences evidenced by a clinician in a potentially adversarial setting may encourage the creation of a therapeutic alliance by assuaging the patient's fear of rejection or discrimination by a representative of the host culture.

Finally, although the role of such cultural factors cannot be minimized in the treatment of these Hispanic sex offenders, we must remember Werbin and Hynes's (1975) caveat not to focus primarily on these "common denominators to the exclusion of unique personality differences" in order "to avoid stereotyping both the Latino and the Anglo" (p. 399).

# References

Abel, G.G. (1976). Assessment of sexual deviation in the male. In M. Hersen & A.S. Bellack (Eds.), *Behavioral assessment: A practical handbook*. Elmsford, NY: Pergamon.

Abel, G.G., Becker, J.V., & Cunningham-Rathner, J. (1984). *Treatment of child molesters*. Atlanta, GA: Behavioral Medicine Laboratory, Emory University.

Abel, G.G., Becker, J.V., & Cunningham-Rathner, J. (1988). Multiple paraphiliac diagnoses among sex offenders. *Bulletin of the American Academy of Psychiatry and the Law 16*, 153–168.

Arce, A.A., & Torres-Matrullo, C. (1982). Application of cognitive behavioral technique in the treatment of Hispanic patients. *Psychiatric Quarterly, 54*, 230–236.

Boulette, T.R. (1975). Group therapy for low income Mexican Americans. *Social Work, 20*, 403–406.

Brehm, J.W. (1972). *Response to loss of freedom: A theory of psychological reactance*. New York: General Learning Press.

Brehm, S.S. (1976). *The application of social psychology to clinical practice*. New York: Wiley.

Brislin, R.W. (1970). Back-translation for cross-cultural research. *Journal of Cross Cultural Psychology, 1*, 185–216.

Brislin, R.W. (1981). Translation and content analysis of oral and written materials. In H.C. Triandis & J.W. Berry (Eds.), *Handbook of cross-cultural psychology: Vol. 2. Methodology* (pp. 389–444). Boston: Allyn & Bacon.

Burgos, N.M., & Perez, I.D. (1986). An exploration of human sexuality in the Puerto Rican culture. *Journal of Social Work and Human Sexuality, 4*, 135–150.

Comas-Díaz, L. (1985). Cognitive and behavioral group therapy with Puerto Rican women: A comparison of content themes. *Hispanic Journal of Behavioral Sciences, 7*, 273–283.

Cullen, K. (1983). Physiologic measurement: Impact on treatment. *Treatment for Sexual Aggressives News, 7*, 7–8.

Delgado, M. (1983). Hispanics and psychotherapeutic groups. *International Journal of Group Psychotherapy, 33*, 507–520.

Delgado, M., & Humm-Delgado, D. (1984). Hispanics and group work: A review of the literature. *Social Work with Groups, 7*, 85–92.

Devore, W., & Schlesinger, E.G. (1987). Contracting: some preliminary considerations. In W. Devore & E.G. Schlesinger (Eds.), *Ethnic sensitive social work practice* (2nd ed., pp. 155–169). Columbus, OH: Merrill.

Earls, M.C., & Proulx, J. (1986). The differentiation of Francophone rapists and nonrapists using penile circumferential measures. *Journal of Criminal Justice and Behavior, 13,* 419–429.

Kolers, P.A. (1968). Bilingualism and information processing. *Scientific American, 218,* 78–86.

Lister, L. (1986). A conceptual framework for exploring ethnoculture and human sexuality. *Journal of Social Work and Human Sexuality, 4,* 135–150.

Lockhart, L.L., Saunders, B.E., & Cleveland, P. (1988). Adult male sexual offenders: An overview of treatment techniques. *Journal of Social Work and Human Sexuality, 7,* 1–32.

Marcos, L.R. (1976). Bilinguals in psychotherapy: Language as an emotional barrier. *American Journal of Psychotherapy, 30,* 502–560.

Marcos, L.R., & Alpert, M. (1976). Strategies and risks in psychotherapy with bilingual patients: the phenomenon of language independence. *American Journal of Psychiatry, 133,* 1275–1278.

Martinez, C. (1977). Group process and the Chicano: Clinical issues. *International Journal of Group Psychotherapy, 28,* 225–231.

McKinley, V. (1987). Group therapy as a treatment modality of special value for Hispanic patients. *International Journal of Group Psychotherapy, 137,* 255–269.

Melella, J., Travin, S., & Cullen, K. (1989). Legal and ethical issues in the use of antiandrogens in treating sex offenders. *Bulletin of the American Academy of Psychiatry and the Law, 17,* 223–232.

Mizio, E. (1979). *Puerto Rican task force report.* New York: Family Service Association of America.

Olarte, S.W., & Masnik, R. (1985). Benefits of long-term group therapy for disadvantaged Hispanic outpatients. *Hospital and Community Psychiatry, 36,* 1093–1097.

Rooney, R.H. (1988). Socialization strategies for involuntary clients. *Social Casework: Journal of Contemporary Social Work, 69*(3), 131–140.

Travin, S., Bluestone, H., & Coleman, E., (1985). Pedophilia: An update on theory and practice. *Psychiatric Quarterly, 57,* 89–103.

Travin, S., Cullen, K., & Melella J. (1988). The use and abuse of erection measures: A forensic perspective. *Bulletin of the American Academy of Psychiatry and the Law, 16,* 235–250.

Tylim, I. (1982). Group psychotherapy with Hispanic patients: The psychodynamics of idealization. *International Journal of Group Psychotherapy, 32,* 339–349.

Werbin, J., & Hynes, K. (1975). Transference and culture in a Latino group. *International Journal of Group Psychotherapy, 25,* 396–401.

# 8 Sex Offender Treatment for Alaska Native Groups

*Roger Graves, Ph.D.*

*I*n late summer of 1997, I was asked to write this chapter and gladly accepted the opportunity to contribute to the worthy effort this book represents. However, about 10 minutes after agreeing to the task, it struck me: Here we go again, another White person writing about what needs to be done to address the needs of Alaska Natives (or American Indians, as is often the case as well). As a good friend and colleague of mine, Dr. Robert Morgan, often says, "With good intent, we often try to find the solutions before we really even understand what the questions are." This predictably results in "solutions" that often have little to do with the actual problem, do not make sense to the intended beneficiary, waste resources, and typically do little to help. This is especially true when individuals or groups of one culture try to "help" those of another. Hence, when it comes to a Euro-American attempting to describe what needs to be done to improve the condition of Alaska Natives, be assured that I am still trying to find out what the question really is.

In order to provide information that readers will find interesting and useful, yet not be disrespectful to the original people of Alaska, I take an approach that may differ from that of my colleagues in this work. First, this chapter briefly reviews the impact of Russians and European Americans on Alaska's first people. In this section, I attempt to illustrate how that contact has changed the lifestyle of people who had been surviving and even flourishing for some 30,000 years. Second, I briefly discuss the serious social and health issues that too many Alaska Natives presently experience. Next, I discuss "traditional" approaches presently used in the treatment of sex offenders in the clinic where I am employed and, more importantly, how they came to be incorporated into the program. Finally, I outline why responsibility for resolving the issues of sexual abuse and offending needs to be given more to Alaska Natives, with assistance provided by the non-Native, majority culture. This is a particularly difficult notion from a moral standpoint because the message then becomes, "Contact with the majority culture is probably the original cause of your problems, but you are going to have to take the leadership in repairing the damage anyway." The reality is that the majority culture will never have the knowledge and expertise to rebuild the culture and heritage of Alaska's first people. And this task is vital if Alaska Natives are to deal effectively with the social and health issues they face, including the one particular to this chapter. I believe, however, that the majority culture has a responsibility to support, in the many forms that this may take, the efforts of Alaska Natives in achieving this end.

Before delving into this topic, there are a few caveats. I have 14 years of experience working with sex offenders and have worked for close to 5 years in a clinic that is the nonprofit health corporation for Cook Inlet Region, Inc. (CIRI), an Alaskan tribal entity. However, I am not of Alaska Native or American Indian descent and claim absolutely no expertise on traditional healing. What I offer is a forum for discussion and an opportunity to research and formulate programs that combine both contemporary and traditional approaches to healing.

Furthermore, it is necessary to acknowledge that "traditional healing" approaches vary widely from culture to culture. Yup'ik elder Alice Abraham (personal communication, 1993) noted during a "healing circle" that although the circle may be a traditional approach for some Native cultures, it was not necessarily a traditional Yup'ik approach. The point is that what is traditional for one Alaska Native group may be alien to another. My intent is to not offend by implying that "traditional" necessarily equates with pan-Indian or pan–Alaska Native approaches to healing. At the same time, I want to support the tremendous work of the Native peoples of Alaska and all of North America in reviving and restoring their heritage, including traditional health practices, a work that has been a major unifying force for tribes across the continent.

# Brief History of Alaska Native Cultures
# and the Impact of Western Influence

Just before his death in 1725, Tsar Peter the Great ordered Vitus Bering, a Danish-born captain-lieutenant in the Russian navy, to sail and explore beyond the Kurile Islands. The mission was to discover whether Asia and North America were connected by land and to search for European settlements (Antonson & Hannable, 1985). Bering failed to find mainland Alaska but did discover the Diomede Islands on the return voyage. On June 4, 1741, Bering, now a captain-commander, again set sail from the east coast of Siberia in his ship the *St. Peter* to again try to determine whether the continents were connected. On July 17 of that same year he sighted snow-covered mountains and a volcano. The Russians named the volcano, known to some Alaska Natives as Waaseita-Shaa, "Saint Elias" because the crew discovered the mountain on the Orthodox Church feast day of Saint Elias.

Between July 17 and July 20 (reports vary), Bering arrived at Kayak Island, located in the southeastern part of what is now known as the Copper River in the Gulf of Alaska. While exploring the region, Bering and his crew discovered evidence of habitation, but no people. They did, however, collect a large quantity of sea otter furs, and their return to Russia with these furs provided economic motivation for continued Russian interest in this region (Hassen, 1978).

It wasn't until the Bering team set sail homeward and passed what is now known as Kodiak Island that Russian and Alaska Native first met on the coast of the Shumagin Islands, off the Alaska Peninsula. Gifts were reportedly exchanged, but none of Bering's interpreters could understand the speech of the Natives (Antonson & Hannable, 1985). Bering's enjoyment of his successful discovery of a bountiful new land would be cut short, however. On December 8, while waiting out harsh winter conditions on the Commander Islands off the coast of Kamchatka, Vitus Bering died of complications of scurvy (Antonson & Hannable, 1985).

Russians began the exploration — and exploitation — of Alaska in earnest beginning in 1745. Russians took Aleuts (as the Russians called the Natives of the region) as hostages and slaves (Antonson & Hannable, 1985). The Aleuts fought back bravely, but by 1780, Aleut resistance had been broken, and they had been effectively subjugated. However, the maritime and hunting skills of the Aleut men were unmatchable and they became — unwillingly — the backbone of the Russian-American Company. These captives were forced to hunt for the Russians as far south as Santa Catalina Island off the coast of southern California (Langdon, 1993).

As Russian explorers and hunters made their way down the southern and then the southeastern coast of Alaska, Europeans began their own exploration and discovery of wealth along the coasts of Alaska, starting with James Cook aboard the *Resolution* and Captain Clark aboard the *Discovery*. As with the Russians, early European interests were initially in the abundance of fur-bearing marine animals, such as otter (Hassen, 1978).

The subjugation and occupation of Alaska was not an easy matter. Besides unpredictable and frequently harsh weather, difficulty obtaining provisions while out on long voyages, and scurvy and other illnesses, the Native peoples of the region were often understandably hostile to the foreign occupation. Russians fought battles on the Aleutian Islands, on the mainland, and on the southeastern coast of Alaska. One group of battles waged by the Tlingit Indians against the Russians and their Aleut captives occurred in 1802 at Sitka, Dry Bay, and Frederick Sound. Emmons (1991) cites reports that the only survivors of this battle were 23 Russians and Aleuts, most of whom were women and children; several hundred other Russians and Aleuts perished.

Despite the courage and efforts of the Alaska Natives to retain control of their lands, the Russian and European invaders were too numerous and the tactics they used too effective. Imported diseases and harsh treatment by the Russian-American Company had a dramatic effect on the Native population. The Aleut population alone, numbering an estimated 16,000 to 20,000 in the early 1700s, had dropped to 7,000 in 1936 and only 4,000 by 1942 (Antonson & Hannable, 1985; Woodhead, 1994).

In 1854 the Crimean War broke out, making Russian shipping a potential target for the more powerful English navy. The depredations of war, losses of ships and furs at sea due to storms, and financial crises at home had destabilized the Russian economy, and on April 4, 1867, the Russians sold Alaska to the United States for about $7.2 million in a deal that, at the time, was referred to as Seward's folly (Antonson & Hannable, 1985; Smith, 1996).

At the time of Vitus Bering's 1741 arrival, Alaska was occupied by an estimated 80,000 people (Langdon, 1993). Today the total number of Alaska Natives residing in the state number between 86,000 (Irwin, 1994, Vol. 1) and 94,000 (Smith, 1996), depending on how Alaska Native is defined. However, contact with outsiders brought diseases for which the Alaska Native had no immunity. The great smallpox epidemic of the 1830s wiped out entire villages and may have killed upward of two-thirds of Alaska Natives in the lower Yukon area (Irwin, 1994, Vol. 1; Woodhead, 1994). The Great Death, a 1900 influenza epidemic that is believed to have originated from Nome, spread like wildfire across the state, killing 60 percent of Eskimos and Athabaskans. The survivors of this tragedy are the grandparents and great-grandparents of today's Alaska Natives (Napoleon, 1996).

Irwin (1994, Vol. 1) reports that in 1910 the Native population of Alaska was only about 25,300, less than one-third the size prior to European contact. The extent and depth of the damage that such death and disruption had on Native culture can only be guessed. Plagues destroyed whole families, tribal and spiritual leaders, elders, artisans, healers, uncles, and those who carried the oral traditions. This massive devastation does not even include the destructive impact that forced acculturation had on survivors. Euro-American control brought a program of cultural annihilation that included the imposition of foreign religious belief systems and languages and a money-based economic system alien to the surviving population and their culture. Napoleon (1996) writes that this catastrophe was the end of the "old culture" (p. 12), with many survivors abandoning their beliefs, losing hope, and developing symptoms similar to those of posttraumatic stress disorder. Napoleon (1996) cites the severity of this psychological trauma as a precursor to the drug and alcohol addiction and associated problems seen today in Alaska Natives, a position supported by Sturtevant and Washburn (1988) for Native Americans as a whole.

## Sexual Abuse and Associated Problems In Alaska's Native Communities

The wide distribution of a relatively small number of people over such a vast area contributes to a variety of health problems in

Alaska, as well as to difficulties with the implementation of intervention programs. With an area of 586,412 square miles, Alaska is roughly one-fifth the size of the lower 48 contiguous states. California would easily fit within Alaska's borders — twice over — and still leave more than enough room for Texas. In proportion to its size, Alaska has a very small population (about 540,000, approximately the same as Vermont, which has an area of only 9,609 square miles). About 40 percent of Alaskans live in the largest city, Anchorage, and fully 66 percent live in Anchorage, in Fairbanks, or along the highway system connecting these two largest cities. The remaining third of Alaskans are spread throughout the state, which is mostly rural; in Alaska, "rural" means remote in a sense that is rarely seen anymore in the lower 48 states.

The harsh physical terrain and weather further complicate the problem of service delivery. Alaska's road system is limited, and even where highways connect towns, travel distances can be extremely long and, in the winter months, considerably dangerous. Air travel connects nearly all villages and towns to the major metropolitan centers. However, flying to villages can be very expensive, often costing considerably more than round-trip airfare for travelers going from Anchorage to New York or even Europe. In addition, harsh weather conditions frequently interfere with arrival and departure times in many locations, sometimes stranding travelers for days at a time.

There are seven primary Native cultural groups within the state, including two separate Eskimo groups (Inupiaq and Yup'ik), four major Indian groups (Athabaskan, Tlingit, Haida, and Tsimshain), and Aleuts (Antonson & Hannable, 1985; Smith, 1996). It should be noted that these distinctions do not reflect the great diversity within the larger Native groups due to geography, dialects, and so forth. In fact, many Alaska Natives may disagree with this breakdown, for example, the Athabaskans, who have numerous subgroups and language dialects.

The final report from the Alaska Natives Commission (Irwin, 1994) contained a series of disturbing figures. Although the Alaska Native segment of the Alaskan population is relatively small (about 16 percent) compared with the non-Native segment, their rates of various health and social problems are comparatively very high. The Native mortality rate from alcohol-related causes is 3.5 times that of non-Natives. The Native infant mortality rate and the rate of fetal alcohol syndrome (FAS) and alcohol-related neurodevelopmental disorder (ARND) are twice the national average. Between 1964 and 1989, the suicide rate among Alaska Natives increased 500 percent, and 79 percent of these suicides were alcohol related. By the 1980s, the suicide rate for Alaska Native males aged 20 to 24 was *30 times* the national rate for all age groups combined. Alaska Natives constitute just over 32 percent of the incarcerated population, despite the fact that they represent only 16 percent of the overall population and just 13.5 percent of the prison-age population. Furthermore, Alaska Natives account for 38 percent of the overall total of those convicted of sexual offenses and 48 percent of those arrested for rape.

Although in recent years a variety of efforts have been made to address the problems in the Alaska Native community, doing so has been difficult. There is currently some sense among those who work in the Alaska Native community that the mainstream Western culture will never be able to address these problems effectively (see Irwin, 1994, Vol. 2). Some professionals have taken the position that all Western interventions should be prohibited and that Native communities need to rely solely on Native healing methods as a means of resolving their problems. Others lean toward a merging of models of healing to include both Western and traditional aspects (Peat, 1994).

To illustrate the difficulty of working with sexual abuse and sexual offenders from the contemporary model, I recount a story I heard several years ago in Anchorage, Alaska. I attended a small meeting at Southcentral Foundation Behavioral Health Services in the summer of 1994 with a group of people who were discussing the problem of sexual abuse in rural villages. One of the attendees described how two mental-health workers had gone to a small Yukon River village, known to have a serious problem with sexual abuse, with the intent of "saving it." These two well-intentioned individuals held public meetings where they described how they were going to end the tragedy of child sexual abuse in the village and make the town a healthier place to raise children. To their dismay, after two days of talks and presentations to nearly everyone in the village, they could not get any support for their efforts from any of the folks in town. They wanted to help and had the means to do so, but it apparently wasn't wanted. Disappointed, frustrated, and more than a little confused, the two headed back to the rooms where they were staying. On the way back, they were stopped by an elderly woman who asked to speak with them. She told them that while almost everyone appreciated their good intentions, they just didn't understand. She told the two individuals that if everyone in the village did what they asked and talked about "the problem" in the community, the Alaska State Troopers would fly out, arrest half the adults in the village, and haul off even more children, that is, the perpetrators and the children who either were their victims or would no longer have care providers. Furthermore, during the following winter the remainder of the village would probably starve because so many of the men (primary providers) would be in jail. Therefore, to do what the well-intentioned clinicians asked could literally spell death.

This experience illustrates how ineffectively the contemporary system is designed to deal with the issue of sexual offending in the village. Interior Alaska, where this village is located, can become as remote as the moon when weather conditions are bad — which is often. Temperatures can drop to 50 degrees or more below zero, and wind, snow, and fog are common. Many of the local residents may not be aware of how to access welfare services for assistance with food and shelter, assuming that food and shelter would be available in such weather and after the social disruptions that would occur if the social workers succeeded. What if the village store owner is one of those arrested and the store is closed? Suppose the village public safety officer, a rough equivalent of the local police officer, is in jail? This example may seem overdramatic, but considering that these small villages often lack the most basic resources that Alaska's larger towns and cities take for granted, the concern for survival can be very real. And even if the town members could survive such an ordeal in a well-intentioned effort to "save them," it is simplistic to think that all that needs to happen is for the village to open up and disclose the offenders and victims and then let the contemporary system do its job.

The social workers' experience illustrates the difficulty often encountered just in determining who has committed a crime and identifying the victims. Even when sexual offenses are successfully prosecuted and offenders enter treatment, village politics and other dynamics often complicate the intervention picture. T. Burns (personal communication, 1997), who has worked with Alaska Natives in many villages, reports situations in which convicted, untreated sex offenders have been invited back to their home villages and back into the family homes where their victims are still residing. In some cases, the victim has even been asked to contribute to the offender's support. At the opposite end of the spectrum, it is not uncommon for Alaska Native sexual offenders, receiving treatment in metropolitan areas, to be told by their home villages that they are not welcome back, even if they successfully complete treatment, and if they decide to return, their safety cannot be guaranteed. Thus, working with sexual abuse and offenders in the Alaska Native population, especially those living in the villages, is a complicated matter with no easy solutions.

## Treatment and the Alaska Native Sexual Offender

To this point, I have tried to convey just how complicated the issue of sexual abuse in the Alaska Native population is, even before one gets to actually providing services to the offenders. Many of these difficulties stem directly from mistrust of the contemporary system — mistrust based on experiences of the very individuals and communities that the system is trying to help. As shown in the story about the Yukon village, individuals and communities fear that asking for help will mean the destruction of the family or even the community — the antithesis of help. Resolution of these issues must occur before sexual abuse treatment, for both offender and victim, can be achieved on the scale needed.

That said, most of the information I discuss regarding treatment of Alaska Native sexual offenders — in this case, all males — is based primarily on experiences obtained while working in my present position with the nonprofit health corporation for an Alaska Native tribal entity.

Southcentral Foundation (SCF) Behavioral Health Services in concert with Dr. Judith Becker (in an Indian Health Service project), Dr. Robert Morgan, and myself, developed the Native Adolescent Healing Project (NAHP) in 1993 as SCF's first pilot project working with sexual offenders. During the development of this program we consulted with a variety of individuals, including various persons of Alaska Native descent, to discuss ways to integrate traditional healing practices into the program. Our intent was to develop a program that incorporated both contemporary, empirically validated approaches to the treatment of sexual offenders and appropriate traditional healing approaches. The challenge before us became clear when I asked elder Walter Austin (personal communication, 1993) about traditional approaches that had been used in the past to treat sexual abuse and sexual offenders. His reply was something to the effect that, "Well, actually it really wasn't much of a problem before you folks arrived on the scene." Later conversations with such highly respected people as Yup'ik elder Alice Abraham (personal communication, 1993) supported this response as she related stories of how sexual abuse, at least as it is defined today, was largely introduced by missionaries, soldiers, and settlers of Russian and later Euro-American origin. The oral reports provided by today's elders seem to suggest that in precontact times when sexual behavior violated norms, there may have been some consequence, including banishment or death (the former usually led to the latter anyway). However, the kinds of offenses and degree to which we see the problem today stem from the contact and forced acculturation imposed on the Alaska Native peoples by others who were essentially invaders.

Not surprisingly, we were asking the wrong question. Our task then became to incorporate into the program the strengths of the heritage of Alaska Natives in general, including their traditional concepts of what healing and health are and what leads to them. To begin work on this process, program staff turned the question over to the program participants while consulting with staff who were Alaska Native. The results proved somewhat more promising.

The process we used to achieve the goals was in many ways more important than the results themselves (recall the earlier comment about the solutions to the wrong questions). Many of the participants in the program were of mixed Alaska Native heritage, and some were not Alaska Native at all; some exhibited a great deal of shame regarding their heritage. The approach we utilized encourages all members of the program, regardless of ethnicity, to examine their own heritage for those values, skills, and tools that are useful and appropriate to help them meet their physical, mental, emotional, and behavioral health goals — including not reoffending sexually. Using this process, each program participant researches his own heritage to bring those strengths to treatment. In many cases, this means finding out for the first time what it means to be Tlingit, Yup'ik, a mix of Alaska Native, a mix of Alaska Native and Russian or European, or something else entirely. This allows each participant to search out his own questions and find his own answers and solutions. This process is being continued in a community-based adolescent sexual offender program for moderate-risk youth who are in intensive outpatient treatment, as well as in our relatively new community-based outpatient program for adult sexual offenders.

A total of eight adolescent and adult sexual offender groups are offered each week at SCF. The results of this approach have varied by program, group, and individual. In the case of the adult programs, which are contracted services with the Alaska Department of Corrections (DOC) and subject to DOC standards of care, progress has been somewhat slower to ensure compliance with contract requirements. However, the following techniques, tools, and processes have been incorporated to varying degrees into sex offender treatment at SCF. Some techniques have been applied with only one individual, some with only one group, some with only one program, and some across the board. Please keep in mind that many of these procedures have been initiated only after consulting with the appropriate tribal member, healer, or elder and receiving his or her approval (often involving training and education).

## "CIRCLE" FORMAT FOR GROUPS (HEALING CIRCLES)

One adolescent group is more "traditional" than others in that at least the first rotation does not allow feedback from other members (the only exception is if the member discloses an additional offense or issue that must be disclosed by law). This practice is more "traditional" to tribes of the lower 48 states, but participants generally report increased feelings of comfort, dignity, and respect using this process.

## EAGLE FEATHERS OR OTHER SACRED OBJECTS OR SYMBOLS

The sacred object is often held by the speaking participant during circles or hung on a medicine wheel to represent the participant or some other belief or value. (This practice was approved by a Tlingit Native who provided the eagle feather.)

## MEDICINE WHEEL

This amazingly powerful tool is constructed by the group participants themselves. When hung, the wheel represents that the group or circle is in progress. In 14 years of practice, I have never found any symbol or opening activity that as effectively transforms a room full of people (in some cases noisy, rambunctious teenagers) *immediately* into a focused working group. (We were assisted in the design and construction by Alaskan and Canadian Natives.)

COLORS

Most of the tribes use particular colors to represent important spiritual meanings. These colors have been incorporated into various items and procedures, such as the medicine wheel and the wrapping around the wheel when it is not hung on the wall.

SMUDGING WITH SACRED HERBS

The herbs — usually sweetgrass, cedar, and sage — are burned and their smoke is used to cleanse the room and prepare the individual for participation in group — and much more. This activity generally begins groups or circles. (We received education regarding this practice from two Tlingit leaders.)

FOODS, BOTH TRADITIONAL
AND CONTEMPORARY

Foods are often a part of social activities and ceremonies, and group is a social activity (though some may disagree with me). Traditional foods, both as a treat at group and especially as a primary source of nutrition for Alaska Natives, appear (anecdotally) to facilitate treatment progress. This outcome may be due to improved physical health that results from a diet that is more consistent with the individual's actual biological needs. It may also act as a powerful key to help reconnect the individual with his culture on a very basic level — through sight, taste, and smell, facilitating memory of past cultural experiences. Finally, food is an important part of meetings for many Alaska Natives.

RESPECT FOR CULTURAL
IDENTITY AND DIFFERENCES

Unfortunately, in the past, this respect has been mistaken for being "soft" on offenders or lacking concern for community safety. All

our sex offender programs have very high compliance requirements and very strict discharge criteria. Program staff are, however, always willing to listen *respectfully* and not automatically
assume that issues that arise during treatment are "sex offender"
issues or thinking errors. For example, respect for culture may
mean allowing a non-Native commercial fisherman to miss a treatment group so he can participate in the 24-hour halibut season or
allowing a Yup'ik offender to miss a group to go berry picking
with his uncle and grandmother who are in town visiting. It also
means not applying Inupiaq values to Yup'ik clients because both
are "Eskimos," and so forth.

## OUTDOOR GROUPS

Alaska Natives have an outdoor, open-air heritage, not a white-
wall, fluorescent light, recirculated-air heritage. In the youth program we have even held overnight camps (and are considering
doing so with the adults). With the youth, camps have also helped
us connect clients with their traditions, with the goal of instilling a
healthy pride in their heritage.

## CULTURAL PRESENTATIONS

Although not a mandated component at this time, program members occasionally present or discuss in group aspects of their
Native culture (and sometimes other cultures that are part of their
heritage as well). This not only encourages participants to research
their heritage but also helps them develop an identity beyond being
just a sex offender to being a human person who has strengths, tal-
ents, abilities, value, and a hopeful future. Because this process has
often resulted in very positive benefits (for example, a healthier
self-image), it is being considered for incorporation as a mandated
part of the program.

## NATIVE WAYS

There is really no English translation for this process. It involves
trying to see the Alaska Native's experiences and healing journey
through a lens that is simply different from the lens of Western
beliefs and values yet undeniably valid, real, and health promoting.
Participants engage in subsistence activities such as fish camp,

attend powwows, engage with elder mentors, and become involved in Native issues. Because of the offending issues that participants have, consultation is important to ensure that the participant's request is consistent with treatment needs and goals.

This list represents a sample of the traditional techniques and processes incorporated into the sex offender programs at SCF at this time. It is important to note that despite some progress in becoming more sensitive to Alaska Native issues and concerns, the SCF programs for individuals who have committed sex offenses are all well grounded in the contemporary model of treatment. If an outside treatment provider attended a group at SCF, he or she would see relapse prevention, work on thinking errors, cognitive restructuring, and everything else expected in a competent program for adults and adolescents who have committed sexual offenses. The primary difference is the variety of ways we present activities and goals and how we address them with clients, as well as the additional activities we do that are not typically seen in contemporary programs. We believe that this approach is defensible and appropriate, given that a primary concern is to ensure community safety. To date, there is no empirical literature supporting the use of traditional (Alaska Native) methods as the sole or even the primary framework for treating sexual offenders. Recall the words of Elder Austin mentioned earlier that sex offending was generally not a problem until after the arrival of Russians and European Americans.

## Future Directions

Our approach to the treatment of Alaska Natives who have committed sexual offenses is valid, sensitive to the needs of the population, defensible, effective, and maybe even innovative — but at best, it is only a beginning. Irwin (1994) makes a number of recommendations regarding a variety of issues concerning Alaska Natives; however, the predominant theme is that Alaska Natives and their tribes must begin to take responsibility and control of the problems facing Alaska Natives. That includes responsibility for health-care needs, including prevention and intervention; mental-health and substance-abuse issues; and the needs of Alaska Natives in the corrections system. While the specifics are far too extensive to discuss in detail here, the final report notes that these needs must be met by Native agencies and the Native community. Irwin (1994, Vol. 1, p. 27) notes, "For tribal councils and village people, expansion of powers and authorities would mean regaining inherent responsibility for village problem-solving in an area where grief and turmoil are the most pronounced."

As proud as we are of our programs for individuals who have committed sexual offenses, they remain basically contemporary programs, tweaked, bent, folded, and molded in the hope of better meeting the needs of and being more sensitive to a population that they were not originally designed for. My hope is that soon an Alaska Native from this agency or elsewhere will lead the work to develop and research a program specifically designed to meet the needs of the Alaska Native community. Such a program would provide both prevention and intervention and would make it safe for communities, such as small Yukon River villages, to begin to resolve the problem of sexual abuse.

# References

Antonson, J.M., & Hannable, W.S. (1985). *Alaska's heritage*. Anchorage: Alaska Historical Commission.

Emmons, G.T. (1991). *The Tlingit Indians*. Seattle: University of Washington Press.

Hassen, H. (1978). *The effect of European and American contact on the Chugach Eskimo of Prince William Sound, Alaska*. Ann Arbor, MI: UMI Dissertation Service.

Irwin, M. (1994). *Alaska Natives Commission: Final Report: Vols. 1 & 2*. Anchorage: n.p.

Langdon, S.J. (1993). *The native people of Alaska*. Anchorage: Greatland Graphics.

Napoleon, H. (1996). *Yuuyaraq: The way of the human being*. Fairbanks: Alaska Native Knowledge Network, University of Alaska, Fairbanks.

Peat, F.D. (1994). *Lighting the seventh fire: The spiritual ways, healing, and science of the Native American*. New York: Birch Lane.

Smith, C. (1996). *The Alaska almanac: Facts about Alaska* (20th anniversary ed.). Anchorage: Alaska Northwest Books.

Sturtevant, W.C. (Gen. Ed.), & Washburn, W.E. (Vol. Ed.). (1988). *Handbook of North American Indians: Vol. 4. History of Indian-White relations*. Washington, DC: Smithsonian Institution.

Woodhead, H. (Series Ed.). (1994). *People of the ice and snow*. Richmond, VA: Time-Life Education.

# 9 Asian-American Cultural Concerns in Sexual Abuser Treatment

*Philip LaClaire, M.A.*

Asian Americans are among the fastest-growing ethnic groups in the United States. They comprise most of the population in certain areas of the United States. Much diversity exists within the various ethnic groups, but many also share "similar characteristics" of behavior and upbringing. An understanding of their cultural behavior and upbringing may clarify the causes of sexual abuse among Asian Americans and help clinicians to devise an effective treatment for perpetrators.

## Cultural Differences

Since 1965, the Asian-American population in the United States has increased from 1 million to more than 7 million (Okamura, Heras, & Wong-Kerberg, 1995). Most of this increase is the result of the admittance of immigrants and refugees from diverse ethnic and national subpopulations. Their languages, cultural backgrounds, and migration experiences vary.

Mental-health professionals should be exposed to cross-cultural information when practicing in sexual abuse treatment. Without information on Asian cultural differences, inaccurate interpretations will hinder the therapeutic process (Gomez, 1992).

For Asians, the family is the central source of identity and emotional security. Within the family are strong interdependent bonds and solidarity. Each member of the family has a clearly defined role (Okamura et al., 1995). A person is obliged to uphold the family name and honor. Personal disgrace or humiliation transcends generations (Tsui, 1985).

A hierarchical organization characterizes most Asian families. The oldest males have the most authority and responsibility. They are expected to maintain the financial well-being of the family and to make the most important decisions. Females maintain the household, attend to the children, and are expected to obey their fathers, husbands, and eldest sons. Older children care for the younger children (Okamura et al., 1995).

Reports of abuse in Asian countries take on a completely different character from those in the United States. A dramatic example of abuse in Japan is a mother killing herself and her children, which reflects the Japanese belief in an inherent bond between parent and child (Ima & Hohm, 1991).

Asians who have been in the United States for more than five years are not as likely to be charged with abuse because they are familiar with abuse laws (Ima & Hohm, 1991). This finding does not mean that child maltreatment charges against refugees are the result of misunderstanding. However, child supervision practices back home may conflict with child-rearing customs in the United States.

According to Okamura et al. (1995), child protection agencies are commonly asked to determine whether several practices are culturally acceptable, stemming from questions such as the following:

(a) Is it true that mothers and fathers use their fingers to wash the genitals of a primary school-aged child?

(b) What about a 13-year-old boy sleeping in the same bed as his mother?

(c) Do family members kiss and touch a baby boy's genitals as a sign of affection for a boy child?

(d) Do fathers of adolescent girls examine their daughters' vaginal areas for medical reasons? (pp. 80–81)

Cultural informants are not in agreement about the acceptability of these behaviors.

The hierarchical structure of Asian families may be mistaken as a high risk for molestation rather than seen as culturally appropriate. This hierarchical structure is in contrast with the definition of a healthy U.S. family: one of democratic relationships. However, culture can be used as a screen to hide abuse (Okamura et al., 1995).

Cambodian teenage boys and girls are never left alone together because sexual urges are considered a powerful force that must be contained by social structure. Kissing and holding hands in public are considered improper social behaviors. When a man rapes a woman, he is considered that woman's husband and becomes financially responsible for her and for any child that results from the incident. It is the family's responsibility to protect a girl from these situations, and it is the family's shame when the family is not successful (Scully, Kuock, & Miller, 1995).

In most cultures, incest is taboo. However, family values often take priority over issues of molestation among people from developing nations. Sexual abuse may become an unfortunate but acceptable incident if the family is financially dependent on the abuser (Heras, 1992). Traditional Asian families have been socialized to behave respectfully toward those in authority. Seeking help outside the family is unacceptable (Okamura et al., 1995).

Tsui (1985) cautions that discussing sexuality with Asians is highly sensitive and may even be taboo. As well, differences among the many different Asian cultures and ethnicities may seem small to the unfamiliar clinician, but distinction is crucial.

## Demographics of Asian-American Sex Offenders

The Union of Pan Asian Communities (UPAC) in San Diego, California, provides counseling services to Asian-Americans and Asian immigrants and refugees who have been accused of child maltreatment. A sample study (Ima & Hohm, 1991) of child maltreatment cases from this agency revealed the following distribution: physical abuse, 53 percent; sexual abuse, 4.9 percent; emotional abuse, 6 percent; and neglect, 36.1 percent. The following distributions of child maltreatment cases are for the general U.S. population: physical abuse, 27.8 percent; sexual abuse, 12.3 percent; emotional abuse, 15.6 percent; and neglect, 44.3 percent (Ima & Hohm, 1991). Whereas physical abuse is greater in the sample than in the general population, the percentage of sexual maltreatment cases within this group of Asians is notably lower than in the general population.

Absent from these figures are Japanese, Chinese, and Asian Indian cases of maltreatment. The likelihood remains that these Asian groups have very low incidences of child maltreatment.

Approximately 7 percent of the U.S. population is Asian; however, this group accounts for less than 2 percent of all child maltreatment cases (Ima & Hohm, 1991).

Vietnamese make up more than 36 percent of the child maltreatment cases involving Asians, though they are only 23 percent of the Asian population in the United States. Cambodians make up 23.6 percent of maltreatment cases, yet they are only 6 percent of the Asian population. Abuse cases among Laotians are proportionately equal to their percentage of the population. Hmong, Korean, and Filipino cases of maltreatment are proportionately less than their percentage of the population (Ima & Hohm, 1991).

In a child sexual abuse study of Asians compared with other populations by Rao, DiClemente, and Ponton (1992), Asians were the most likely group to be abused by a male relative. In contrast, White children were least likely to be abused by a male relative but most likely to be abused by an acquaintance.

Ima and Hohm (1991) found that half the Asian sexual abuse perpetrators were fathers. The other half were individuals other than the parents. In the general population, fathers were only 36 percent of the perpetrators, and 21 percent were fathers and mothers acting together. Mothers acting alone accounted for 10 percent, and 33 percent were individuals other than parents. However, according to Okamura et al. (1995), an Asian nonoffending parent will often align with the offending parent against the child in an attempt to maintain the respectability of the family.

In maltreatment cases involving Asians, a greater proportion of victims are female and younger children than in the general population. Physical abuse is more prevalent than other forms of abuse, and Asian parents are more likely to be charged as abusers individually rather than jointly (Ima & Hohm, 1991).

Poorer Asian groups, such as Cambodians, are under closer watch by social service agencies because they are more dependent on public welfare. Because of their social status, they may be more likely to be reported to Child Protective Services. Poorer persons tend to be reported for child maltreatment more than people of higher social ranking (Ima & Hohm, 1991).

When compared with the general U.S. population, Asians were less likely to be charged with sexual abuse (Ima & Hohm, 1991). Asians were, however, more likely to be abused by a male relative, which may be related to the fact that a male relative was more likely to be living in the home. Asians may be more vulnerable to abuse by a male relative in the home setting (Rao et al., 1992).

## Cultural Effects of Sexual Abuse

Recently arrived Asian immigrants and refugee families, whose energies are focused on adjustment and survival in the United States, are at a higher risk for family dysfunction and incidents of child abuse (Okamura et al., 1995). Maltreatment stems from adjusting to a new society and from traumas experienced before migration. Refugees from war-torn countries such as Vietnam have experienced the most trauma. Circumstances that undermine parents' ability to care for their young are related to increased maltreatment (Ima & Hohm, 1991).

Documented incidents of other forms of family violence, such as wife and child battering in Southeast Asian communities, stem from the high state of distress caused by the refugee experience (Wong, 1987). Often Asian immigrants and refugees encounter hostile racist behaviors but do not protest the discriminatory encounters. However, the feelings of anger and powerlessness can result in a higher risk for violence within the home. Okamura et al. (1995) believe that "incest among immigrant and refugee families occurs more often than community members themselves wish to acknowledge" (p. 78). Data regarding the extent of child sexual assault in Southeast Asian countries are limited (Wong, 1987).

Children of Cambodian and Vietnamese refugees are more likely to be maltreated than the children of other Southeast Asian refugee groups, such as Hmong and Laotian. One reason may be that Hmong and Laotians were not affected by war-related experiences to the extent that Cambodians and Vietnamese were. For example, Cambodians suffered agonizing oppression, including torture, under the Pol Pot regime. The results of the war-related trauma include emotional depression, posttraumatic stress syndrome, and physical illness. With more than 50 percent of Cambodians experiencing severe emotional crisis, they have the highest recorded measure of depression (Ima & Hohm, 1991).

Khmer male survivors, helpless to deal with the destruction all around them and full of survival guilt, often became obsessed with sexuality. Cambodian men, outnumbered by Cambodian women, had sexual relationships with many women and often their children. In the Khmer communities of the United States, alcohol would exacerbate the sexuality and violence (Scully et al., 1995).

Scully et al. (1995) generalize that sexual abuse among Cambodians falls into the following categories:

1. Rape as torture, which occurred during the civil war and again in the Pol Pot regime and in the camps in Thailand.
2. Sexual abuse as exploitation in the refugee camps and in post–Pol Pot Cambodia, which includes the forced prostitution of women and children for survival of the family.
3. Sexual abuse as the acting out of rage and violence in today's communities.
4. Sexual abuse as a dysfunctional attempt by survivors to meet sexual needs or deal with psychological symptoms.
5. The sexual abuse of Cambodian children and teens in foster homes. (p. 111)

Asian children are often targeted by pedophiles because of their physically small bodies and submissive responses. Asians value being inconspicuous, which contributes to the stereotype of Asian passivity. The victim of sexual abuse risks emotional rejection from the family if he or she does not remain silent (Okamura et al., 1995).

Ethnic enclaves, such as Chinatowns and Little Vietnams, serve as refuges for social and language access. Because of the low wages earned by immigrants, housing is poor and crowded. With relatives and non-related boarders in the home, the risk of sexual abuse increases. Parents are away from the home working long hours and attempt to reduce stress by using drugs and alcohol (Okamura et al., 1995).

Discussing sexually related issues in Asian communities is highly taboo. As a result, a child's ability to tell adults about a sexual assault and the family's ability to report it to outsiders are obstructed. If a girl were raped, she would be considered damaged goods, prompting a family not to tell anyone about the sexual assault for fear of community rejection and blame (Wong, 1987).

## Effective Modes of Treatment

Psychotherapy with Asian Americans includes an understanding of cultural differences, assimilation, and immigration history. Because of the cultural norms concerning resistance and shame in the sharing of problems with mental health professionals, the Western therapeutic process is not as likely to be effective with Asian Americans (Chan, 1988). The cultural and social barriers to those seeking help must be addressed (Wong, 1987).

Heras (1992) suggests that ethnic families rely on nonverbal ways of communicating. This indirect communication style is frequently judged as dysfunctional. Making Asian individuals directly express their feelings, whether positive or negative, in order for them to become healthier would be inappropriate for a therapist. For example:

> Mrs. S's therapist had insisted that she get angry with Mr. S by calling him a bastard or a son of a bitch in session. This client only felt more inadequate at not being able to call her husband a bastard the way her therapist wanted her to, and felt uncomfortable about swearing in the presence of an authority figure. (Heras, 1992, p. 124)

To Western-oriented therapists what is viewed as "repression of feeling" is among Asians a virtue to be cultivated (Tsui, 1985). A culturally competent therapist would not require Asian clients to express anger and grief openly. A therapist must also display a control of his or her own emotions in the beginning phases of therapy (Okamura et al., 1995).

Different cultural styles of expressing feelings should be considered in determining a client's progress. Therapists can make serious errors if they are not aware of these cultural differences. A lack of outward emotion can be mistaken for resistance or poor motivation. Accepting responsibility and making changes needed for successful reunification of the family are the core treatment issues. The perpetrator's family and cultural values should match these changes (Okamura et al., 1995).

Cultural groups that tend to have a low literacy rate, such as Laotians and Cambodians, may learn more effectively through visual presentations rather than written text, when it is applicable (Wong, 1987). A family member or nonprofessional translator should never be used to provide treatment for any trauma issue. When trauma memories are evoked, a client becomes highly suggestible and compliant. In these instances ensuring the high quality of a translator's skills and integrity becomes imperative.

Unfortunately, it is often easier for a social worker to arrange foster care than to find a translator (Scully et al., 1995).

Discussing family problems outside the family is considered shameful and creates a culture clash between Western-trained therapists and traditional clients (Rao et al., 1992). As a result, there is a high rate of premature termination. Many seek professional help only when the problem has reached crisis proportions.

The primary impediment to Asians seeking counseling is shame, followed by a lack of knowledge on human sexuality (Tsui, 1985). Because shame is not supposed to be discussed with an outsider, to discuss this disgrace with a therapist would intensify the guilt.

The impersonal and nondirective approach of Western counseling is often ineffective with Asian clients. When an Asian individual seeks sexual counseling, he or she is usually at the point of desperation. It is a crisis in which the individual feels humiliated and at a total loss. The therapist needs to be able to take control of the situation and lead the individual to the appropriate course of action (Tsui, 1985).

A solid, behaviorally oriented approach to treatment is most effective. A directive, practical approach is well suited for Asians, whereas exploring the psychodynamics of the individual only enhances the shame (Tsui, 1985).

The therapeutic task of Asian perpetrators is to break the denial and move toward change (Okamura et al., 1995). They may make cultural excuses for inappropriate behavior in the initial phases of therapy. This resistance needs to be reframed. Asian perpetrators may minimize the trauma of sexual abuse. Although minimizing trauma is a culturally adaptive response, it needs to be worked through in therapy.

Because deep feelings of shame and loss of face are associated with an admission of guilt, the therapist should understand that the perpetrator will resist repeated admissions in future sessions. However, it is crucial that he or she accept responsibility for the molestation. If a therapist pressures the perpetrator to discuss his or her remorse at every session, that pressure may increase the shame and destroy the ego resources of the perpetrator. Outward displays of empathy will likely be subdued. In addition, the perpetrator is frightened about losing familial and social standing (Okamura et al., 1995). According to Tsui (1985), "It must be made clear that the suggestion of options does not indicate the therapist's choice nor his or her opinion" (p. 360).

Group therapy is usually ineffective with Asian clients. Sharing problems with a therapist is shameful enough. Sharing them with a whole group is extremely aggravating. The damage it does to self-esteem far outweighs the potential benefits gained from group support (Tsui, 1985).

Discussing sexual matters with strangers is highly taboo. To do so with someone of the opposite sex is unthinkable (Tsui, 1985). It will enhance a client's feelings of humiliation and disgrace.

The primary goal of the therapeutic process should be to rebuild trust in the family. Simply stopping the problem and not rebuilding trust will provide only short-term relief (Scully et al., 1995).

# References

Chan, C.S. (1988). Asian-American women: Psychological response to sexual exploitation and cultural stereotypes. *Women and Therapy,* 6(4), 33–38.

Gomez, M.V. (1992). Some suggestions for change regarding culturally appropriate interventions in child sexual abuse: A reaction to Heras. *Journal of Child Sexual Abuse,* 1(3), 125–131.

Heras, P. (1992). Cultural considerations in the assessment and treatment of child sexual abuse. *Journal of Child Sexual Abuse,* 1(3), 119–124.

Ima, R., & Hohm, C.F. (1991). Child maltreatment among Asian and Pacific Islander refugees and immigrants. *Journal of Interpersonal Violence,* 6(3), 267–285.

Okamura, A., Heras, P., & Wong-Kerberg, L. (1995). Asian, Pacific Island, and Filipino Americans and sexual child abuse. In L.A. Fontes (Ed.), *Sexual abuse in nine North American cultures: Treatment and prevention* (pp. 67–96). Thousand Oaks, CA: Sage.

Rao, R., DiClemente, R.J., & Ponton, L.E. (1992). Child sexual abuse of Asians compared with other populations. *Journal of the American Academy of Child and Adolescent Psychiatry, 31,* 880–886.

Scully, M., Kuock, T., & Miller, R. (1995). Cambodians and sexual child abuse. In L.A. Fontes (Ed.), *Sexual abuse in nine North American cultures: Treatment and prevention* (pp. 97–127). Thousand Oaks, CA: Sage.

Tsui, A.M. (1985). Psychotherapeutic considerations in sexual counseling for Asian immigrants. *Psychotherapy, 22,* 357–362.

Wong, D. (1987). Preventing child sexual assault among Southeast Asian refugee families. *Children Today,* 16(6), 18–22.

# 10 Conceptual Issues in Therapy with Sexually Abusive Māori Men

Paul Robertson, Ph.D. (Kai Tahu, Kati Mamoe,
   Waitaha, Kati Celt)
Jillian Larsen, Ph.D.
David Hillman, Ph.D. (Tuhoe)
Stephen M. Hudson, Ph.D.

There is a relatively strong foundation in the literature for the development of successful programs for adult men who have been convicted of sexually offending against children. In Aotearoa/New Zealand this body of knowledge has provided the basis for the development of the Kia Marama treatment unit in Christchurch described by Hudson, Marshall, Ward, Johnston, and Jones (1995). In turn, Kia Marama has provided the blueprint for the Te Piriti treatment unit in Auckland (Larsen, Robertson, Hillman, & Hudson, 1998). However, another dimension has been added to the original blueprint at Te Piriti through the development of a cultural perspectives policy that focuses on meeting the needs of Māori, the indigenous people of Aotearoa. These developments coincide with an increasing recognition of the need to address cultural factors in therapy, both in Aotearoa and overseas (e.g., Durie, 1995; Sawrey, 1991; Yutrzenka, 1995). In developing its program, Te Piriti has begun to answer the challenge to develop sexual offender programs for groups with specific needs.

The focus of this chapter is on some of the central conceptual issues facing those seeking to develop programs to meet the needs of the indigenous people of Aotearoa and potentially those of other countries. We begin with consideration of the unique elements of the New Zealand context, notably the Treaty of Waitangi (see Appendix 1) and key concepts traditionally considered central to the well-being of Māori. The latter leads us to discussion of the question "Who is Māori?" and the impact of individuals' varied levels of connectedness with traditional aspects of Māori culture.

Then we identify some of the limits of conventional approaches to the treatment of sexual offenders. We also describe the application of some of the previously outlined concepts that have provided the basis for extending existing treatment models to facilitate the delivery of more effective treatment to Māori.

In summarizing, we suggest some major principles for working effectively with Māori men who have sexually offended against children, as well as making suggestions for further research and evaluation and potential difficulties related to these processes. Although the focus of this chapter is on the indigenous people of Aotearoa/New Zealand, it is likely that the principles and themes presented may be applicable to other indigenous peoples and minority ethnic groups

First the much-debated question of who should deliver treatment (i.e., Māori or non-Māori) needs to be considered. This question has proved vexatious for both Māori and non-Māori in Aotearoa, with many Māori advocating that only Māori can deliver effective treatment for Māori. It is certainly true that in important ways it would be very difficult, if not impossible, for non-Māori to work optimally with Māori, given the importance of *whānaungatanga* (making kin links). It is also true that many Māori come into contact with non-Māori service providers and that some members of this group have little if any contact with or knowledge of their own culture. In fact, some Māori, for a variety of reasons, including embarrassment about lack of knowledge and the impact of negative stereotypes, choose to see Pakeha (non-Māori; more specifically, New Zealanders of European descent) rather than Māori clinicians. Another important factor related to the question of who should provide treatment is the fact that there are a limited number of skilled Māori practitioners, from both Western and traditional Māori perspectives. Therefore, practical demands dictate that non-Māori will work with Māori in therapeutic contexts. So, the answer to "How do non-Māori work optimally with Māori?" is likely to depend on a range of issues.

## Aotearoa/New Zealand Context

In New Zealand, the Treaty of Waitangi creates a unique focus on the relationship between the Tangata Whenua (indigenous people, i.e., Māori) and the Crown, represented by the government. Consideration of the role of the treaty in New Zealand's history, and its place in present-day society, is beyond the scope of this chapter; however, we present a brief description to provide a context for the issues discussed herein.[1]

The Treaty of Waitangi was signed in 1840 by representatives of many of the *hapu* (subtribes) of Aotearoa (New Zealand) and representatives of the queen of England. Bringing whalers, seamen, escaped convicts, and other settlers under control was a significant motivating factor for Māori signing the treaty. Preempting the French and facilitating settlement of a new colony provided significant motivation for the English.

Problems arose following the signing of the treaty and continue today as a result of different interpretations of the document and, relatedly, the failure of successive governments to honor it. The different understandings have been due in part to differences in the Māori and the English translations, particularly related to the issue of sovereignty. The colonists considered that the Māori had ceded sovereignty, while the latter considered that they had agreed only to governance. Given their superior numbers at the time of signing and their intimate relationship with the land, it is highly unlikely that Māori would have ceded sovereignty to the English. Differing perceptions of people's relationship with the land, including the concept of ownership, have also been key factors in subsequent difficulties.

The debate over the provisions of the treaty and arguments over the failure to honor it continue today. It has been argued that successive governments have continually manifested and reinforced monoculturalism and impeded the progress of biculturalism in Aotearoa (Ministerial Advisory Committee, 1988). In addition, a number of New Zealanders view the treaty as irrelevant and wish to consign it to the history books. The current implementation of the principles of the treaty depends considerably on the attitude of those involved in the development of policies and practices that impact on Māori. Despite ongoing debate, the treaty is seen as providing a positive basis for change to a more bicultural society. It is certainly central to the development of effective programs for the treatment of Māori who sexually offend and/or experience a range of other difficulties. Several fundamental principles embodied in the treaty provide guidance for program development, including

---

1. For fuller coverage of treaty issues Orange (1987) and Yensen, Hague, and McCreanor (1989) provide a useful start point.

partnership, equity, and *tino rangatiratanga* (power over resources, self-determination).

## The Impact of Colonization, Urbanization, and Modernization

In common with other indigenous peoples, colonization has had a significant impact on the well-being of Māori. In addition to the arrival of diseases against which they had little defense, loss of land and undermining of belief systems and social structures have contributed to the decline of Māori society. Loss of land not only eroded the economic base of Māori but also undermined central aspects of well-being and identity for a people who have an intimate relationship with the land. Acts of Parliament, such as the Tohunga[2] Suppression Act, also contributed to undermining the belief systems that provided not only a social framework but also guidance for day-to-day activity, for example, in relation to maintaining food hygiene and productivity. Missionaries further contributed to the deterioration of social structures by attacking spiritual beliefs integral to day-to-day functioning. In combination, these factors seriously undermined the well-being of Māori, and at one stage it was thought inevitable that the Māori race would die out. It was suggested at the time that the only obligation of the settlers and their government was to smooth the pillow of a dying race (Durie, 1994).

Māori did not die out, but their social structures and belief systems continue to be eroded by assimilationist policies. Movement to urban areas in search of work after the Second World War has also contributed to the difficulties of Māori. This urbanization involved separation from traditional settlements and from *whānau* (family) support. Separation from these areas also reduced the opportunity for passing on and maintaining skills and knowledge central to the upkeep of social structures and belief systems. A lack of a sense of belonging and a less strongly developed sense of identity also emerged. Problems related to having to adapt to the demands of the mainstream culture, that would be less pressing in rural settings, also began to emerge.

---

2. Tohunga is a term often roughly translated as "medicine man" but is more correctly described as a expert with a high level of training, skills, and knowledge in a particular area, for example, spiritual matters, genealogy, natural medicines, harvesting of food.

## Aotearoa Today

Today in New Zealand there are a number of Māori who have little if any contact with their traditional *marae* (gathering place), have little if any knowledge of their culture, and are unable to speak their own language. Loss of language, a vital means of communicating the central elements and values of any group, has been hugely damaging for Māori. Their problems are exacerbated by negative stereotypes of Māori, which affect the behavior and thinking of Māori as well as non-Māori. Clearly these psychological burdens and the damage sustained through continued undermining of social structures and belief systems have contributed to increased susceptibility to unwellness.

Even for those Māori who are functioning well, there are increased demands as they seek to live within the parameters of two often conflicting cultures. Renfrey (1992) talks of "bicultural competence" and the need for indigenous people to acquire this skill in order to survive. It has been suggested that, to add insult to injury, Pakeha get all the glory for being bicultural, while Māori, who are bicultural by necessity, not by choice, get none (Stanley, 1993). A number of authors (e.g., Beauvais, 1992; Oetting & Beauvais, 1990–1991; Renfrey, 1992) propose that acculturation and deculturation are key issues that need to be addressed when working with indigenous and other ethnic peoples. It is suggested that failure to acculturate into the mainstream and/or one's own society leaves individuals marginalized and susceptible to a range of difficulties, including poor health and imprisonment. It is also suggested that failure to acculturate and deculturation contribute to chronic low self-esteem, difficulties with formal education in dominant-culture schools, difficulty in communicating, and a generalized sense of resentment, frustration, and aggression (Jackson, 1987, 1988; Renfrey, 1992).

## Practical Considerations

In addition to obligations under the treaty, developments in the area of culturally responsive therapy have been driven by practical demands. While Māori make up less than 15 percent of the population, they constitute nearly 50 percent of the prison population and are overrepresented in other areas of the criminal justice system (Braybrook & Southey, 1992; Mason, Ryan, & Bennett, 1994). They are also increasingly being admitted and readmitted to mental-health institutions, primarily in relation to substance use and psychotic disorders (Te Puni Kokiri, 1996). These rates reflect trends for indigenous peoples and minorities in other countries (LaFromboise, 1988; Tonry, 1994). Biased policies and practices within criminal justice systems may also have contributed to this situation (Fergusson, Horwood, & Lynsky, 1993), but the factors contributing to the overrepresentation of indigenous peoples in these areas are still being clarified. However, there are numerous indications that conventional treatment modalities have not served Māori well and that there is a need to develop programs that are more responsive to the needs of Māori and more compatible with the beliefs and values that guide the behavior of many Māori.

## Concepts Central to the Well-being of Māori

This section does not purport to provide a definitive statement on concepts central to the well-being of Māori but rather seeks to give the reader a basic idea of some beliefs and values that need to be considered in the development of culturally responsive treatments. In doing so we have drawn upon an emerging literature focused on the description of models of Māori health (e.g., Durie, 1994; Peri, 1995). A more exhaustive explication of the central aspects of Māori society is also beyond the scope of this chapter, but those interested in exploring this area further are referred to Durie (1994) and Salmond (1991) as a starting point. In addition, it should be noted that as is the case with any translation, the English version of Māori concepts often does not capture the complete nature of phenomena. In spite of these caveats, we hope to be able to provide a description of a model based on the integration of Māori and Western knowledge bases.

### Holism and Collectivism

A holistic view of people, including a spiritual dimension and their intimate relationship with the land and nature in general, is central to a Māori model of wellness. The importance of kin ties, extending to ancestors who have passed on, is indicative of both the holistic and the collective nature of Māori society and their concept of wellness. The focus for traditional Māori and many contemporary Māori is on the collective rather than the individual, a focus that is shared with many other non-Western peoples. There is a clear implication that the well-being of the group is seen as being an integral part of the health of the individual, and there is a collective responsibility for the individual's well-being and vice versa.

Following appropriate protocols in various situations, such as the collection of food, birth, death and the first encounter with other people, is viewed as vital to the ongoing well-being of the individual and the collective. Central to these rituals is acknowledgment of the both the spiritual and the temporal dimensions. Engagement in such situations is facilitated through drawing links with others present (*whakawhānangatanga*) and discussion of the reason for the gathering (*kaupapa taka*, or agenda). Following appropriate protocols is seen as vital for the creation of a safe situation in which the *take* (task) can be successfully undertaken. However, while all *iwi* (tribes/clans) may hold general beliefs in common, there is variation in their detail and expression. In addition, although fundamental aspects of the Māori world are enduring, their expression has altered over time, especially with the influence of outside groups. An example of such change can be seen in the giving of a *koha* (gift) as part of rituals of encounter. Traditionally, *koha* would be food or a particular *taonga* (treasure) from the visitors' area, but today it is usually money.

## Key Concepts

A number of the key concepts in *te ao Māori* (the Māori world) relate to the division between *tapu* and *noa*, which roughly translate as the sacred and the profane, or the ordinary and the extraordinary. These concepts, which permeate Māori myth and legend, have traditionally been central pillars of social organization and have provided the basis for behavior in all realms of life, from interactions with the spiritual dimension to arrangements for domestic activities. These concepts have been set out in *tikanga* (protocols and practices) that provide the general framework for action, the specifics of which are contained within *kawa*, or the rules for a particular situation. *Pono* (right thought) and *aroha* (variously translated as compassion, sympathy, empathy, or love) are also cited as central guiding principles of behavior and action. *Mana*, roughly translated as status, standing, or esteem, is another central concept for Māori, with much emphasis placed on its protection, increment, and decrement. It is impossible to convey the complexity of these concepts even in a series of books, let alone a short paragraph, but it is hoped that this brief discussion will alert readers to some differences and similarities between peoples and to the potential barriers to providing effective therapy.

Similar to other peoples, Māori describe their values and beliefs, as well as guidelines for appropriate behavior, in their myths and legends. Of particular relevance to the treatment of men who sexually offend is the story of Tane (god of the forest) who had an incestuous relationship with his daughter Hinetitama, whom he married. When she found out that her husband was also her father, she fled with shame and became Hinenui Te Po (goddess of death/the underworld).

### Māori Models of Health

A number of people and groups have sought to incorporate the central aspects of Māori society into models of health (e.g., Durie 1994; Pere, 1984). One of the most widely disseminated models is the *te whare tapa wha* (the four walls of the house) model, which presents health as a structure made up of four *taha* (sides); *taha wairua* (spirituality), *taha hinengaro* (mental health), *taha tinana* (physical health), and *taha whānau* (family health). Other models have included a number of other *taha*, including *taha whenua* (environment), *taha tikanga* (rules), *taha tangata* (self), and *taha pakeha* (new world). The latter is seen as important by some, as many Māori have some pakeha kin or ancestors. Recently, more dynamic models have been developed to allow for the consideration of process variables in achieving wellness, for example, the *powhiri* (ritual of encounter) and *poutama* (developmental stages) models (Cassidy, personal communication, 1997; Huriwai, personal communication, 1997). Many of the Māori involved in the development of these models have qualifications from Western institutions as well as knowledge and skills acquired in *te ao Māori* (the Māori world). These people and others have a critical role as Māori take control, or at least take a leading role, in the delivery of health services.

## Who Is Māori?

An important part of developing any therapy or treatment program is identifying the people for whom the program is being developed. The impact of colonization, urbanization, modernization, and intermarriage has complicated the process of identifying who is Māori. Uncertainty about this issue has primarily resided with non-Māori, as most Māori readily identify who is Māori through *whakapapa* (genealogy). Difficulty has come as Māori have been traditionally identified in official statistics and research by non-Māori. Identification was characteristically based on the assumption that anyone who looked Māori (e.g., had brown skin) was Māori. However, using such rudimentary criteria failed to account for the myriad factors that contribute to the development and maintenance of cultural identity. For example, a number of people who look Māori actively reject such an identity, while others who look Pakeha strongly identify as Māori. A common current approach to this dilemma, which is not without limitations, is that anyone with Māori ancestry who chooses to identify as such is Māori. However, because there is no simple answer to the question of who is Māori, it is likely that addressing the question of ethnic/cultural identity will be an integral aspect of any therapy program for indigenous and possibly other minority peoples.

Questions related to the identity issue include who should have access to interventions developed from a Māori basis and who is likely to benefit from such intervention. The first question evokes a strong response from many Māori who are angered by past appropriation of this culture, land, and art by non-Māori and who are wary of scarce resources being removed from the control of Māori. In answer to the second question, it has been suggested by Māori, and by some Pakeha, that programs developed from a *kaupapa* Māori perspective (agenda) would benefit both Māori and non-Māori. It has been proposed that such programs fill significant gaps in narrowly focused conventional services that fail to account for the range of variables that contribute to a person's well-being.

# Limits of Conventional Approaches to Treatment of Sexual Offenders

The approaches to the treatment of men who have sexually offended thus far have been developed primarily from a Western epistemological base. While programs developed from this basis have been of some benefit, there is evidence that this approach has not provided optimal treatment for Māori and that programs based on it have failed to attract some individuals in need of treatment (Jones, 1993; Larsen & Hillman, 1996). Impediments to delivering effective treatment arise from both the theoretical underpinnings and the clinical application of theory. In addition, defining of issues by non-Māori, for example, designation of identity, has failed to facilitate investigation of crucial factors likely to contribute to a person's difficulties.

*Theoretical Issues*

Theoretically, research and treatment development could be a powerful vehicle for change; however, it can also be used to perpetuate structures and systems that may not provide effective treatment for those outside of the dominant culture (Jackson, 1987; Stanley, 1993). It has been suggested that the positivist approach to research and psychology, the methodologies of which are based on Western beliefs and values, emphasizing culture-dependent variables and deficits, has contributed to maintaining the status quo (Smith, 1991). This approach has helped facilitate the dominant culture's "superior" position by definition and justified subjugation of "inferior" peoples, using its standards to judge and draw conclusions about other cultures. Use of this framework has contributed to the development of a hierarchy that considers Western knowledge, values, and beliefs by definition as superior to that of indigenous peoples (Jones, 1993). These processes were not necessarily intentionally disempowering, but rather were often the result of the difficulty researchers had in seeing the impact of their own values and beliefs on their work.

Fortunately, work is emerging from various disciplines within the social sciences that is more cognizant of the cultural issues and the power dynamics of the research process. Clark (1987), for example, proposes that any comprehensive psychological theory necessarily accounts for cultural factors. She suggests that such factors need to be considered not just as categorical variables but as part of a complex structure that is integral to a person's functioning. Such approaches as critical theory and scientific realism may more readily facilitate development of a knowledge base that is freer from the intellectual imperialism inherent in the positivist approach. However, even these approaches may implicitly place indigenous knowledge bases in a position that is secondary to the dominant epistemological discourse. This ongoing debate is not easily resolved, but at least at this stage a single perspective of what constitutes science and knowledge no longer presides unchallenged.

### Clinical Issues

At an applied level, many clinicians are seeking to adapt therapeutic interventions so that they are more meaningful for the clients they are working with. Several non-Māori have reported using a range of methods, often using stories or action techniques to create a more meaningful context in which the therapeutic process can be more readily facilitated (e.g., Slattery, 1987). There has also been a move away from more individualistic modes of therapy and increased involvement of family in an effort to acknowledge and make use of the more collective focus of many non-Western peoples (Medland, 1988). Although these efforts may be seen as positive, there is concern about the role of nonindigenous people providing treatment for indigenous peoples. Some of this concern has been alleviated to a degree by the increase in the number of Māori professionals and the greater influence of Māori on policy and practice. However, autonomy and maintaining control over resources remain an area of serious concern for many Māori.

Some of these concerns have also been alleviated by models of wellness developed by Māori, which have provided frameworks for developing more effective therapy for Māori in Aotearoa. These approaches have characteristically focused more heavily on the process of engagement and making connections than do conventional therapies and have more actively sought involvement from family members and significant others. Concepts of significant value and meaning such as *mana* (standing), *tapu* (sacredness), and *whānaungatanga* (kin links) have also been used to provide the basis and focus of therapeutic interventions being developed by and for Māori. It is proposed that the incorporation of central aspects of Māori society in therapy helps reverse the negative impact of colonization by validating traditional beliefs and attitudes, thus facilitating acculturation into *te ao Māori* (the Māori world) in parallel with increasing acculturation into Pakeha society. In addition, such therapy does not contribute to alienation for those who are secure in their identity as Māori. The use of such approaches in the treatment of men who have sexually offended against children is discussed later.

## Adaptation of Existing Programs

There is debate whether existing programs should be adapted or whether it is more effective to develop programs from a Māori base and incorporate Western theory and methods as appropriate. This debate represents the latest stage in attempts to address the needs of Māori, which may be traced back to "add-on" approaches that included "culture" as just another module in programs underpinned by dominant therapeutic paradigms (Glover & Robertson, 1997). Since that time, there have been moves toward a more integrated approach, especially as more Māori have developed expertise in research, psychology, and other relevant fields. This has allowed for a greater understanding of how aspects of Western and traditional models may be integrated and presented in ways more meaningful to Māori. In addition, as more Māori become involved in the research process, a greater understanding of the impact of cultural variables is emerging.

The following section outlines some of the ways concepts of central importance to Māori have been incorporated into a treatment program for sexual offenders. The developments at Te Piriti represent steps along the pathway to the development of more effective programs for Māori clients. The program remains embedded in a Western psychological context, but extensive efforts have been made to maximize the impact of input from Māori, primarily via the employment of a cultural consultant, but also through input from local Māori and the *whānau* (extended family) of men undertaking the program. A key element is that Māori at least in part control the process in terms of allowing certain processes to occur and actively supporting the program. This means that the program is more acceptable to many Māori, even though it is based in a Pakeha institution.

A central assumption underpinning the Te Piriti program is similar to that of other programs for sexual offenders, that is, that sexual aggression is determined by a combination of social, cultural, developmental, biological, and conditioning processes (Marshall & Barbaree, 1990). A further central assumption underlying developments at Te Piriti is that cultural issues are not discrete entities, but rather run as a thread through people's entire lives and are inextricably interwoven into all aspects of their behavior. The corollary of this assumption is that culture is a thread that runs through the entire therapeutic process and is an integral part of the entire program at Te Piriti.

### Te Piriti: Theory in Practice

Te Piriti's mission statement provides the basis for practice within the unit (see Appendix 2). It makes explicit the bicultural emphasis of the program and its adherence to central principles of the Treaty of Waitangi, especially partnership and *tino rangatiratanga* (self-determination). In this way, Māori values and beliefs are supported, and the rights and responsibilities of both parties (i.e., Māori and the Crown) are acknowledged. A cultural perspective policy with clear goals and aims in specifically defined areas has been developed to facilitate delivery of a more culturally responsive program. The first three goals of the policy relate to establishing a bicultural context, including employing an ethnically diverse and informed staff, creating a culturally supportive environment, and developing processes for consultation with local *iwi* (tribe/clan) and other Māori. The fourth goal relates more directly to bicultural service delivery. Each goal and its impact on practice is outlined below.

Goal one focuses on creating an environment that is culturally supportive of all staff. This involves three main tasks: (1) developing appropriate methods of welcoming Māori and other cultures; (2) ensuring that all staff of Māori descent have the opportunity to attend network *hui* (meetings); and (3) requiring that all staff have the opportunity to attend bicultural and cross-cultural *hui*.

Development of rituals of welcome has extended from the welcoming of new staff and visitors to include the welcoming of new groups starting the program. In conjunction with local *iwi kaumatua* (elders) and Psychological Service staff of Māori descent, the cultural consultant has established protocols for *powhiri* (welcome). Development and maintenance of relationships with local *kaumatua* (elders) and Māori service providers have been integral to putting the cultural perspectives policy into practice. The positive outcomes of this practice have included demonstration of respect for *tangata whenua* (indigenous people) and facilitation of fuller understanding of the processes and practices of people of other cultures. In addition, the *powhiri* process conveys a warm welcome that facilitates dialogue and receptivity to the program. Artwork and posters depicting Māori people and values are present throughout the unit and create a more welcoming environment. The three group therapy rooms have been given names in both Māori and English, conveying positive values of Māori and Pakeha (non-Māori) cultures.

*Powhiri* to welcome new therapy groups take place in the therapy unit immediately before the commencement of the therapy program. Inmates from the Māori cultural group participate with staff in welcoming new program participants as well as visitors to the unit. This is an opportunity for them to practice language and *powhiri* protocols. Rituals of encounter are also extended to the process of therapy, with all groups finishing with a *poroporoaki* (ritual of departure). All groups decide on their own methods for opening and closing group sessions, which provides an opportunity to acknowledge the spiritual dimension. Some groups choose to have *karakia* (prayer), *waiata* (song), or *whakatauaki* (proverbs) relevant to the program.

Developments in this and other areas have been assisted by efforts to recruit appropriately skilled Māori staff. During the planning stages for the unit, a decision was made to include therapy staff from disciplines other than psychology, as there is still a shortage of Māori psychologists. The rehabilitation workers in the unit typically have a social-work background. A major focus of their work is establishing links with the clients' families and other supporters, as well as becoming the liaison with agencies that contribute to the external management phase of relapse prevention.

Goal two is focused on increasing the knowledge and skills of staff in the cultural arena. This has been achieved in a variety of ways, from in-house training to external *hui* (meetings) and study at tertiary institutions. In addition, psychologists at the unit are currently participating in a bicultural therapy project, which includes examining attitudes and beliefs about the impact of culture, promoting acceptance of differences, and addressing other relevant issues regarding assessment and treatment. In-house training has included consideration of the influence of the Treaty of Waitangi on the Department of Corrections and how the treaty affects the participants' work. It is proposed that if staff are to meet obligations in the department, it is important that they look at themselves and their way of working so that they can endeavor to provide better service to Māori.

The cultural consultant, who has played a central role in the training of staff, has presented a series of lectures on the foundations of Māori psychology. The topics have included important concepts such as Māori cosmology, genealogy, kinship and social structures, *whānau hui* (family meetings), change and progress, sources of knowledge, and the different aspects of the person. The cultural consultant also provides advice regarding appropriate *powhiri* (welcoming) and *poroporoake* (farewell) processes for staff, visitors, and clients. This has involved teaching *waiata* (Māori songs) and *mihi* (formal introductions).

Goal three is concerned primarily with developing and maintaining relationships with local Māori and Māori service providers. A healthy relationship with *tangata whenua* (Māori from the local area) is considered vital to the success of any culturally based program, as demonstration of respect for the *mana* (standing) of the local people has been a consistent ingredient of successful relationships throughout Māori history. The emphasis at Te Piriti has been on developing ongoing reciprocal relationships that are mutually beneficial to both parties. A weakness of past partnership attempts with Māori in many arenas has been the tokenistic nature of the relationship. Te Piriti staff were very conscious of this history and eager to ensure that the mistakes of the past were not repeated. Achieving goal three has involved several tasks, including establishing a register of Māori resources and providing all staff with opportunities to establish ongoing contact with members of the local *iwi* and Māori service providers. This has been achieved by giving presentations about the program, attending *hui* (meetings) on *marae* (gathering place), and involvement in research projects. In addition, *iwi* representatives have been involved in evaluating the Te Piriti program, especially with regard to cultural initiatives.

Goal four rests on the foundations of the preceding goals and is focused on developing the program so that it is more responsive to the needs of Māori. It involves attention to both policy and practice. This goal involves (1) the department cultural advisory officer, consultants, and *kaumatua* (elders) being consulted on all matters pertaining to unit cultural polices; (2) consistent funding for the cultural consultant being secured; (3) *powhiri* (welcome) and *poroporoake* (farewell) being conducted for each treatment group; (4) all Māori inmates having the opportunity to undergo cultural assessment by the cultural consultant and to receive ongoing input as required; (5) adaptation of treatment group process; (6) adaptation of program content; (7) for each individual Māori resident, contact being made with appropriate *whānau* (family), *hapu* (subtribe), and *iwi* (tribe) representatives to facilitate post-release reintegration to the tribal region; and (8) all Māori sexual offenders in the Te Piriti catchment area being actively encouraged to attend the program.

The Te Piriti catchment area consists of all the prisons north of Wellington. Two dedicated sexual offender programs (Te Piriti and Kia Marama) essentially split the population in half. And as the North Island is warmer, a greater proportion of the population lives there; there is also a greater proportion of Māori on the North Island, hence the specialized unit. At the Te Piriti unit there are 60 beds, with 40 to 50 men involved in treatment at any one time. The program is funded by the Department of Corrections — the treatment staff are employed under the Psychological Services division of the department, with the custodial aspects being covered as part of the prison budget.

In terms of the treatment process, the cultural consultant has a significant role in culturally assessing Māori clients. Issues considered include the potential contribution of the effects of colonization/urbanization, as well as the potential contribution of deculturation to the clients' offending. The assessment covers familiarity and comfort with aspects of both Māori and Pakeha cultures and concludes with recommendations to address deficits (e.g., English or Māori language classes, instruction in *marae* [gathering place] protocols). It is hypothesized that addressing symptoms of deculturation (e.g., poor interpersonal skills, lack of identity, lack of self-efficacy) will contribute to reducing the risk of reoffending.

Recommendations from the cultural assessment are discussed with the client's therapist and integrated with other treatment goals.

When a Māori client is experiencing difficulties that cannot be resolved in the group setting, the cultural consultant may meet with him individually, with or without his therapist. Clients are referred to Māori healers and teachers when appropriate for further assistance with cultural issues. In addition, the cultural consultant convenes a weekly Māori caucus in which aspects of therapy may be discussed. In this group, instruction is also given in *tikanga* (practice and protocols), *marae* (gathering place) protocol, *haka* (war dance), *waiata* (songs), and related areas in order to increase individuals' sense of connectedness and confidence within their own culture.

A comprehensive reintegration protocol has been developed for all participants in the Te Piriti program. For Māori clients, it is particularly important to organize *hui* (meetings) with *whānau* (family) and *hapu* (subtribe)/*iwi* (tribe) representatives, as the concept of *whānaungatanga* (interconnectedness) permeates Māori society. Whenever possible, *whānau hui* (family meetings) are arranged between the participant's family and the cultural consultant and other staff. When necessary, staff assist inmates in contacting *whānau* members for support.

The cultural consultant plays a role in organizing and facilitating these *hui* (meetings) and ensures that the visitors understand the goals and methods of the program and how they might best support the client on his release. To date, several reintegration *hui* have been organized where clients returned to their home *marae* and met with *whānau* and representatives of support agencies. These *hui* were considered by all present to be worthwhile and signaled a positive development in the relationship between Māori and the Department of Corrections. Te Piriti intends to conduct these reintegration *hui* whenever possible to increase Māori community support and understanding of the program.

The cultural consultant position at Te Piriti is now permanent and full-time, after initially being a two-year contract. It is clear that without such a position many aspects of the culture perspective policy could not have been implemented. This position has been central to developments, and it would have been impossible to adapt the content and processes of the program without it. The cultural consultant has also had a key role in assessing the veracity of claims by clients who have attempted to use so-called cultural factors as an excuse for their offending. His knowledge and expertise in *te ao Māori* have been crucial in this area, as has his *mana* and acceptance by the Māori community.

The cultural consultant has also played an important role in motivating Māori offenders, who had previously been reluctant to volunteer for treatment. He has been part of the recruitment team that visits other prisons throughout the North Island. In presenting information about Te Piriti, he guides the team in following Māori processes, thus increasing the credibility of the program. He has been able to clearly explain the content and processes of the program, decreasing the suspicion of potential participants and challenging rumors about the nature of the treatment provided at Te Piriti.

In summary, the mission statement and cultural perspectives policy have been integral in the development of a more culturally responsive program at Te Piriti. While not always able to be smoothly implemented, the policy and the statement have provided a consistent reference point for program development. Recruiting Māori staff and raising the bicultural skills of non-Māori staff have been an essential part of developing the program so that it is more responsive to the needs of Māori. The inclusion of cultural assessment information in the formulation phase of assessment has facilitated more appropriate and effective treatment, as has the delivery of key concepts of the program in ways that are more meaningful to Māori clients, for example, via myth, legend and *whakatauaki* (proverbs). Reintegration processes to assist in reconnecting with *whānau* and home *marae* have been critical in developing a more responsive program. Ongoing relationships with local *iwi* and Māori service providers have provided a solid foundation for the developments at Te Piriti by providing a line of accountability back to the community. These relationships have also been an important source of feedback for program development. The cultural consultant has been a critical element in these developments; it is doubtful that the progress made thus far could have been achieved without the input of the person in this position.

### Training

A critical aspect of providing a culturally responsive program has been the development of training for staff. An integral part of this process has been facilitating application of psychological and other health models in ways that are meaningful to Māori (McFarlane-Nathan, 1994; Peri, 1995). Concepts of acculturation and deculturation have been central, as they allow formulation of a broad range of issues likely to contribute to Māori offending. In addition, training has focused on assisting Pakeha workers to develop relationships with "experts" in the Māori world, to whom they can refer clients when issues are beyond the scope of their own expertise. The training model developed at Te Piriti promotes explicit acknowledgment of the ethnicity of the client. It also acknowledges Māori resources present in the community, as well as the value of traditional and neo-traditional healing processes.

*Research and Evaluation*

Research is obviously an essential basis for program development, and a number of issues need to be considered in undertaking research with Māori. It has been argued that traditionally the position of Pakeha and other Western psychologists has allowed them to create knowledge that reflects the values and beliefs of the mainstream culture (Gilgen, 1994; Smith, 1989, 1991). Further, it has been proposed that the resulting knowledge has often been used to justify and continue the subjugation of a particular group rather than to contribute to the resolution of difficulties (McCreanor, 1993; Smith, 1991).

A number of Māori and non-Māori have sought to rectify this situation through analysis of existing research paradigms and development of strategies that more readily facilitate addressing the needs of Māori (e.g., Robertson & Larsen, 1995; Smith, 1991; Te Awekotuku, 1991; Warwick, 1980). A number of Māori are also seeking to define an approach to research that embodies central elements of Māori culture (Glover, 1997). These developments represent efforts to build a knowledge base that reflects the realities of Māori culture, rather than the biases of particular research methodologies. The aim is not to abandon scientific rigor or merely to change the faces of researchers; rather, the focus is on developing models that facilitate consideration of variables that have tended to be invisible in much past research and clinical work with Māori. These efforts also provide guidance for the development of culturally responsive policies and practices in treatment programs, such as the one described in this chapter. As this area develops, we are gaining a clearer understanding of the factors likely to contribute to the resolution of health issues for Māori.

## Central Principles for Working Effectively with Māori

We propose several key principles for the development of programs that are more responsive to the needs of Māori. It is likely that many of the principles will also apply to programs for other indigenous people and minority groups, but we caution against their wholesale application without full assessment of the particular needs of the group to which they may be applied.

First, Māori need to be in control of the resources and processes that provide the basis for treatment development. This principle is in line with the concept of *tino rangatiratanga*, which is central to the provisions of the Treaty of Waitangi. Arguably, Māori are in the best position to determine their needs and the means by which those needs are best met. This does not preclude input from non-Māori, but it clearly locates control of the process and choices regarding therapeutic frameworks with Māori.

Second, where Māori do not have complete control over resources, it is necessary to develop and maintain an equal and reciprocal relationship with Māori who have a stake in the project. It is especially important to maintain an ongoing relationship with *tangata whenua* (Māori from the local area). Partnership necessarily involves acknowledgment of the equal validity of the Māori worldview and epistemological foundations of Māori models of health.

Third, it is important to consider the wider context within which individuals exist and the impact of their offending behavior on both the *whānau* of their victims and on their own *whānau*. Sexual offending obviously infringes on the *mana* (status) of victims and their *whānau*, and these issues need to be considered in the treatment of offenders. Addressing the impact of the offending on the perpetrator's own *whānau* is also critical to his successful reintegration into the community.

Fourth, in order to allow for different and often conflicting values and beliefs, practitioners need to remain flexible in their approach and maintain a willingness to adapt their practice to ensure that therapy is meaningful. Such flexibility requires that practitioners not only have knowledge of central concepts of *te ao Māori*, especially those that relate to health, but also are aware of the underlying assumptions of their own culture and profession. It also requires partnership with Māori who have sufficient expertise to enable them to determine what is likely to be therapeutically meaningful and efficacious for Māori clients.

Fifth, working within the limits of one's training and knowledge is central not only to ethical practice but also to providing optimal service to Māori. Increasingly it is recognized that there are limits to what psychology and related disciplines have to offer, especially to people who are not from Western societies and do not subscribe to the values and beliefs that underlie psychological theory and practice. Developing awareness of professional and personal limits is essential in the delivery of effective treatment to Māori. However, it is important not to merely abdicate responsibility at the edge of those limits, which is where the principle of partnerships emerges. When professional limits are reached, relationships with Māori experts provide the means for referral to more appropriate services and the opportunity to develop optimal treatment through shared care.

Finally, it is essential to remember that not all Māori are the same in terms of their connectedness with and knowledge of *te ao Māori* (the Māori world). Individual Māori have a diverse range of experience and knowledge of *te ao Māori*, just as they do of *te ao Pakeha*. The processes of colonization, urbanization, and modernization have contributed to the alienation of many Māori from significant aspects of their culture. In the past, many Māori actively rejected their own culture in order to pursue the trappings of the Pakeha world because no value was attributed to being Māori by the society in which they lived. In some cases, individuals might even be actively negative about being Māori. Such alienation is likely to be significant in terms of maintaining dysfunctional behavior and inhibiting the development of a satisfying and constructive lifestyle. Therefore, it behooves practitioners to develop a knowledge base and skills to be able to assess and respond to such issues if they are to provide effective treatment. In such situations, non-Māori practitioners potentially have a role in facilitating reconnection of these individuals to *te ao Māori*. However, it is vital that they do not act in ways that exacerbate clients' alienation.

# Appendix 1: *Te Tiriti o Waitangi/ The Treaty of Waitangi*

The Treaty of Waitangi is made up of four articles, the first three of which were presented in both the Māori and the English language. The fourth article is usually not cited when reference is made to the treaty as it was included only in the Māori translation.

### *Article the First*

ENGLISH VERSION

The Chiefs of the Confederation of the United Tributes of New Zealand, and the separate and independent Chiefs who have not become members of the Confederation, cede to Her Majesty the Queen of England, absolutely and without reservation, all the rights and powers of sovereignty which the said Confederation of individual Chiefs respectively exercise or possess, or may be supposed to exercise or possess, over their respective territories as the sole Sovereigns thereof.

MĀORI VERSION

The Chiefs of the Confederation and all the Chiefs who have not joined the Confederation give absolutely to the Queen of England forever the complete government over their land.

### *Article the Second*

ENGLISH VERSION

Her Majesty the Queen of England confirms and guarantees to the Chiefs and Tributes of New Zealand, and to the respective families and individuals thereof, the full exclusive and undisturbed possession of their lands, estates, forests, fisheries, and other properties they may collectively or individually possess, so long as it is their wish and desire to retain the same in their possession; but the Chiefs of the United Tribes and the individual Chiefs yield to Her

Majesty the exclusive right of preemption over such lands as the proprietors thereof may be disposed to alienate at such prices as may be agreed upon between the respective proprietors and persons appointed by Her Majesty to treat with them in that behalf.

MĀORI VERSION

The Queen of England agrees to protect the Chiefs, the subtribes, and all the people of New Zealand in the unqualified exercise of their chieftainship over their lands, villages, and all their treasures; but on the other hand the Chiefs of the Confederation and all the Chiefs will sell land to the Queen at a price agreed to by the person owning it and by the person buying it (the latter being) appointed by the Queen as Her purchase agent.

## Article the Third

ENGLISH VERSION

In consideration thereof Her Majesty the Queen of England extends to the Natives of New Zealand Her royal protection and imparts to them all the rights and privileges of British subjects.

MĀORI VERSION

For this agreed arrangement therefore concerning the Government of the Queen, the Queen of England will protect all the ordinary people of New Zealand and will give them the same rights and duties of citizenship as the people of England.

## Article the Fourth

MĀORI VERSION

The Governor says that the several faiths (beliefs) of England, of the Wesleyans, of Rome, and also Māori custom shall alike be protected by him.

---

English translation from the Treaty of Waitangi Act (1975). Maori translation by Sir Hugh Kawharu.

# Appendix 2: Brief Outline of
# Te Piriti Program

The treatment program involves attention to cognitive, behavioral, and social learning concepts and consists of two phases. In the first three to four months, the primary focus is on enabling the men to understand the facts that motivated their offending, challenging distorted beliefs concerning the offending, encouraging them to take responsibility for their offending, and developing empathy for their victims. The core of this part of the program is the "understanding your offense chain" module. It involves the man presenting his offending process in a series of steps. We base this process on the understanding we have developed as to what are typical pathways (Ward, Louden, Hudson, & Marshall, 1995).

We strive to maintain an atmosphere of collaboration, and with the help of group members, we aim to have the man develop an understanding of how factors such as low mood, lifestyle imbalances, and sexual and intimacy difficulties, set the scene for offending. We then encourage him to move on to issues such as distal planning, where high-risk situations are set up, as well as the steps he typically goes through in carrying out his offending. Finally, his reactions to having offended are explored. This module is seen as being fundamental to the remainder of the program, as other treatment modules are designed to decrease motivational components (sexual reconditioning), increase motivation both for treatment and for avoidance of risk (victim harm and empathy), and provide skills to manage mood, enhance appropriate intimacy, and manage the early precursors of the relapse process.

Treatment is provided in a group format (10 men plus one or two therapists) over a nine-month period. The first and last weeks of the program are devoted to assessment. During the remaining weeks, the groups meet for 2.5 hours per day, three days per week. All participants in the program have voluntarily entered treatment for their offending and related issues. They remain at the unit for the duration of their treatment program and on completion of their therapy are released or returned to another prison to await release. For Māori men, reintegration *hui* in their community of origin is becoming an increasingly important part of the program.

# References

Abbott, M.W., & Durie, M.H. (1987). A whiter shade of pale: Taha Māori and professional psychology training. *New Zealand Journal of Psychology, 16,* 58–71.

Beauvais, F. (1992). An integrated model for prevention and treatment of drug abuse among American Indian youth. *Journal of Addictive Diseases, 11,* 63–80.

Braybrook, B., & Southey, P. (1992). *Census of prison inmates 1991.* Wellington, NZ: Department of Justice.

Clark, L.A. (1987). Mutual relevance of mainstream and cross-cultural psychology. *Journal of Consulting and Clinical Psychology, 55,* 461–470.

Durie, M. (1994). *Whaiora: Māori health development.* Auckland, NZ: Oxford University Press.

Durie, M. (1995). *Māori in New Zealand: Purchasing effective mental health services.* Department of Māori Studies, Massey University, New Zealand.

Fergusson, D.M., Horwood, L.J., & Lynsky, M.T. (1993). Ethnicity and bias in police contact statistics. *Australia & New Zealand Journal of Criminology, 26,* 193–206.

Gilgen, M. (1994, August). *Ethnocentrism and its contribution to skewed research.* Paper presented to the Psychological Services Bicultural Research Hui, Auckland, NZ.

Glover, M. (1997, December). *Kaupapa Māori research.* Paper presented to Health Research Council Hui Whakapiriri, Otara, NZ.

Glover, M., & Robertson, P. (1997). Facilitating development of kaupapa Māori psychology. In H. Love & W. Whitaker (Eds.), *Practice issues for clinical and applied psychologists in New Zealand* (pp. 136–146). Wellington, NZ: New Zealand Psychological Society.

Hudson, S.M., Marshall, W.L., Ward, T., Johnston, P.W., & Jones, R.L. (1995). Kia Marama: A cognitive-behavioural program for incarcerated child molesters. *Behaviour Change, 12,* 69–80.

Jackson, M. (1987). *The Māori and the criminal justice system a new perspective: He whaipanga hou, part 1.* Wellington, NZ: Department of Justice.

Jackson, M. (1988). *The Māori and the criminal justice system a new perspective: He whaipanga hou, part 2.* Wellington, NZ: Department of Justice.

Jones, R. (1993, March). *Cross-cultural psychology: Some implications for psychological practice within New Zealand.* Paper presented at the Department of Justice Psychological Services annual conference, Wellington, NZ.

LaFromboise, T.D. (1988). American Indian mental health policy. *American Psychologist, 43,* 388–397.

Larsen, J.J., & Hillman, D. (1996, April). *Te Piriti: A bicultural approach to treating sex offenders in Aotearoa, New Zealand.* Paper presented at the Management and Treatment of Sexual Offenders: An International Perspective Conference, Perth, Australia.

Larsen, J., Robertson, P., Hillman, D., & Hudson, S. (1998). Te Piriti: A bicultural model for treating child molesters in Aotearoa/New Zealand. In W. Marshall, S. Hudson, T. Ward, & Y. Fernandez (Eds.), *Sourcebook of treatment programs for sexual offenders* (pp. 385–398). New York: Plenum.

Marshall, W.L., & Barbaree, H.E. (1990). An integrated theory of the etiology of sexual offending. In W.L. Marshall, D.R. Laws, & H.E. Barbaree (Eds.), *Handbook of sexual assault: Issues, theories, and treatment of the offender* (pp. 257–275). New York: Plenum.

Mason, K., Ryan, B., & Bennett, H. (1994). *The committee of inquiry in procedures used in certain psychiatric hospitals in relation to admission, discharge, or release on leave of certain classes of patients.* Wellington, NZ: Department of Health.

McCreanor, T. (1993, March). Pakeha psychology and its resistance to the Māori challenge. *Bulletin of the New Zealand Psychological Society,* 27–30.

McFarlane-Nathan, G. (1994, March). *Cognitive behaviour therapy and the Māori client.* Paper presented at the Psychological Services annual conference, Rotorua, NZ.

Medland, J. (1988). Therapy with the whamere. *Australia & New Zealand Journal of Family Therapy,* 9, 33–35.

Ministerial Advisory Committee. (1988). *Puau Te AtaTu (Daybreak), the report of the ministerial committee on a Māori perspective for the Department of Social Welfare.* Wellington, NZ: Department of Social Welfare.

Oetting, E.R., & Beauvais, F. (1990–1991). Orthogonal cultural identification theory: The cultural identification of minority adolescents. *International Journal of Addictions, 25,* 655–685.

Orange, C. (1987). *The Treaty of Waitangi.* Wellington, NZ: Allen & Unwin in association with Port Nicholson Press.

Pere, R.R. (1984). The health of the family. *New Zealand Health Review, 4,* 17.

Peri, M. (1995, September). *Dynamics of whānaungatanga.* Paper presented at the Psychological Services Bicultural Training Program and Māori Psychologists Roopu, Auckland, NZ.

Renfrey, G. (1992). Cognitive behavior therapy and the Native American client. *Behavior Therapy, 23,* 321–340.

Robertson, P., & Larsen, J. (1995, March). *Research on or research? Developing guidelines for undertaking "Māori research" in the Department of Justice.* Paper presented at the annual divisional conference, Psychological Services, Rotorua, NZ.

Salmond, A. (1991). *Two worlds: First meetings between Māori and Europeans 1642–1772.* Auckland, NZ: Viking.

Sawrey, R. (1991, August). *A survey of psychologists' opinions and behaviour on aspects of Māori mental health.* Paper presented at the annual conference of the New Zealand Psychological Society, Wellington, NZ.

Slattery, G. (1987). Transcultural therapy with aboriginal families: Working with the belief system. *Australia & New Zealand Journal of Family Therapy, 8,* 61–70.

Smith, L.T. (1989, August). *On being culturally sensitive: The art of gathering and eating kina without pricking yourself on the finger.* Paper presented at the annual conference of the New Zealand Psychological Society, Auckland, NZ.

Smith, L.T. (1991). Te Rapunga I Te Ao Marama (The search for the World of Light): Māori perspectives on research in education. In T. Linzey & J. Moiss (Eds.), *Growing up: The politics of human learning* (pp. 46–55). Auckland, NZ: Longman Paul.

Stanley, P. (1993, January). *The power and the glory and the great white hunter.* Paper presented at the Psychological Services Hui on Bicultural Issues in Psychology, Auckland, NZ.

Te Awekotuku, N. (1991). *He tikanga whakaro: Research ethics in the Māori community.* Wellington, NZ: Manatu Māori.

Te Puni Kokiri. (1996). *Nga ta o te ora nga hine nagaro Māori (Trends in Māori mental health).* Wellington, NZ: Te Puni Kokiri/The New Zealand Mental Health Foundation.

Tonry, M. (1994). Racial politics, racial disparities, and the war on crime. *Crime and Delinquency, 40,* 475–494.

Ward, T., Louden, K., Hudson, S.M., & Marshall, W.L. (1995). A descriptive model of the offense chain for child molesters. *Journal of Interpersonal Violence, 10,* 452–472.

Warwick, D. (1980). The politics and ethics of cross-cultural research. In H.C. Triandis & W.W. Lambert (Eds.), *Handbook of cross-cultural psychology Vol. 1: Perspectives* (pp. 319–371). Boston: Allyn & Bacon.

Yensen, H., Hague, K., & McCreanor, T. (Eds.). (1989). *Honouring the treaty: An introduction for pakeha to the Treaty of Waitangi.* Auckland, NZ: Penguin.

Yutrzenka, B.A. (1995). Making a case for training in ethnic and cultural diversity in increasing treatment efficacy. *Journal of Consulting & Clinical Psychology, 63,* 197–206.

# 11  Summary and Future Directions

*Saundra D. Johnson, B.A.*
*Eric Cuestas-Thompson, M.A.*

This book represents a beginning with respect to cultural considerations in the assessment and treatment of sexual offenders. The various authors have dealt with an area of sexual offender treatment overlooked for many years. Each focused on a population that he or she has treated or studied and offered the reader insight in how to best work with specific groups cross-culturally.

The challenge to each person in the field of sex offender treatment who has read this book is to be an explorer and to make practical application of the information gleaned from this text. For too long, all sexual perpetrators received the same cookie-cutter assessment and treatment. There is a dearth of sex offender research and treatment programs that directly and efficiently address cultural awareness and sensitivity issues germane to successfully treating clients of color. This omission is no longer acceptable and does a disservice to the offender and his or her family. This book offers practical ways of assessing clients cross-culturally that affirm their differences. It is a handy reference for social workers, psychologists, psychiatrists, and other mental-health professionals who work with sex offenders. The do's and don'ts should serve the veteran as well as the newcomer with respect to treatment of this population. We hope that every reader has found an array of tools that can be used again and again for all the vexing and perplexing challenges of doing cross-cultural sex offender work.

The aim of this final chapter is to examine each chapter briefly and leave readers with several key ideas to remember and use in their daily work with sex offenders of color. The overall objective is to suggest ways in which therapists can modify existing approaches or create new ones that will better serve their clients of color.

215

In Chapter 1, Jones, Loredo, Johnson, and McFarlane-Nathan provide an overview of the current state of assessment and treatment on a global level. They address the critical concept that unrecognized and unaddressed ethnocentrism on the part of practitioners can blind them from providing effective and compassionate treatment to their clients of color. They make a passionate plea to counselors and therapists to get cross-cultural training and experience if they plan to work with special populations.

The authors also note that overcoming the barriers is essential to effective cross-cultural sex offender treatment. They point out in particular the need for policy changes within organizations and systems. They also assert that in spite of existing gaps, the sex offender treatment field is in a strong position to address the clinical and research issues in the enhancement of cultural competence.

Lewis, in Chapter 2, points out that it is important to be an explorer, one who is willing to form hypotheses and test them. One aspect of being such an explorer as a clinician may be to find in the client a source of culturally relevant information that can be used to provide effective and culturally reflective treatment. Such an approach is likely to result not only in the clinician receiving information necessary for him or her to provide effective treatment to the client but also in the client becoming emotionally invested in the treatment process, feeling that he or she plays a valuable role in the treatment experience. The author also suggests that treatment providers must become aware of taboo subjects and bring them up in the context of treatment when the client seems ready to discuss them. Examples of taboo subjects may include masturbation, premarital same-sex and opposite-sex behavior, and incest. The author also discusses cultural resistance to pharmacological intervention.

Minasian and Lewis, in Chapter 3, give weight to the importance of gender issues and differences. Issues of underreporting and the frequent difficulty of detecting female perpetration are addressed. The authors emphasize the need to train professionals to ask the right questions that will aid in the detection of sexual abuse by females. Clearly, understanding the discrete differences in male and female sex offenders is necessary to be successful in the assessment and treatment of female perpetrators. Examples of this enhanced perspective include considering the kind of previously existing relationship between the perpetrator and the victim, motives and reasons underlying the offender's abusive behavior, and kinds of behavior involved in the abuse. The chapter also addresses some of the distinctions between adult and adolescent female sex offenders. Salient assessment and treatment issues regarding this population are also presented. The authors go on to relate the need to develop treatment models for females based on empirical research rather than simply replicating models developed for male offenders.

Wyse and Thomasson, in Chapter 4, point out that one critical element in working with Native American sex offenders is understanding and appreciating the fact that their cultural history is one of brutalization and dehumanization. Although this brutalization and dehumanization have been perpetrated by the dominant Anglo culture, as a result, there exists what the authors term "lateral abuse" that occurs between and among Native Americans. The authors state that therapy should be designed that is more need and result oriented than time oriented. This approach provides treatment that is more reflective of the values, mores, and traditions of the population being served. As a result, clients will be more open and receptive to the treatment being offered. There must also be knowledge of and respect for traditional healers in working with this population, as well as incorporation of traditional healing concepts and practices into the treatment. Clinicians working with Native American clients need to fully accept and respect Native American cultural paradigms that are fundamentally and radically different from the traditional Western worldview. The authors address the importance of knowing that a single Native American identity does not exist and that clinicians need to become knowledgeable about and sensitive to the customs, traditions, history, and nuances of the tribal affiliation represented by the particular Native American client.

In Chapter 5, Broadfield and Welch address the powerful impact of historical abuse and personal devaluation perpetrated by the dominant Anglo culture, starting with the advent of slavery. Despite this damaging and painful backdrop, adaptive strengths that transcend all differences among African-American families exist. Such strengths incorporated into the treatment process can result in empowering the client and making treatment more effective and successful. These strengths include kinship bonds, role flexibility, religion, work and industry, education, and extended kinship network (Boyd-Franklin, 1989). The chapter also addresses some of the cultural beliefs and attitudes, such as homophobia, the keeping of family secrets, and a distrust of the law-enforcement and judicial system, that may play significant roles in the reporting of abuse and the client's receptiveness to treatment. These authors urge readers to recognize diversity within the African-American culture and to deliver therapeutic services based on an Afrocentric worldview.

Loredo, in Chapter 6, provides a number of salient concepts necessary to effectively work with Hispanic sex offenders. In order for the clinician to be interculturally competent, he or she must have knowledge of his or her own culture's patterns of sex and gender, similar knowledge of the other culture, and knowledge of that culture's history of discrimination and power inequalities, and must be cognizant of his or her own discomfort and uneasiness while being committed to redressing cultural prejudices at the individual, agency, and institutional levels. The author points out the importance of familiarity with key words and concepts that are unique to a culture in order to establish rapport with clients. Knowing specific words that are unique to a culture can make it easier for the clinician to make these connections. For example, in the Latino culture, the word *respeto* is very important. A practitioner who is unfamiliar with this and other key concepts will fail to reach and effectively counsel a Latino sex offender.

Loredo is clear that Spanish-speaking ability on the part of the practitioner is not necessary to treat Hispanic sex offenders who speak English. What is necessary is that the practitioner be familiar with and sensitive to vital cultural and linguistic concepts germane to that culture. One must, however, recognize the importance of language and its nuances while conducting assessments and intervention and should be aware when one's linguistic limitations do not serve the clients and the intervention.

Similarly, Cullen and Travin, in Chapter 7, address assessment and treatment issues of Spanish-speaking sex offenders. They address the lack of existing scholarly literature on treating Hispanic sex offenders. The authors also recognize the obstacles to treating all sex offenders, regardless of ethnic background, who have been coerced legally or otherwise into an offender treatment program. The majority of offenders receiving such treatment fall into this category. In addition to their perception that treatment is a continuation of punishment, clients fear that being more forthcoming may result in more punishment. Thus Spanish-speaking offenders are more likely to be resistant to a culturally insensitive clinician who, in addition, may lack the necessary linguistic skills. It is also important for the clinician to be aware that many Hispanic cultures feature specific behavioral expectations when dealing with authority figures, which may include avoidance of eye contact and refusal to show disrespect by displaying anger or disagreeing or making any other negative display of emotion. In addition, Hispanics are a very diverse group whose level of acculturation varies. While certain cultural values may be consistent across Hispanic groups, such as the premium placed on family and the role of the Catholic Church, there is tremendous diversity among various Hispanic groups. For example, language and ethnic identity among Puerto Rican–Americans in New York City are vastly different from those of Mexican Americans living in Tucson, Arizona. Even with a specific Hispanic group within a specific setting, there is tremendous diversity, including factors such as which generation the individual belongs to, the region of origin, and the individual's personal level of acculturation. Further, respect for the nuances of culture differences may facilitate the creation of a therapeutic alliance, assuaging the client's fears of rejection or discrimination by a representative of the host culture.

Graves, in Chapter 8, begins by addressing the negative historical impact of early Russian exploration and exploitation on the Alaskan Native peoples. This exploitation began a long and painful history of societal problems experienced by the many indigenous peoples, including substance abuse, domestic violence, and sexual abuse at levels tremendously higher than those of non-Native peoples. As a result, there is often great distrust of non-Native peoples, especially those in positions of authority. Furthermore, in remote Native communities, where there are high incidences of sexual abuse, community members are often afraid to address this issue for fear that the resulting arrest and imprisonment of the community's members would paralyze and damage the community, possibly with tragic consequences for the literal survival of the remaining members. Graves stresses the importance of Alaska Native sex offenders researching their own culture and heritage as part of their treatment. Through increased knowledge and pride in their culture, the perpetrators will be able to take more responsibility. They also will be able to develop an identity other than as a sex offender, which often leads to a healthier self-image.

LaClaire, in Chapter 9, examines the role and structure of the traditional Asian familiy and how that affects the occurrence of sexual abuse and the responses of family members. The author posits that because of the cultural tenet of many Asians to avoid explicit expression of feelings and other such emotional displays, a solid, behaviorally oriented approach to treatment seems to be optimally effective with Asian sex offenders. Asian perpetrators may minimize the trauma of sexual abuse for various reasons. Family members may feel obligated to accept the abuse if they are financially dependent on the perpetrator. If the perpetrator is an authority figure, inside or outside of the family, there is a powerful injunction to respect authority. In addition, it is often seen as unacceptable to seek help from outside the family. Although minimizing trauma is a culturally adaptive response, it needs to be worked through in therapy (Okamura, Heras, & Wong-Kerberg, 1995). It is also important to note the role of stress resulting from the immigration or refugee experience of many Asians residing in the United States. Asian immigrants and refugees are less likely to report racist and discriminatory treatment by non-Asians as well as by other Asians outside of their ethnic group. As a result, internalized anger and rage and feelings of powerlessness and helplessness may be vented in the form of domestic violence and sexual abuse within the family.

Robertson, Larsen, Hillman, and Hudson, in Chapter 10, look at ways to adapt treatment for sexual offending behavior among the Māori, the indigenous people in New Zealand. The authors identify the damaging results of holding Western values as superior and emphasize the use of a cultural consultant to train staff and to be available to meet the clients outside of their traditional therapy. The authors also discuss the impact of the 1840 Treaty of Waitangi between tribal representatives and representatives of the queen of England. This was seen by both sides as being cooperative, yet historically there have been problems regarding its interpretation and enforcement. The authors feel that in keeping with the bicultural spirit of the treaty, effective treatment of Māori sex offenders needs to incorporate Māori traditions and customs into the treatment process. Te Piriti is the name of the psychological treatment program in Auckland Prison, New Zealand, that combines traditional modes of treatment with traditional Māori modes of healing. The treatment staff consists of Māori individuals as well. Examples of incorporating Māori culture into the treatment process include use of Māori vocabulary, work with Māori elders, and use of Māori healing and other spiritual practices. The treatment process also involves the family, subtribes, and tribes. The program employs a full-time Māori cultural consultant. In addition, the Māori clients plan and implement certain Māori elements in the treatment process.

Progressing through *Cultural Diversity in Sexual Abuser Treatment*, the reader becomes aware of a few prominent themes. Clearly, each culturally diverse population has its own unique and distinct qualities, attributes, and explicit and implicit rules of conduct. However, there are some themes and guidelines for treatment that will be helpful in treating sex offenders of color.

One emerging theme is that many of these populations have experienced exploitation at the hands of either the dominant cultural group of their region of residence, as was the case with African Americans and the Māori of New Zealand, or an invading force, as was the case with the Alaskan Native peoples. Another emerging theme is the importance of family both in terms of playing a resistant role regarding the reporting and treatment of abuse and in terms of being a valuable element of the treatment process.

With regard to the treatment process, a common theme that emerges throughout the chapters is the importance of the clinician being well trained in the cultural traditions, values, critical linguistic concepts, and nuances of the culture of his or her clients. It is also stressed that the clinician must be well aware of his or her own biases, discomfort, and ignorance before beginning to treat sex offender clients from other ethnic groups. Finally, another common theme is the tremendous value and importance of directly incorporating elements from healing and other spiritual practices germane to that culture's identity into the treatment process. It is very important that members of the particular minority group be directly involved in the planning, decision making, and implementation of these elements into the treatment process. It is strongly believed that if the clinician implements these concepts and awareness into his or her practice, the result will be the provision of effective treatment to sexual offenders of culturally diverse populations that is compassionate, respectful, and empowering.

As we continue to develop models for the assessment and treatment of sex offenders, we must consider the whole element of culturally sensitive treatment. It is hoped that the following recommendations will lead to more responsive assessment and treatment for sex offenders of color.

1. Increased emphasis, through agencies and organizations, on staff development and training in the area of culturally competent sex offender treatment.

2. Research and program development, design, and implementation for work with minority sex offenders.

3. Development of college- and university-level certificate and continuing education programs to address issues regarding minority sex offenders.

4. Continued encouragement and active solicitation by professional organizations (such as the Association for the Treatment of Sexual Abusers) of papers to be presented at conferences that focus on the assessment and treatment of sex offenders of color.

5. Publishers (such as the Safer Society Press, Sage, and Guilford, among others) that encourage and support scholarly papers and books being published that deal with sex offenders of color.

Not everything that is faced can be changed but nothing can be changed until it is faced.

— James Baldwin

# References

Boyd-Franklin, N. (1989). *Black families in therapy: A multi-system approach.* New York: Guilford.

Okamura, A., Heras, P., & Wong-Kerberg, L. (1995). Asian, Pacific Island, and Filipino Americans and sexual child abuse. In L.A. Fontes (Ed.), *Sexual abuse in nine North American cultures: Treatment and prevention* (pp. 67–96). Thousand Oaks, CA: Sage.

# Index

Abel, G. G., 117, 156, 157

Abraham, Alice, 165, 173

Acculturation: in the assessment and treatment process, 46, 49–50; Hispanics and acculturation issues, 132–33, 145; Māori and, 192; socio-historical factors, racism, and, 12–15

Adolescents: ethnocentric bias in juvenile sexual offenders, 6–7; female adolescent sex offenders, 71–73, 75–80; National Task Force on Juvenile Sex Offending, 121, 134–36; providing food to juvenile sexual offenders, 34

Adults: adult female sexual offenders/abusers, 71–73, 74–75; ethnocentric bias in adult sexual offenders, 6

African Americans: experience with racism and prejudice, 59; language differences, 22; legacy of slavery, 13, 29, 59, 108–9, 112; role flexibility in family structure, 49; spiritual beliefs, 52, 57, 61–62, 110–11; storytelling with, 58, 59

African-American family, sexual offending behavior in the, 108; African-American culture and homosexual lifestyles, 54, 116; assessment, 115–18; attitudes toward sexuality, 112–13; extended kinship network, 111–12; the family, 109–12; historical and cultural contexts, 108–9; kinship bonds and role flexibility, 110; religion, 110–11; sexual abuse and misconduct, 113–15; sexual aggression and violence in Black communities, 14; work and industry, 111

Alaska Department of Corrections, 174

Alaska Native groups, sex offender treatment for, 164–65; brief history of Alaska Native culture and the impact of Western influence, 166–68; future directions, 177–78; sexual abuse and associated problems in Alaska's Native communities, 167–72; treatment and the Alaska Native sexual offender, 172–77

Alaska Natives Commission, 169

Alkali Lake project (British Columbia), 104

Allen, C., 72, 73

Alpert, M., 137, 153

American Psychological Association, 30

# Select Safer Society Publications

*Roadmaps to Recovery: A Guided Workbook for Young People in Treatment* by Timothy J. Kahn (1999). $18.

*Web of Meaning: A Developmental-Contextual Approach in Sexual Abuse Treatment* by Gail Ryan and Associates (1999). $22.

*Feeling Good Again* by Burt Wasserman (1999). A treatment workbook for boys and girls ages 6 and up who have been sexually abused. $18.

*Feeling Good Again Parents & Therapists Guide* by Burt Wasserman (1999). $8.

*Female Sexual Abusers: Three Views* by Patricia Davin, Ph.D., Teresa Dunbar, Ph.D., & Julia Hislop, Ph.D. (1999). $22.

*Sexual Abuse in America: Epidemic of the 21st Century* by Robert E. Freeman-Longo & Geral T. Blanchard (1998). $20.

*Personal Sentence Completion Inventory* by L.C. Miccio-Fonseca, Ph.D. (1998). $50, includes 10 inventories and user's guide. Additional inventories available in packs of 25 for $25.

*When You Don't Know Who to Call: A Consumer's Guide to Selecting Mental Health Care* by Nancy Schaufele & Donna Kennedy (1998). $15.

*Tell It Like It Is: A Resource for Youth in Treatment* by Alice Tallmadge with Galyn Forster (1998). $15.

*Back on Track: Boys Dealing with Sexual Abuse* by Leslie Bailey Wright & Mindy Loiselle (1997). $14. A workbook for boys ages 10 and up. Foreword by David Calof.

*Assessing Sexual Abuse: A Resource Guide for Practitioners* edited by Robert Prentky & Stacey Bird Edmunds (1997). $20.

*Impact: Working with Sexual Abusers* edited by Stacey Bird Edmunds (1997). $15.

*Supervision of the Sex Offender* by Georgia Cumming & Maureen Buell (1997). $25.

*STOP! Just for Kids: For Kids with Sexual Touching Problems* adapted by Terri Allred & Gerald Burns from original writings of children in a treatment program (1997). $15.

*A Primer on the Complexities of Traumatic Memories of Childhood Sexual Abuse: A Psychobiological Approach* by Fay Honey Knopp & Anna Rose Benson (1997). $25.

*The Last Secret: Daughters Sexually Abused by Mothers* by Bobbie Rosencrans (1997). $20.

*Men & Anger: Understanding and Managing Your Anger for a Much Better Life* by Murray Cullen & Rob Freeman-Longo. Revised and updated, new self-esteem chapter (1996). $15.

*When Children Abuse: Group Treatment Strategies for Children with Impulse Control Problems* by Carolyn Cunningham & Kee MacFarlane (1996). $28.

*Adolescent Sexual Offender Assessment Packet* by Alison Stickrod Gray & Randy Wallace (1992). $8.

*The Relapse Prevention Workbook for Youth in Treatment* by Charlene Steen (1993). $15.

*Pathways: A Guided Workbook for Youth Beginning Treatment* by Timothy J. Kahn (Revised Edition 1997). $15.

*Pathways Guide for Parents of Youth Beginning Treatment* by Timothy J. Kahn (Revised Edition 1997). $8.

*Man-to-Man, When Your Partner Says NO: Pressured Sex & Date Rape* by Scott A. Johnson (1992). $6.50.

*From Trauma to Understanding: A Guide for Parents of Children with Sexual Behavior Problems* by William D. Pithers, Alison S. Gray, Carolyn Cunningham, & Sandy Lane (1993). $5.

*Empathy and Compassionate Action: Issues & Exercises: A Workbook for Clients in Treatment* by Robert Freeman-Longo, Laren Bays, & Euan Bear (1996). Fourth workbook in a series of four for adult sex offenders. $12.

*When Your Wife Says No: Forced Sex in Marriage* by Fay Honey Knopp (1994). $7.

*Female Adolescent Sexual Abusers: An Exploratory Study of Mother-Daughter Dynamics with Implications for Treatment* by Marcia T. Turner & Tracey N. Turner (1994). $18.

*Protocol for Phallometric Assessment: A Clinician's Guide* by Deloris T. Roys & Pat Roys (1994). $10.

*Assessments of Sex Offenders by Measures of Erectile Response: Psychometric Properties and Decision Making* by William D. Murphy & Howard Barbaree (1988; updated for Safer Society & bound 1994). $10.

*Who Am I & Why Am I in Treatment? A Guided Workbook for Clients in Evaluation and Beginning Treatment* by Robert Freeman-Longo & Laren Bays (1988; 8th printing 1997). First workbook in a series of four for adult sex offenders. Also available in Spanish. $12.

*Why Did I Do It Again? Understanding My Cycle of Problem Behaviors* by Laren Bays & Robert Freeman-Longo (1989; 6th printing 1997). Second in the series. $12.

*How Can I Stop? Breaking My Deviant Cycle* by Laren Bays, Robert Freeman-Longo, & Diane Montgomery-Logan (1990; 5th printing 1997). Third in the series. $12.

*The Relapse Prevention Workbook for Youth in Treatment* by Charlene Steen (1993). $15.

The Safer Society Press is part of The Safer Society Foundation, Inc., a 501(c)3 nonprofit national agency dedicated to the prevention and treatment of sexual abuse. We publish additional books, audiocassettes, and training videos related to the treatment of sexual abuse. To receive a catalog of our complete listings, please check the box on the order form (next page) and mail it to the address listed or call us at (802) 247-3132. For more information on the Safer Society Foundation, Inc., visit our website at http://www.safersociety.org.

# ORDER FORM

**Date:**_____

All books shipped via United Parcel Service.
Please include a street location for shipping
as we cannot ship to a Post Office address.

**SHIPPING ADDRESS:**

Name and/or Agency _____

Street Address (no PO boxes) _____

City _____ State_____ Zip_____

**BILLING ADDRESS** (if different from shipping address):

Address _____

City _____ State_____ Zip_____

Daytime phone (____)_____ P.O.#_____

Visa or MasterCard # _____ Exp. Date _____

Signature (for credit card order)_____

☐ Please send me a catalog.      ☐ Do not add me to your mailing list.

| QTY | TITLE | UNIT PRICE | TOTAL COST |
|-----|-------|------------|------------|
|     |       |            |            |
|     |       |            |            |
|     |       |            |            |
|     |       |            |            |
|     |       |            |            |
|     |       |            |            |
|     |       |            |            |
|     |       | **SUBTOTAL** |          |
|     | VT RESIDENTS ADD SALES TAX |  |          |
|     | SHIPPING (SEE BELOW) |      |          |
|     | **TOTAL** |            |            |

No returns.
All prices subject to change without notice.

Bulk discounts available, please inquire.
All orders must be prepaid.

Make checks payable to:
**SAFER SOCIETY PRESS**

Mail to:

### Shipping and Handling

| | | | |
|---|---|---|---|
| 1–5 items | $5 | 16–20 items | $20 |
| 6–10 items | $10 | 21–25 items | $25 |
| 11–15 items | $15 | 26–30 items | $30 |
| | 31+ items | $35 | |

call for quote on rush orders

**Safer Society Press**
P O  B O X  3 4 0 • B R A N D O N • V T  0 5 7 3 3

Phone orders accepted with MasterCard or Visa.
Call (802) 247-3132.